THEOLOGY AND HISTORY IN THE FOURTH GOSPEL

THEOLOGY AND HISTORY IN THE FOURTH GOSPEL

Tradition and Narration

Jörg Frey

BAYLOR UNIVERSITY PRESS

The Library of Congress has cataloged this title under the ISBN 978-1-4813-0989-9.

Printed in the United States of America on acid-free paper with a minimum of 30 percent recycled content.

CONTENTS

EXPANDED CONTENTS

PREFACE

The present book is a reworked and expanded version of the lectures I was invited to present in January 2018 in the distinguished series of the Yale Shaffer Lectures at Yale Divinity School. Since the donor has designed the Shaffer Lectures to focus on the life, character, and teachings of Jesus, I was able to choose a topic from my predominant field of research, the Gospel of John, and from the considerations that are implicit within my larger project of a comprehensive commentary on this work, a text which has attracted my fascination for more than thirty years. How is information about the life and teaching of Jesus adopted and processed in the Fourth Gospel, how is it transformed under the influence of the Gospel's thorough interest in Christology and in the awareness of the presence of the Spirit, and how can we still decipher historically valid information despite the intense theological retouches?

The considerations presented here draw on a history of research, in which the Fourth Gospel has long been considered largely invalid for the quest for the Jesus of history, while, on the other hand, the image of the "Historical Jesus" has mostly been drawn without reference to the strongly theologized and allegedly spiritualized depiction of Jesus in John. Whereas the quest for historical tradition in John was often dismissed, with the famous exception of C. H. Dodd's magisterial work

Historical Tradition in the Fourth Gospel, the past two decades have seen a number of countermovements, initiated mainly from conservative scholars who would like to find more reliable historical information not only in the Synoptic Gospels but also in John. Thus, the quest for "John, Jesus, and History" has attracted considerable interest in the discussions of the Society of Biblical Literature.

The present book reacts to those recent debates and to the governing desire of more closely bringing together the Jesus of history and his Johannine depiction. It raises the questions of whether such a scholarly inclination is historically and theologically appropriate to the Fourth Gospel or whether it possibly underestimates its theological and interpretive intentions. Do our views and prejudices of how historically valid "the Bible" should be actually miss the views and editorial procedures of the biblical authors? And should we not try to grant John his own right and his own perspective, and simply "let John be John" (J. D. G. Dunn)? The approach suggested here, therefore, tries to embed the quest for historical tradition into the overall theological framework of the Fourth Gospel. It departs from theology to end up with some aspects of history and, again, theology. The title is deliberately phrased with reference to J. Louis Martyn's famous book *History and Theology in the Fourth Gospel*, albeit it is a reversal of the two terms. Whereas for us the historical contextualization is necessary for an appropriate theological understanding (and this is the legacy of Martyn's title), the evangelist begins with theology or, rather, Christology as theology, and expresses the aim of providing a deeper and more truthful understanding of the nature and meaning of Jesus, the glorified crucified one. We will, therefore, have to observe how the evangelist utilizes and reshapes the traditions available to him, and how he himself justifies his approach. The results will differ from our image of a "historically truthful" author and give reason to rethink our views of factuality and fictionality, of "truth" in historical and theological terms.

It is more than appropriate here to express my sincerest thanks for the honorable invitation to deliver the 2018 Shaffer Lectures at Yale Divinity School. It is particularly humbling for me to appear in a series of most distinguished scholars including C. H. Dodd (1935) and J. Louis Martyn (2000); distinguished Johannine scholars such as

Raymond E. Brown (1978); and also the most honorable names from my German scholarly tradition such as Martin Dibelius (1937), Rudolf Bultmann (1951), Oscar Cullmann (1955), Ernst Käsemann (1966), and my revered academic mentor Martin Hengel (1992), who passed away nine years ago on July 2, 2009, and whose contributions to theology and history, not only in the Fourth Gospel, are still worthy of consideration. This book is dedicated to his memory.

I am also grateful to all my dear friends at Yale who made our stay enjoyable, in particular my colleagues Greg Sterling, Adela and John Collins, Judith Gundry, Harry Attridge, Michal-Beth Dinkler, and Yii-Jan Lin, as well as Emma McHugh and Elaine Rancato in the administration. I am also grateful for the steady confidence of Carey Newman, the director of Baylor University Press, an author from the other side of the world, for his indefatigable encouragement, and for the invaluable support of his team at BUP, in particular Kingsley East, Cade Jarrell, and Jenny Hunt, as well as copyeditor Dan Khan. Last but not least I would like to thank my valuable collaborator in all matters of English language and style, Jacob Cerone (Munich), for his great help in shaping the lectures and the present book.

Jörg Frey
Zurich, June 2018

INTRODUCTION

J. Louis Martyn: History and Theology or Theology and History?

Exactly fifty years ago, in 1968, the great American New Testament scholar J. Louis Martyn (1925–2015) from Union Theological Seminary published his famous study on *History and Theology in the Fourth Gospel*.[1] This small book turned out to be nothing less than a milestone in Johannine scholarship. Together with the larger works of his Union colleague Raymond E. Brown (1928–1998), the magisterial Anchor Bible commentary on the Gospel and the Epistles of John[2] and the shorter comprehensive study on *The Community of the Beloved Disciple*,[3] published roughly in the same period, Martyn's book has changed the

[1] J. Louis Martyn, *History and Theology in the Fourth Gospel* (New York: Harper & Row, 1968; 2nd enl. ed., Nashville: Abingdon, 1979). In the following I quote the third edition: *History and Theology in the Fourth Gospel*, NTL (Louisville: Westminster John Knox, 2003).

[2] Raymond E. Brown, *The Gospel according to John*, 2 vols., AB 29/29A (New York: Doubleday, 1966/1970); Raymond E. Brown, *The Epistles of John*, AB 30 (New York: Doubleday, 1982).

[3] Raymond E. Brown, *The Community of the Beloved Disciple: The Loves and Hates of an Individual Church in New Testament Times* (New York: Paulist Press, 1979). This was in a certain manner Brown's answer to Martyn's book, acknowledging the progress in scholarship over against the first volume of his own commentary.

views about the Fourth Gospel in North American scholarship and beyond.[4] Expanded in its second edition in 1979 and republished again in the New Testament Library series in 2003, Martyn's brief study opened up new paths to understanding the Fourth Gospel beyond the classical interpretations of Rudolf Bultmann (1884–1976) and C. H. Dodd (1884–1973), the champions of Johannine studies in Germany and England in the mid-twentieth century.[5] "For all of its brevity," Martyn's book "is probably the most important single work on the Gospel since Bultmann's commentary."[6] Its main achievement is that it has not only reinscribed John into a more Jewish context but also rephrased the historical issues around John with a new focus on the situation and history of the Johannine community and its theological development.

In contrast with the then-widespread explanation of John within a Hellenistic or even gnostic context, as advocated by Bultmann[7] and

[4] Cf. D. Moody Smith, "The Contribution of J. Louis Martyn to the Understanding of the Gospel of John," in *The Conversation Continues: Studies in Paul and John in Honor of J. Louis Martyn,* ed. Robert T. Fortna and Beverly R. Gaventa (Nashville: Abingdon, 1990), 275–94; repr. in the 3rd ed. of Martyn, *History and Theology,* 1–19; see also idem, "Postscript for Third Edition of Martyn, *History and Theology in the Fourth Gospel,*" in Martyn, *History and Theology,* 19–23; see also William Baird, *History of New Testament Research,* vol. 3: *From C. H. Dodd to Hans Dieter Betz* (Minneapolis: Fortress, 2013), 604–22. For Brown's impact on Johannine scholarship, see Francis J. Moloney, "The Gospel of John: The Legacy of Raymond E. Brown and Beyond," in *Life in Abundance: Studies of John's Gospel in Tribute to Raymond E. Brown*, ed. John R Donahue (Collegeville: Liturgical Press, 2005), 19–39.

[5] Cf. Rudolf Bultmann, *Das Evangelium des Johannes,* KEK 2 (Göttingen: Vandenhoeck & Ruprecht, 1941); ET: *The Gospel of John: A Commentary,* trans. George R. Beasley-Murray (Oxford: Blackwell, 1971); C. H. Dodd, *The Interpretation of the Fourth Gospel* (Cambridge: Cambridge University Press, 1953); see also idem, *Historical Tradition in the Fourth Gospel* (Cambridge: Cambridge University Press, 1963).

[6] John Ashton, *Understanding the Fourth Gospel* (Oxford: Oxford University Press, 1991), 107. Joel Marcus expresses it similarly: "No postwar monograph has done more to determine the direction of subsequent Johannine studies" (Joel Marcus, "Tribute to J. Louis Martyn," *NT Blog*, http://ntweblog.blogspot.ch/2015/06/tribute-to-j-louis-martyn-by-joel-marcus.html).

[7] From the mid-1920s, Rudolf Bultmann developed the view that the history-of-religions background of the Fourth Gospel (the evangelist and some of his sources) lay in gnosticizing Baptizer circles of the Transjordan region. The alleged gnostic redeemer myth, as reconstructed predominantly from later Mandaean and Manichaean sources,

Dodd,[8] Martyn explained the Gospel within a Jewish or Jewish Christian background.[9] With this remarkable shift of perspective, Martyn took into consideration new insights gained through the discovery of the Dead Sea Scrolls[10] at a time when the leading forces in Johannine scholarship were still following different tracks of historical explanation

---

was considered the background of Johannine Christology. Hermeneutically, the supposed gnostic background could support an interpretation wherein the Johannine proclamation was articulated in critical opposition to the predominant philosophical worldview of the time. For the relevance of the gnosis paradigm for Bultmann's hermeneutics and interpretation, see Jörg Frey, *Die johanneische Eschatologie,* vol. 1: *Ihre Probleme im Spiegel der Forschung seit Reimarus,* WUNT 97 (Tübingen: Mohr Siebeck, 1997), 86–157; for Bultmann's interpretation, see also Jörg Frey, "Johannine Christology and Eschatology," in *Beyond Bultmann: Reckoning a New Testament Theology,* ed. Bruce W. Longenecker and Mikeal C. Parsons (Waco: Baylor University Press, 2014), 101–32; and Richard Bauckham, "Dualism and Soteriology in Johannine Theology," in Longenecker and Parsons, eds., *Beyond Bultmann,* 133–54.

[8] Like the majority of British scholarship, Dodd did not follow Bultmann in his source criticism and his theological existentialism, nor did he accept his reference to an alleged pre-Christian Gnosticism. Dodd, instead, explained the Fourth Gospel in a Platonizing tradition against the background of Hellenistic syncretism, as present, e.g., in the Hermetic corpus, but also in Hellenistic Judaism, particularly in the writings of Philo. His second main work on John (*Historical Tradition*) then addressed the issue of historical traditions in or behind the Gospel, i.e., the questions that will also be discussed in the present volume. On Dodd's interpretation of the Johannine writings, see also Frey, *Die johanneische Eschatologie,* 1:247–51; and Baird, *History of New Testament Research,* 3:45–52.

[9] This is already prefigured in Martyn's Yale PhD dissertation from 1957 on "The Salvation-History Perspective in the Fourth Gospel" where he argues that the original setting of the Gospel or its formative tradition was the synagogue (cf. Smith, "The Contribution of J. Louis Martyn," 9).

[10] Among the early comparisons between the newly discovered texts and the Fourth Gospel, the presentation by Raymond E. Brown, "The Qumran Scrolls and the Johannine Gospel and Epistles," *CBQ* 17 (1955): 403–19 and 559–74, provides the most balanced perspective. Although the early claims of a direct influence of Qumran texts and thought on the Fourth Gospel were overstated, the lasting effect of the discoveries has been deeper insight into the Jewish character of John's language and thought. See also the more recent evaluation of the relationship between Qumran and the Johannine writings in Jörg Frey, "Recent Perspectives on Johannine Dualism and Its Background," in *Text, Thought, and Practice in Qumran and Early Christianity,* ed. Ruth Clements and Daniel R. Schwartz, STDJ 84 (Leiden: Brill, 2008), 127–57.

or rather neglecting historical inquiry in favor of a merely theological, existential reading.[11]

In *History and Theology in the Fourth Gospel*, Martyn decidedly readdresses the historical issues, with a particular focus on the time and situation of the Gospel's composition. The first task "is to say something as specific as possible about the actual circumstances in which John wrote the Gospel."[12] The most specific problem or process behind the composition of the Gospel is then identified in the miracle story of the man born blind in John 9, in which it is even said that members of the synagogue community do not openly confess Jesus because the Jews had decided to expel those who would confess him (John 9:22). Thus, the process of separation between the synagogue and the group of Jesus followers, the "parting of the ways,"[13] is presented as the back-

[11] This is characteristic for the interpretation of Bultmann and his school. It is not insignificant that Bultmann's commentary on John, the most influential work of Johannine scholarship in the twentieth century, did not include an introduction but presented all its daring hypotheses about the literary development, the sources, alleged relocations, and ecclesiastical redaction only in the footnotes, whereas the main text of the commentary presents a "supposedly contextless" theological interpretation (thus John Painter, *Theology as Hermeneutics: Rudolf Bultmann's Theology of the History of Jesus* [London: Bloomsbury, 2015], 67) without any references to the historical situation at the time of the earthly Jesus, nor to the situation of the evangelist or his community. Likewise, Bultmann's student Ernst Käsemann, in his provoking rejection of Bultmann's interpretation (Ernst Käsemann, *The Testament of Jesus according to John 17* [London: SCM Press, 1966]), did not depart from the historical contextualization of John, but rather drew on formal and, in particular, theological criteria. Concerning Käsemann's interpretation, cf. Frey, *Die johanneische Eschatologie*, 1:160–70.

[12] Martyn, *History and Theology*, 29.

[13] The term was introduced into recent scholarship by James D. G. Dunn, *The Partings of the Ways: Between Christianity and Judaism and Their Significance for the Character of Christianity* (London: SCM Press, 1991; 2nd rev. ed., 2006). See also the criticism by Judith M. Lieu, "'The Parting of the Ways': Theological Construct or Historical Reality?" in *Neither Jew nor Greek: Constructing Early Christianity* (London: T&T Clark, 2002), 11–29; the questioning of the paradigm in *The Ways That Never Parted: Jews and Christians in Late Antiquity and the Early Middle Ages*, ed. Annette Yoshiko Reed and Adam H. Becker, TSAJ 95 (Tübingen: Mohr Siebeck, 2003); and the more recent discussions in Jörg Frey, "Towards Reconfiguring Our Views on the 'Parting of the Ways': Ephesus as a Test Case," in *John and Judaism: A Contested Relationship in Context*, ed. R. Alan Culpepper and Paul N. Anderson, RBS 87 (Atlanta: SBL 2017), 221–41; and Adele Reinhartz, *Cast Out of the*

ground upon which the development of the Johannine community and the composition of the Gospel can be explained. Thus, Martyn also addresses the challenge posed by the polemic against the *Ioudaioi* (Judeans or Jews)[14] uttered by the Johannine Jesus, a problem that made reading John so troublesome particularly after the Shoah.[15] The hostility between Jesus and the *Ioudaioi* in John is historically explained as a result of the tragic history of the Johannine community and the separation between Jewish Jesus followers and the synagogue. Consequently, these polemical passages are definitely not words of the Jesus of history[16] but rather triggered by the history and situation of the evangelist and his community. With regard to this dark side of John, it is obvious that the Fourth Gospel needs a critical interpretation, which could not be established as long as scholars continued to explain the Gospel in a rather timeless pattern[17] or to derive its legacy from an eyewitness testimony and defend its historical accuracy or the substantial authenticity of the words of the Johannine Jesus.

Covenant: Jews and Anti-Judaism in the Gospel of John (Lanham, Md.: Rowman & Littlefield, 2018).

[14] The appropriate translation of the Greek term *Ioudaioi* in John is disputed. The attempt to render the term with "Judeans" (in order to distinguish them from contemporary Jews) does not work in all passages. The Galileans in John 6:41 and 6:52 cannot be called "Judeans" without difficulties, and Jesus is not a "Judean" according to John 4:9 but is rather a Jew from Galilee. With regard to the problems in Josephus, cf. Daniel R. Schwartz, "'Judaean' or 'Jew'? How Should We Translate *Ioudaios* in Josephus?" in *Jewish Identity in the Greco-Roman World*, ed. Jörg Frey, Stephanie Gripentrog, and Daniel R. Schwartz, AGJU 71 (Leiden: Brill, 2007), 3–27.

[15] Cf. also the discussion in Jörg Frey, *The Glory of the Crucified One: Christology and Theology in the Gospel of John*, trans. W. Coppins and C. Heilig, BMSEC 6 (Waco: Baylor University Press, 2018), 39–72.

[16] Recent claims that such a separation could already have happened at the time of Jesus (cf. Jonathan Bernier, *Ἀποσυνάγωγος and the Historical Jesus in John: Rethinking the Historicity of the Johannine Expulsion Passages*, BibInt 122 [Leiden: Brill, 2013]) are inspired too much by wishful thinking about the historical validity of New Testament texts, and do not solve the historical and hermeneutical problems.

[17] In Bultmann's interpretation, the Johannine *Ioudaioi* (clearly rendered as "Jews") are not considered in their historical context but as a cipher for the attitude of unbelief. Such a generalizing interpretation, however, has been rightly criticized for uncritically continuing the anti-Jewish rhetoric of the Gospel and traditional paradigms of anti-Judaism.

From today's perspective, fifty years later, Martyn's landmark study is characteristic for a period of scholarship that was still rather optimistic about its ability to reconstruct the literary history of the Fourth Gospel and the development of the Johannine community. After the primarily theological interpretations of Bultmann and Dodd, scholars in the 1960s gradually returned to historical issues.[18] They started asking about the Johannine community, its historical situation and its development. But their optimism about reconstructing sources or redactional layers was probably overstated, as scholarship came to discover in the 1980s through the influence of literary and narrative approaches which were introduced through the seminal study on the "anatomy" of the Fourth Gospel by R. Alan Culpepper and other works on John's narrative unity and literary design.[19]

Therefore, Martyn's reconstruction of the history of the Johannine community from its Jewish Christian origins through the separation

[18] On the revival of Johannine redaction criticism (*Literarkritik*) in that period, see Frey, *Die johanneische Eschatologie*, 1:266–97. The most prominent reconstructions were presented by Jürgen Becker (cf. his commentary: Jürgen Becker, *Das Evangelium nach Johannes*, 2 vols., ÖTK 4/1–2 [Gütersloher and Würzburg: Echter, 1978/1980; 3rd ed., 1991]); Georg Richter, *Studien zum Johannesevangelium*, ed. J. Hainz, BU 13 (Regensburg: Pustet, 1977); and Robert T. Fortna, *The Gospel of Signs: A Reconstruction of the Narrative Source Underlying the Fourth Gospel*, SNTSMS 11 (Cambridge: Cambridge University Press, 1970). In the later editions of his book, Martyn associates himself with the literary pattern established by Fortna, cf. J. Louis Martyn, "Glimpses into the History of the Johannine Community: From Its Origin through the Period of Life in Which the Gospel Was Composed," in *The Gospel of John in Christian History: Essays for Interpreters* (New York: Paulist, 1979), 90–121 (included as an additional chapter since the 2nd ed. of *History and Theology*; see in the 3rd ed. pp. 145–67).

[19] R. Alan Culpepper, *Anatomy of the Fourth Gospel: A Study in Literary Design* (Philadelphia: Fortress, 1983); for an evaluation of the effects, see Tom Thatcher, "Anatomies of the Fourth Gospel: Past, Present, and Future Probes," in *Anatomies of Narrative Criticism: The Past, Present and Future of the Fourth Gospel as Literature,* ed. Tom Thatcher and Stephen D. Moore, RBS 55 (Atlanta: SBL, 2008), 1–35. Cf. also the historical argument for a relative literary unity of the Gospel by Martin Hengel, *The Johannine Question* (London: SCM Press, 1989), 88–94; the thorough criticism of the signs-source theory by Gilbert van Belle, *The Signs Source in the Fourth Gospel: Historical Survey and Critical Evaluation of the Semeia Hypothesis,* BETL 116 (Leuven: Peeters, 1994); and the evaluation of Johannine *Literarkritik* from the perspective of style analysis in Frey, *Die johanneische Eschatologie,* 1:429–45.

from the synagogue until the elaboration of its high Christology[20] appears all too novelistic in its details. In his *Introduction* to the Fourth Gospel, in which he began to update the views expressed in his commentary, the late Raymond E. Brown took a much more cautious approach by only distinguishing between an origin of the tradition in the public activity of Jesus and the developments in the post-resurrection context of the community's history.[21]

In particular, the key "event" singled out by Martyn (a general expulsion of Jewish Jesus followers from the synagogue, sparked by the rabbinic decision to rephrase the so-called *Birkat ha-Minim*, the "curse on the heretics," in the daily prayer of the Eighteen Benedictions, supposedly issued by the sages at Yavneh/Jamnia in the late first century CE[22]) has been decisively questioned by specialists in Jewish literature and history.[23] Apart from the problem that even such

[20] Thus summarized in Martyn, "Glimpses into the History of the Johannine Community." Here, Martyn reads the Gospel like an archaeological site with various "strata" (145), distinguishing (a) the stratum of a messianic group within the synagogal community, (b) its later excommunication from the synagogue, including traumatic experiences of martyrdom, and (c) a later development toward firm social and theological configurations. For a discussion of these matters, cf. Frey, *Glory of the Crucified One*, 52–54. Raymond E. Brown has developed an even more detailed pattern of the theological development of the circle in five stages; cf. Brown, *Gospel according to John*, 1:xxxiv–xxxix; idem, *The Community of the Beloved Disciple*; for discussion, cf. Frey, *Die johanneische Eschatologie*, 1:269–73.

[21] Raymond E. Brown and Francis J. Moloney, *An Introduction to the Gospel of John*, ABRL (New York: Doubleday, 2003), 66–69 and 85–86 (with the excursus on pp. 69–85 written by Francis Moloney).

[22] Cf. Martyn, *History and Theology*, 46–66. Cf. also the critical reflection by Robert Kysar, "Expulsion from the Synagogue: A Tale of a Theory," in *Voyages with John: Charting the Fourth Gospel* (Waco: Baylor University Press, 2005), 234–45.

[23] Cf. Günter Stemberger, "Die sogenannte 'Synode von Jabne' und das frühe Christentum," *Kairos* 19 (1977): 14–21; Peter Schäfer, "Die sogennante Synode von Jabne: Zur Trennung von Juden und Christen im ersten/zweiten Jh. n. Chr," in *Studien zur Geschichte und Theologie des Rabbinischen Judentums*, AGJU 15 (Leiden: Brill, 1978), 45–64; Reuven Kimelman, "Birkat Ha-Minim and the Lack of Evidence for an Anti-Christian Jewish Prayer in Late Antiquity," in *Jewish and Christian Self-Definition*, ed. E. P. Sanders, Albert I. Baumgarten, and A. Mendelson (London: SCM Press, 1981), 2:226–44; Steven T. Katz, "Issues in the Separation of Judaism and Christianity After 70 C. E.: A Reconsideration," *JBL* 103 (1984): 43–76; and Daniel Boyarin, "Justin Martyr Invents Judaism," *Church History* 70 (2001): 427–61. See also

an explanation cannot completely whitewash the Gospel from the charge of anti-Judaism or, at least, its anti-Jewish effects, the main historical objections are (a) that the "synod" or "school" of Yavneh is a rabbinic construct integrating a greater number of decisions of the sages; (b) that the extant texts from the early siddurim are quite late, and the term "nozerim" (= Jewish Christians) was probably only added at a later stage of the tradition to the earlier term "minim" (= heretics); (c) that Jewish Jesus followers would not have considered themselves "heretics," so they would not necessarily have applied the revised prayers to themselves; (d) that there is no evidence of a formal expulsion; and, finally, (e) that it is unclear how far and how quickly decisions in Jewish Palestine would have affected the communities in the diaspora.[24] Even if it is probably true that the otherwise unattested term ἀποσυνάγωγος (John 9:22; 12:42; 16:2-3) points to processes of the separation between Jewish Jesus followers and the synagogal community, these processes cannot be attributed to a central act of the rabbis in Palestine but rather a local split between Jewish (Johannine) Jesus followers and the local synagogal communities.[25]

In particular, Martyn's stimulating paradigm that the Gospel can actually be read as a "two-level drama"[26] deserves some reconsideration.

---

the most recent summary of the criticism in Adele Reinhartz, *Cast Out of the Covenant: Jews and Anti-Judaism in the Gospel of John* (Lanham, Md.: Rowman & Littlefield, 2018), chap. 6.

[24] Jörg Frey, "Von Paulus zu Johannes: Die Diversität 'christlicher' Gemeindekreise und die 'Trennungsprozesse' zwischen der Synagoge und den Gemeinden der Jesusnachfolger in Ephesus im ersten Jahrhundert," in *The Rise and Expansion of Christianity in the First Three Centuries of the Common Era,* ed. Clare K. Rothschild and Jens Schröter, WUNT 301 (Tübingen: Mohr Siebeck, 2013), 235–78 (266–75). In this article, I focus on the influence of political factors such as the newly imposed taxation on Jews after 70 CE, the *fiscus iudaicus*. The new taxation is considered with respect to its triggering effects for the separation between the diaspora synagogue and Jesus followers. Another important perspective has been expressed by John Kloppenborg with regard to disaffiliation processes in voluntary associations; see John S. Kloppenborg, "Disaffiliation and the ἀποσυνάγωγος of John," *HTS* 67 (2011), 159–74.

[25] Cf. D. Moody Smith, "Judaism and the Gospel of John," in *Jews and Christians: Exploring the Past, Present, and Future,* ed. James H. Charlesworth (New York: Crossroad, 1990), 76–96 (85); and also idem, "Postscript for Third Edition of Martyn."

[26] Martyn, *History and Theology in the Fourth Gospel*, 46.

Martyn developed that paradigm from his reading of the episode in John 9 which, in his view, simultaneously narrates an incident from the time of the earthly Jesus and another one from the temporal context of the community, where the healer is actually a Christian preacher, and the Pharisees interrogating the healed man are the Jewish authorities. Such a "doubling" of the events, however, is unconvincing: when John 9 narrates that Jesus heals a man born blind, we cannot really assume that the narrative actually mirrors an analogous event from the Johannine community, such as the healing of a blind man through a Christian charismatic or preacher. The episodes narrated in John are still part of the story of the earthly Jesus, even though the image of "the Jews" and the Pharisees, their judicial power, and also the expressions of Christology, community affiliation, and faith are obviously shaped by insights and experiences from the post-Easter period and particularly from the Johannine community.

On the other hand, the paradigm of the two-level drama is quite perceptive and stimulating. There are, indeed, two levels in John's narration of the Jesus story: the level of the narrated story of the earthly Jesus and the level of the narration, of the author telling his story to his readers or hearers. It is widely accepted that the Johannine narrative is shaped by insights, challenges, and theological terms from the context of the community of addressees. It is also quite likely that some of the elements in the Johannine narration are inspired by experiences from the time between Jesus and the composition of the Gospel.

But how are these two (or even more) levels connected in the Johannine text? Can we still separate them and determine what is historically true and what is mere interpretation or theology? Or are they connected in an almost inseparable unity so that the insights and fears of the community of addressees are introduced into the narration of the history of Jesus, and, consequently, the earthly Jesus is presented in the light of later christological insights as a divine being? And if this is true, what is the function of that fusion of levels or horizons[27] which makes John and his representation of the history of Jesus so unique among the Gospels? These are the questions to be considered

[27] On the term "fusion of horizons" (= *Horizontverschmelzung*), see the references to Hans-Georg Gadamer's philosophy of history below, n. 31.

in the present book. And it is no coincidence that, for this investigation, I have reversed Martyn's title: instead of *History and Theology in the Fourth Gospel*, the present book is entitled *Theology and History in the Fourth Gospel.*

Martyn departed from the quest for *history* (or, more precisely, the history of the community of addressees) to explain the *theology* of the Gospel. John's high Christology is then explained as the product of and answer to the separation of Johannine Jewish Christians from the synagogue.[28] But what if the reconstruction of the history and in particular the history of thought development is fragile and questionable? While acknowledging and actually presupposing a number of fundamental insights from Martyn's approach, I will make my inquiry in the reverse, from *theology* to *history*. How (and how far) can we investigate the history behind John's Gospel if its priority is theology or rather Christology as theology? How can Johannine theology explain the unique representation of the appearance, history, and message of Jesus in this gospel? And how far can we still hope to discover or even isolate historical traditions[29] or splinters of historical information in John? In this reversed perspective, I will critically discuss more recent tendencies of looking for historiography or historically valid traditions in John and ask about the character of the "history" we can find in the Gospel. I will, therefore, depart from the insights of more recent scholarship in which the Gospel is primarily read as a coherent narrative unity[30] that is kept together by a dense web of metaphors. I intend to do this without ignoring the task of the interpreter to ask about historical traditions and their possible value and to understand how and why the evangelist adopted, reshaped, rearranged, and interpreted his materials.

[28] Martyn, *History and Theology*, 101–13.

[29] Here, the most important scholarly contribution is Dodd, *Historical Tradition in the Fourth Gospel.* The fact that this work has set the standard for a long period with only a few followers in subsequent decades is remarked upon by D. A. Carson, "Historical Tradition in the Fourth Gospel: After Dodd, What?" in *Gospel Perspectives*, vol. 2: *Studies of History and Tradition in the Four Gospels,* ed. R. T. France & David Wenham (Sheffield: JSOT Press, 1981), 83–145.

[30] For an account of my exegetical approach on John, see Frey, *Glory of the Crucified One,* 3–38.

A key insight for this approach is derived from the philosophy of history of Hans-Georg Gadamer.[31] In his main work, *Truth and Method*, Gadamer develops the idea that history is better understood in retrospect. In the narrative process of understanding history from a later viewpoint, the fusion of the two horizons of the story told and of the storyteller creates a new intellectual space in which a better understanding is developed. The Gospel of John is such a retrospective narration of the story of Jesus, a narrative "memory"[32] from a post-Easter viewpoint. This is explicitly acknowledged in the narrative commentaries, which note that the disciples did not understand Jesus' words and deeds during his earthly life but arrived at a true understanding only later, after his glorification (John 2:22; 12:16) in remembrance through the Spirit (cf. 14:25-26; 16:13-15).

Consequently, the Gospel author is well aware that he does not simply present the "historical truth" as was accessible to the contemporaries of Jesus. It is not simply a representation of the history of the earthly Jesus, and, thus, a historicizing approach to John must necessarily fail.[33] But on the other hand, the Gospel is not merely a theological allegory that simply mirrors the insights and situation of the author and his contemporaries. Instead, John is a complex web in which both levels are fused with the result that the story of the Word incarnate, freshly narrated and interpreted, leads to a new understanding of the present. The present insights, gained in the post-Easter time, are used for a true understanding of Jesus, his fate, and his words. Thus, the interpretation of John can neither simply stay on the

[31] See Hans-Georg Gadamer, *Wahrheit und Methode: Grundzüge einer philosophischen Hermeneutik*, 5th ed. (Tübingen: Mohr Siebeck, 1986), 296–312; for its adoption in Johannine scholarship, see the hermeneutically groundbreaking work by Takashi Onuki, *Gemeinde und Welt im Johannesevangelium: Ein Beitrag zur Frage nach der theologischen und pragmatischen Funktion des johanneischen 'Dualismus,'* WMANT 56 (Neukirchen-Vluyn: Neukirchener Verlag, 1984), 10–12; and Jörg Frey, *Die johanneische Eschatologie*, vol. 2: *Das johanneische Zeitverständnis*, WUNT 110 (Tübingen: Mohr Siebeck, 1998), 249–68; see also idem, *Glory of the Crucified One*, 73–100.

[32] Cf. Jörg Frey, "The Gospel of John as a Narrative Memory of Jesus," in *Memory and Memories in Early Christianity*, ed. Simon Butticaz and Enrico Norelli, WUNT 398 (Tübingen: Mohr Siebeck, 2018), 261–84.

[33] On the historicizing approach, see my considerations in Frey, *Glory of the Crucified One*, 7–11.

level of Jesus' history nor on the level of the Johannine community and theology. As readers, we are left with the two horizons and with a new space for understanding the in-between. Herein, we are better off than Peter and the other contemporaries of Jesus who steadily misunderstand things during his earthly life. Only when their standpoint is left behind and the post-Easter insights are taken seriously can the story of Jesus be understood truthfully; on the other hand, the truth can never be told without reference to the history of Jesus, the incarnate and crucified one.

1

CHRISTOLOGY AS THEOLOGY

The Johannine Approach as a Challenge Then and Now

1. Jesus as "God": Christology as Theology

In ancient Christianity, the Apostle John, considered to be the author of the Fourth Gospel, the three Johannine Epistles, and Revelation,[1] was not only characterized as the "eagle evangelist"[2] who soared to particular spiritual heights but was also given the honorary title "the theologian" (ὁ θεόλογος). This term, attested already in Origen and used

[1] Concerning the reception history and the "myth" of John the Apostle, see R. Alan Culpepper, *John the Son of Zebedee: The Life of a Legend* (Edinburgh: T&T Clark, 2000); for the problems related to Johannine authorship, see Jörg Frey, "Das Corpus Johanneum und die Apokalypse des Johannes: Die Johanneslegende, die Probleme der johanneischen Verfasserschaft und die Frage der Pseudonymität der Apokalypse," in *Poetik und Intertextualität der Apokalypse*, ed. S. Alkier, T. Hieke, and T. Nicklas, WUNT 346 (Tübingen: Mohr Siebeck, 2015), 71–133.

[2] In Rev 4:7, the eagle is one of the four beings next to God's throne, which were interpreted by Irenaeus (*Haer.* 3.11.8) as a reference to the unity of the fourfold gospel (on this, see Bernhard Mutschler, *Das Corpus Johanneum bei Irenäus von Lyon*, WUNT 185 [Tübingen: Mohr Siebeck, 2006], 67–70). Irenaeus assigned the human being to Matthew, the eagle to Mark, the ox to Luke, and the lion to John. Augustine (*Cons.* 1.6) assigns the lion to Matthew, the human being to John, and the eagle to John. The later standard assignment—with the correlation of the human being with Matthew, the lion with Mark, the ox with Luke, and the eagle with John—which determines the presentation of the evangelists in Christian art, was presented and firmly established through Jerome (*Hom.* 75; *Comm. Ezech.* 1.1) and Gregory the Great (*Hom. Ezech.* 2.1 and 4.1). See Culpepper, *John the Son of Zebedee*, 167–68; and Francis Watson, *Gospel Writing: A Canonical Perspective* (Grand Rapids: Eerdmans, 2013), 553–56.

in Orthodox theology until today,[3] does not point to "theology" in the modern sense of the word, as a particularly rational "talk about God," but to the fact that it is John who most clearly expresses the divinity of Christ. Here, not only the primordial Logos (John 1:1-2) but also the incarnate Jesus (20:28; cf. 1:18) is said to be θεός (God) or even "the true God" (17:3; cf. 1 John 5:20), who is "one with the Father" (cf. John 10:30). Unlike Mark, where readers are confronted with a "messianic secret,"[4] John presents Jesus from the very beginning (1:1-2, 14, 18) in his divine glory, which is said to be revealed in the signs (2:11) and the deeds of his earthly ministry. Therefore, the Gospel of John became the most important biblical source for the later development of the doctrines about the Trinity and about Christ's two natures.

To be sure, John is not the only New Testament author to express the divinity of Christ.[5] Such a divine dignity of Jesus is also expressed in other late writings of the New Testament, such as the Pastorals (Titus 2:13), Second Peter (2 Pet 1:1), or Revelation,[6] and likewise in the Apostolic

[3] Origen, *Comm. Jo.*, frg. (Preuschen 1903, 483.14; see also 484.7 from later catena); see further Christoph Markschies, *Christian Theology and Its Institutions in the Early Roman Empire: Prolegomena to a History of Early Christian Theology*, trans. W. Coppins, BMSEC 3 (Waco: Baylor University Press, 2015), 13–14.

[4] Cf. the influential view by William Wrede, *Das Messiasgeheimnis in den Evangelien: Zugleich ein Beitrag zum Verständnis des Markusevangeliums* (Göttingen: Vandenhoeck & Ruprecht, 1901); ET: *The Messianic Secret*, trans. J. C. Greig (London: James Clark, 1987). The idea is, of course, not uncontested by scholars.

[5] On John's high Christology, its NT precursors, and the development of the idea of the divinity of Christ, see also Frey, *The Glory of the Crucified One: Christology and Theology in the Gospel of John*, trans. W. Coppins and C. Heilig, BMSEC 6 (Waco: Baylor University Press, 2018), 359–64.

[6] Cf. in particular the similar "I am" sayings of God and Christ: Rev 1:8 (God) and 1:17 (Christ); 21:6 (God); and 22:13 (Christ); see further Rev 2:23; 22:16. The fusion of the words of God on his throne and those of his (still subordinate) throne mate Christ is significant for the Christology of Revelation. Although the theocentricity of God is clear, the claims made for Christ show that he participates in his divine status. The parallel but different usage of the ἐγώ εἰμι formula also forms an interesting link between the Fourth Gospel and Revelation; on this, cf. Jörg Frey, "Erwägungen zum Verhältnis der Johannesapokalypse zu den übrigen Schriften im Corpus Johanneum," in Martin Hengel, *Die johanneische Frage: Ein Lösungsversuch, mit einem Anhang zur Apokalypse von Jörg Frey*, WUNT 67 (Tübingen: Mohr Siebeck, 1993), 326–429 (399–402).

Fathers,[7] although these writings focus on the exalted Christ, not on the incarnate one or on his earthly ministry. In earlier New Testament writings, things are somewhat more difficult. In Hebrews 1:8, the predication "God" comes only from a biblical quotation (Ps 45:7 LXX), and in the disputed passage in Romans 9:5[8] the predication is taken from a doxology where it most likely referred to the one God of Israel. Accordingly, these two writings cannot be counted as testimony for a direct reference to Jesus as "God."

Although recent scholarship has increasingly supposed that a "high Christology"—which considered Jesus to be a superhuman or a divine being—developed from a Jewish paradigm quite early within the Jesus movement,[9] it is obvious that it took a certain amount of time

[7] See 2 Clement (2 Clem. 1.1), the letters of Ignatius (*Eph.* inscr; 1.1; 7.2; 18.2; 19.3; *Trall.* 7.1; *Rom.* 3.3; *Smyrn.* 10.1; *Pol.* 8.3), and the letter of Polycarp (*Phil.* 12.2).

[8] Cf. the discussion in the commentaries, e.g., R. Jewett, *Romans*, Hermeneia (Minneapolis: Fortress, 2007), 567–69. In any case, Paul can mention Christ as Lord in one line with (and on the same level as) God in the confession formula of 1 Cor 8:6, where the *Shema Yisrael* is "unfolded" and applied to God and Christ in a "binitarian" manner; cf. Otfried Hofius, "'Einer ist Gott—Einer ist Herr': Erwägungen zu Struktur und Aussage des Bekenntnisses 1 Kor 8,6," in *Paulusstudien 2*, WUNT 143 (Tübingen: Mohr Siebeck, 2002), 167–80.

[9] See the comprehensive study by Larry W. Hurtado, *Lord Jesus Christ: Devotion to Jesus in Earliest Christianity* (Grand Rapids: Eerdmans, 2003); see further the important studies on Christology by Martin Hengel, collected in idem, *Studien zur Christologie: Kleine Schriften IV*, ed. Claus-Jürgen Thornton, WUNT 201 (Tübingen: Mohr Siebeck, 2006); and partly in English in Martin Hengel, *Studies in Early Christology* (Edinburgh: T&T Clark, 1995). See also the important contributions by William Horbury, *Jewish Messianism and the Cult of Christ* (London: SCM Press, 1998); idem, "Jewish Messianism and Early Christology," in *Contours of Christology in the New Testament*, ed. Richard N. Longenecker (Grand Rapids: Eerdmans, 2005), 3–24; idem, "Jüdische Wurzeln der Christologie," *Early Christianity* 2 (2011): 5–21; Carey C. Newman, *Paul's Glory Christology: Tradition and Rhetoric*, NovTSup 69 (Leiden: Brill, 1992); Richard Bauckham, *God Crucified: Monotheism and Christology in the New Testament* (Carlisle: Paternoster, 1998); Andrew Chester, *Messiah and Exaltation: Jewish Messianic and Visionary Traditions and New Testament Christology*, WUNT 207 (Tübingen: Mohr, 2007). For a more recent overview, see Andrew Chester, "High Christology—Whence, When and Why?" *Early Christianity* 2 (2011): 22–50; and Jörg Frey, "Eine neue religionsgeschichtliche Perspektive: Larry W. Hurtados *Lord Jesus Christ* und die Herausbildung der frühen Christologie," in *Reflections on Early Christian History and Religion—Erwägungen zur frühchristlichen Religionsgeschichte*, ed. Cilliers Breytenbach and Jörg Frey, AJEC 81 (Leiden: Brill 2012), 117–68.

until Jesus followers would dare speak about Jesus explicitly as "God." Mark's Gospel already expresses Jesus' divine dignity and power in narrative terms (e.g., Mark 4:36-41) and presents a prologue or rather a "prelude in heaven" (1:2-3)[10] in which God, or at least the Scriptures, address Jesus as the Lord, that is, the biblical name of God is applied to him. Furthermore, since this predication is clearly located before his earthly appearance and his baptism in the river Jordan, one might even consider it to be an expression of the idea of Jesus' preexistence.[11] In any case, the passage demonstrates that Mark's Christology is far from being "low": Jesus is not simply "adopted" to be God's Son in his baptism. Instead, he is already addressed as "the Lord" before his earthly appearance, and this scriptural voice "foreshadows the heavenly voice that only he hears in 1:11."[12] Nevertheless, Mark still avoids the predicate θεός with regard to Jesus, as do Luke and Matthew, who both present Jesus as the Son of God and as the eschatological judge to whom all power "is given" (Matt 28:18). And yet, they still limit the use of the term θεός to the one God of Israel.

With John, this has changed. Jesus—not only the preexistent one or the divine Logos, but also the incarnate, crucified, and risen one—is called the μονογενής, the Son, and even explicitly θεός (John 1:18;

[10] Thus the title of Hans-Josef Klauck, *Vorspiel im Himmel? Erzähltechnik und Theologie im Markusprolog*, BThS 32 (Neukirchen-Vluyn: Neukirchener, 1997), alluding to the famous heavenly prologue in Johann Wolfgang von Goethe's *Faust*.

[11] Thus Simon J. Gathercole, *The Pre-existent Son: Recovering the Christologies of Matthew, Mark, and Luke* (Grand Rapids: Eerdmans, 2006), 249–52; cf., even more boldly, Otfried Hofius, "Jesu Zuspruch der Sündenvergebung: Exegetische Erwagungen zu Mk 2,5b," in idem, *Neutestamentliche Studien*, WUNT 132 (Tübingen: Mohr Siebeck, 2000), 38–56 (54–55): "Als höchst bedeutsam erweist sich . . . der Charakter des in V. 2 zitierten Gottesspruchs: Wie das zweimalige σου anzeigt, ist der Prophet Zeuge eines Wortes geworden, das Gott—in der himmlischen Welt—in direkter Anrede an ein Gegenüber gerichtet hat. Dieses Gegenüber ist der 'Sohn,' dessen reale und personale Praexistenz mithin in V. 2b in aller Deutlichkeit ausgesagt wird." Cf., however, the more cautious interpretation in Klauck, *Vorspiel im Himmel?* 106–8; and Adela Yarbro Collins, *Mark: A Commentary*, Hermeneia (Minneapolis: Fortress, 2007), 135–6.

[12] Thus Joel Marcus, *Mark 1–8*, AB 27 (New York: Doubleday, 2000), 147. Cf. also Jörg Frey, "How Could Mark and John Do without Infancy Stories? Jesus' Humanity and His Divine Origins in Mark and John," in *Infancy Gospels: Story and Identity*, ed. Claire Clivaz et al., WUNT 281 (Tübingen: Mohr Siebeck, 2011), 189–215 (199–202).

20:28).[13] It is of great importance that Thomas confesses Jesus' divinity just when he sees the marks of the nails on Jesus' hands, that is to say, in view of Jesus being the incarnate and crucified one.[14] Jesus' divinity is expressed not merely in regard to his premundane or exalted postmundane status, but also in regard to his bodily appearance, even in view of the marks of his death on the cross.[15] In light of the marked expression of high Christology in John, it is obvious that the conception of Christ, particularly that of Christ during his earthly ministry, has undergone a change with respect to the unfolding of early Christology.

Of course, this poses hermeneutical and theological questions. Who was, and who is, Christ "really"? Does the creed claim that he is something different from what he was? And is the concept of development appropriate for describing those issues? The theological legacy of such a reconstruction has been disputed, with conservatives of all denominations demanding that we should just follow the testimony of the Gospels that Jesus was indeed God.[16] But where such a claim is made, there is the danger of some hermeneutical pitfalls. First of all, the differences between the language and terms used in the various writings cannot be denied. In historical perspective, we cannot do without a certain idea of development, at least

[13] In John 1:18, the reading θεός should be preferred as *lectio difficilior* over against the reading υἱός.

[14] On the interpretation of the Thomas episode, cf. Jörg Frey, "Die *theologia crucifixi* des Johannesevangeliums," in *Kreuzestheologie im Neuen Testament,* ed. Andreas Dettwiler and Jean Zumstein, WUNT 151 (Tübingen: Mohr Siebeck, 2002), 169–238 (231–36); see also idem, *Glory of the Crucified One*, 227–35.

[15] This is also valid if the marks of the nails in John 20:19-23, 25-27 can be interpreted as scars, as Candida R. Moss ("The Marks of the Nails: Scars, Wounds and the Resurrection of Jesus in John," *Early Christianity* 8 [2017]: 48–68) has recently argued.

[16] Thus, most prominently, Joseph Ratzinger (Pope Benedict XVI), *Jesus of Nazareth*, vol. 1: *From the Baptism in the Jordan to the Transfiguration,* (New York: Doubleday, 2007) where, in spite of the acceptance of historical research, a dogmatic approach based on the creed of the early church is chosen. In the introductory preface, Ratzinger explains that he wants to see "the Jesus of the Gospels" (without further differentiation) "as the real, historical Jesus in the strict sense of the word" (xxii). Even if the criticism of the exegetical search for "the Historical Jesus" is conceded, Ratzinger cannot escape the problem that his approach papers over the differences and tensions between the early Christian traditions and ultimately arrives at a "spiritualizing" view that can only insufficiently include the true humanity of Jesus. For criticism, see Jörg Frey, "Der Christus der Evangelien als der 'historische Jesus': Zum Jesus-Buch des Papstes," in *Der Papst aus Bayern: Protestantische Wahrnehmungen*, ed. Werner Thiede (Leipzig: Evangelische Verlagsanstalt, 2010), 111–29.

with regard to the language used and the predicates attributed to Jesus. Of course, the dogmatic issue of who Jesus "really was" cannot be decided from historical reconstruction. In historical perspective, we can merely observe what the various testimonies and authors actually confess about Jesus or which claims are implied in the words that can be reasonably attributed to the earthly Jesus. And even if we are not too pessimistic about those sayings and concede that there are quite high claims about the eschatological function and importance of his person,[17] historical research cannot decide whether these claims are actually true. It would be too naive to say that the early church transformed a mere human being into a divine being, or reversely to accuse historians of having reduced the Son of God to a merely human figure. But the hermeneutical circle in these issues is unavoidable, and this is quite visible in the scholarly debate. While one group of scholars tries to distance the divine being of the Christian creed as much as possible from the Jesus of history, the Jewish prophet, or wisdom teacher,[18] others instead prefer a Jesus informing his disciples about his divinity from the very beginning, at best on Easter day,[19] in order to avoid the purportedly "heretical" idea of a historical "development." However, considering that we only deal with various linguistic testimonies that are embedded in a history of memory, we do not need to decide for either of those extreme views but can concede that there was at least a *linguistic* development with an increasing willingness to attribute a divine status to Jesus, and such a willingness is most distinctively visible in John.

The tension between historical and dogmatic reasoning only mirrors the other tension which is in the Johannine text: the paradox between

[17] Cf. Jörg Frey, "Continuity and Discontinuity between 'Jesus' and 'Christ': The Possibilities of an Implicit Christology," *RCT* 36, no. 1 (2011): 69–98. See also the important studies by Martin Hengel, "Jesus, the Messiah of Israel," in *Studies in Early Christology*, 1–72; idem, "Jesus as Messianic Teacher of Wisdom and the Beginnings of Christology," in *Studies in Early Christology*, 73–118. For a comprehensive discussion, cf. the monograph based on Martin Hengel's 1992 Shaffer Lectures, Martin Hengel and Anna Maria Schwemer, *Jesus und das Judentum*, vol. 1 of *Geschichte des frühen Christentums* (Tübingen: Mohr Siebeck, 2007).

[18] Thus the tradition of liberal theology, as famously represented by Adolf von Harnack and others. In more recent times, this tradition has been represented by, e.g., Maurice Casey in his book *From Jewish Prophet to Gentile God* (Louisville: Westminster John Knox, 1992).

[19] Thus, e.g., Bauckham, *God Crucified*; and, in a more dogmatic manner, Otfried Hofius, "Jesu Leben, Tod und Auferstehung nach dem Zeugnis des Neuen Testaments," in idem, *Neutestamentliche Studien*, WUNT 132 (Tübingen: Mohr Siebeck, 2000), 3–18 (3).

Jesus' true, uncontested humanity[20] and the divine authority attributed to him throughout the Gospel. In John, *Christology is expressed as theology*, while on the other hand, *theology is inseparably linked with Christology*. That is, just as the invisible God is exclusively disclosed in his only image, the earthly figure of Jesus of Nazareth (1:18) in and through whom the Father can be seen (14:7, 9), so also the human figure of Jesus of Nazareth, whose father and mother are well known (6:42), is presented as "God" from the beginning of the Gospel (the introductory prologue of 1:1f., 18) until the end of the narrative (the pivotal confession of Thomas: "My Lord and my God!," 20:28).

2. The Twofold Challenge of the View of Jesus' Divinity

We can hardly imagine the challenge of such a claim, to regard as divine a human being who lived and acted in the "flesh" (cf. John 1:14; see also 1 John 2:22; 4:2) and even died the death of an accursed criminal by means of Roman crucifixion.[21] While the idealistic reading of the Gospel, from Ferdinand Christian Baur to Ernst Käsemann, undervalued and downplayed the relevance of Jesus' real humanity in John, these aspects are consistently retained:[22] He is the Word that became "flesh" and did not merely appear in an epiphany,[23] he is a Jew (4:9), has a father and a mother (6:41), and acts within a precisely defined region, at named places, and at a particular time. He even grows tired and thirsty (4:6-7), weeps (11:35), has zeal (11:33, 38; cf. 2:17), and ultimately dies a human death, one that is far from being a "noble" death[24] but is

[20] Cf. Marianne Meye Thompson, *The Humanity of Jesus in the Fourth Gospel* (Philadelphia: Fortress, 1988). See also Jörg Frey, *Glory of the Crucified One,* 204–14.

[21] On crucifixion as the most shameful death in antiquity, cf. M. Hengel, *Crucifixion: In the Ancient World and the Folly of the Message of the Cross*, trans. John Bowden (Philadelphia: Fortress, 1977). Cf. more recently John Granger Cook, *Crucifixion in the Mediterranean World*, WUNT 327 (Tübingen: Mohr Siebeck, 2014); and David W. Chapman and Eckhard J. Schnabel, *The Trial and Crucifixion of Jesus: Texts and Commentary,* WUNT 344 (Tübingen: Mohr Siebeck, 2015).

[22] Cf. Frey, *Glory of the Crucified One,* 199–214.

[23] Cf. Frey, *Glory of the Crucified One,* 268–72.

[24] On that category, cf. *Martyrdom and Noble Death: Selected Texts from Graeco-Roman, Jewish and Christian Antiquity,* ed. Jan Willem van Henten and Friedrich

instead a shameful death: the crucified one is mocked and beaten by the soldiers (19:1-3) and is exposed by having his last shirt stripped off.[25] Jesus' divinity is not accomplished by a reduction of his humanity. The paradox of the author's portrayal of Jesus' true human flesh, emotion, suffering, and death, while at the same time depicting him in divine colors and even calling him "God," constitutes the strongest theological challenge of the Fourth Gospel.

This presentation of not only the exalted but also the incarnate, earthly Jesus as "God" meant a twofold challenge for John's contemporaries, Greco-Roman and Jewish readers alike.

a) Within a Greco-Roman pattern of thought, it was commonly presupposed that gods are immortal, and that a person who has really died cannot be truly considered a god. Thus, if the Logos and also the incarnate Jesus truly was a heavenly, divine being, Greco-Roman readers had immense difficulties in understanding his true humanity, his human nature, his human emotions, suffering, or, especially, death. Interpreters in the second century developed a large variety of strategies to negotiate those problems. Some inserted a distinction between the truly divine Logos and the one that actually created or shaped the material world,[26] or distinguished between a heavenly Christ who stayed in

---

Avemarie (London: Routledge, 2002). Although the features of human suffering do recede in comparison with the other Gospels, this is not due to an interest in a "euphemistic" narrative but to strong theological reasons. The category of "noble death" is ultimately insufficient for interpreting the death of Jesus; cf. Frey, *Glory of the Crucified One*, 177–81.

[25] See Frey, *Glory of the Crucified One*, 206–12.

[26] Thus, e.g., Heracleon, in his exposition of John 1:3 (frg. 1; Origen, *Comm. Jo.* 2.14.100–103), claims that δι' αὐτοῦ is not necessarily to be understood in the sense that the Logos himself created (that is, that God created the world through the Logos), but could also be read in the sense that another created through the power of the Logos: αὐτοῦ ἐργοῦτος ἕτερος ἐποίει. In such a reading, the divine Logos only gave reason to another one, possibly a demiurge, to create the cosmos. This means that the physical cosmos is not a creation of the Logos himself but of another being, and that the divine Logos is not responsible for the material world as it is. Likewise, Ptolemaios, in his *Letter to Flora* (cited by Epiphanius, *Pan.* 33.3–7), inserts a distinction between the perfect God who is still said to be the creator and a "mediator" different from him who carried out the actual work of creation. On these interpretations, cf. Jörg Frey, "The Johannine Prologue and the References to the Creation of the World in Its Second Century Receptions," in *Les judaïsmes dans tous leurs états aux Ier—IIIe siècles (Les Judéens des synagogues,*

heaven and another one who appeared on earth.[27] Others felt the need to reconsider the nature of Jesus, speculating about the material quality of his body[28] or whether he actually left footprints on the ground. Most scandalous for the church were interpretations according to which the divine power departed from the human Jesus prior to crucifixion.[29] All these readings, somewhat imprecisely labeled as "docetic,"[30] only point to the challenge that the paradox of the "incarnation" and the death of

les chrétiens et les rabbins): Actes du colloque de Lausanne 12–14 décembre 2012, ed. C. Clivaz, S. C. Mimouni, B. Pouderon, Judaïsme ancien et origines du christianisme 5 (Turnhout: Brepols, 2015), 221–44; see also Titus Nagel, *Die Rezeption des Johannesevangeliums im 2. Jahrhundert: Studien zur vorirenäischen Aneignung und Auslegung des vierten Evangeliums in christlicher und christlich-gnostischer Literatur,* ABG 2 (Leipzig: Evangelische Verlagsanstalt, 2000), 294–99; and Tuomas Rasimus, "Ptolemaeus and the Prologue's Valentinian Exegesis," in *The Legacy of John: Second-Century Reception of the Fourth Gospel,* ed. Rasimus, NovTSup 132 (Leiden: Brill, 2010), 145–72 (146–58).

[27] Thus Theodotus, in the fragments presented by Clement of Alexandria (*Exc.* 7.3; cf. Frey, "The Johannine Prologue," 238; and Titus Nagel, *Die Rezeption des Johannesevangeliums,* 341–57), distinguishes between a heavenly Christ who stays in the bosom of the Father (= the Monogenes, John 1:18) and another one, who appeared on earth (ὀφθείς), about whom John 1:14 only says "as/like the Monogenes" (ὡς μονογενοῦς).

[28] Thus, Irenaeus reports that Saturninus conceived of the Savior as incorporeal and only seemingly a human (*Haer* 1.24.2: "Salvatorem autem innatum demonstravit et incorporalem, et sine figura, putative autem visum hominem . . ."), and, according to Ps.-Tertullian (*Haer.* 6.1), Cerdo taught that Christ came not in the substance of flesh but only in appearance, and that he had not really died or really been born of a virgin. According to the Acts of John, John, sometimes reclining at Jesus' breast (cf. John 13:23), perceived his breast sometimes smooth and tender, sometimes hard as stone (Acts John 89), and as he tried to see him "as he was," he observed that his eyes were never closed. Likewise, Jesus' body was "sometimes . . . a material and solid body; and at other times again . . . the substance was immaterial and bodiless and as if it were not existing at all" (93). The Acts of John can even say that Jesus' body did not leave any footprints in the soil (93). On these interpretations, see Jörg Frey, "'Docetic-like' Christologies and the Polymorphy of Christ: A Plea for Further Consideration of Diversity in the Discussion of 'Docetism,'" in *Docetism in the Early Church: The Quest for an Elusive Phenomenon,* ed. Joseph Verheyden et al., WUNT 402 (Tübingen: Mohr Siebeck, 2018), 27–49 (41, 47–48).

[29] Thus, according to Irenaeus, Cerinthus (*Haer.* 1.26.1) and Carpocrates (*Haer.* 1.25.2).

[30] The category was shaped only from a dogmatic (chalcedonic) perspective when Ferdinand Christian Baur introduced it into the discourse of early Christian history, so caution and more differentiation is needed; cf. Frey, "'Docetic-like' Christologies," 27–49 (on the problem of definition, see in particular 30–33).

a divine being necessarily meant for most of the Greco-Roman (and in particular Platonic) readers of John. And although we cannot prove that it was already necessary for the evangelist to react to some kind of "docetism,"[31] the wording in John 1:14 suggests that he was well aware of the challenge implied in the idea that the truly divine, eternal Word did not merely appear in an epiphany, as Greek gods could appear among humans for a certain limited time, but that he underwent a change when entering humanity in the human figure of Jesus, who died on the cross. But this is the implication of σὰρξ ἐγένετο ("became flesh"): The scholarly attempts to explain this remarkable phrase from a Greco-Roman context of divine epiphanies[32] is insufficient. The context of the entire Gospel story suggests that σὰρξ ἐγένετο implies the full humanity of Jesus, including mortality and the way toward the cross.

The abstract idea of "incarnation" is only slightly illustrated by the adoption of the biblical concept of God's "dwelling" among his people: "The word became flesh *and dwelled among us*" (John 1:14ab).[33] But as this "tabernacling" of the Logos is considered not only a temporal epiphany but a permanent presence that remains even in the passion and death of Jesus,[34] the challenge of God's eschatological presence in a mortal human being is by no means removed.

[31] Scholars have suggested that the opponents rejected in the Johannine Epistles (and perhaps also in the Gospel) were "docetists"; cf. Udo Schnelle, *Antidocetic Christology in the Gospel of John: An Investigation of the Place of the Fourth Gospel in the Johannine School*, trans. Linda M. Maloney (Minneapolis: Fortress, 1992), but this is just a conjecture from the Epistles (and the epistles of Ignatius), with no further evidence. On the problems, see Jörg Frey, "Die johanneische Theologie zwischen 'Doketismus' und 'Antidoketismus': Auseinandersetzungen und Trennungsprozesse im Hintergrund der johanneischen Schriften und ihrer Rezeption," in *Erzählung und Briefe im johanneischen Kreis*, ed. Uta Poplutz and Jörg Frey, WUNT 2/420 (Tübingen: Mohr Siebeck, 2016), 129–56.

[32] Cf. Frey, *Glory of the Crucified One*, 268–72.

[33] Cf. Frey, *Glory of the Crucified One*, 272–84; see also idem, "God's Dwelling on Earth: '*Shekhina*-Theology' in Revelation 21 and in the Gospel of John," in *John's Gospel and Intimations of Apocalyptic*, ed. Christopher Rowland and Catrin Williams (London: Bloomsbury T&T Clark, 2013), 79–103.

[34] This is suggested from the background of the Jewish wisdom tradition (in particular Sir 24) where Wisdom seeks and finds a place to rest, and this resting place (in Zion, or in the temple cult) is not a temporary but a permanent one. Against this plausible reconstruction of the prologue's background, Bultmann's interpretation in

b) Even more obviously, John's high Christology provided a challenge for contemporary Jewish readers. Compared with Greco-Roman thought, the biblical and Jewish tradition felt much more obliged to observe the line of demarcation between gods and humans, or rather between the one God and his creatures. While in Greco-Roman tradition gods could appear on earth and humans could eventually become heroes or receive a share in the divine nature, biblical monotheism made contemporary diaspora Judaism distinctive in its exclusion of the veneration of any being apart from the one God.[35] There is no idea of a real incarnation of God the creator, nor of one of his agents, angels, archangels, Lady Wisdom, or his Logos. Nor can we presuppose that ideas about the enthronement of Moses, the patriarchs, or other eschatological agents were universally known in contemporary Judaism. Even if some texts speak about enthroned patriarchs, principal angels, or mediatorial figures and so give a clue to understanding the Jewish origins and early development of a high Christology,[36] the most widespread view about the messiah was that he is a basically human, political figure.[37] Only in a few texts do messianic or eschatological figures adopt superhuman traits.[38] In any case, the veneration of Jesus as a divine being or even his explicit categorization with the term θεός ("God") could be considered a threat to monotheism and thus rejected by the majority of contemporary Jews, not only in the land of Israel but also in the diaspora.

---

his commentary, wherein he draws the conclusion from the notion of a "tent" that the Logos' dwelling on earth was merely of a temporary character, is clearly erroneous.

35 We cannot enter a detailed discussion of biblical monotheism here; for the present purpose, cf. Larry W. Hurtado, *One God, One Lord: Early Christian Devotion and Ancient Jewish Monotheism*, 3rd ed. (London: Bloomsbury, 2015); cf. also idem, *How on Earth Did Jesus Become a God?* (Grand Rapids: Eerdmans, 2005), 111–33.

36 Most of these traditions are presented and discussed in Hurtado, *One God, One Lord*, 41–96.

37 This is prominently expressed by Trypho in Justin Martyr's *Dialogue with Trypho* (*Dial.* 49.1): πάντες ἡμεις τὸν Χριστὸν ἄνθρωπον ἐξ ἀνθρώπον προσδοκῶμεν γενήσεσθαι ("we all expect the Messiah to be born as a human from humans").

38 Thus, e.g., the messiah in the LXX version of Ps 110 (= 109 LXX) or As. Mos. 10.1–2; some texts from the Parables of Enoch (1 En. 37–71); the Melchizedek text from Qumran (11QMelch); and the so-called Self-Glorification Hymn 4Q491, etc. Those texts require a special study, which is being prepared by my doctoral student Ruben Bühner.

This reaction is also confirmed in the Fourth Gospel. John's narrative provides evidence that contemporary Jews actually considered the Johannine claims about Jesus blasphemy (John 10:33, 36; cf. Mark 14:64).[39] Jesus is accused of "making himself equal with God" (John 5:18), or claiming to be "the Son of God" (19:7), and this most probably reflects debates from the time of the community or the evangelist. Furthermore, John repeatedly narrates that "the Jews" attempt to kill Jesus when he makes claims about acting or even being in unity with the one God (5:18; 8:39; 10:39). Finally, the Jewish authorities decide to kill Jesus not because of his messianic confession (as in Mark 14:64) but because of his claim of divine authority. This is confirmed by the fact that the decision of the authorities is narrated immediately after the greatest demonstration of his divine, life-giving power, the raising of Lazarus (John 11:47-53). Their reason for demanding the death sentence from Pilate is precisely that "he has made himself God's Son" (19:7).

These claims and charges obviously come not from the time of the earthly Jesus but mirror later debates about Jesus, his status, and the christological claims about him from the time of the Johannine community and the composition of the Gospel.[40] The high christological views of the Johannine community were strictly rejected by the contemporary synagogue, and the Gospel narrative reflects this rejection.

The decisive question, however, is not whether the Gospel claims divine authority and dignity for Jesus. This is clear and all the attempts to reduce these claims exegetically for the sake of some political correctness are mistaken. The issue between the Johannine community and its Jewish contemporaries is only whether this claim is true.

[39] On blasphemy in the Judaism of the first century, see Darrell L. Bock, *Blasphemy and Exaltation in Judaism and the Final Examination of Jesus*, WUNT 2/106 (Tübingen: Mohr Siebeck, 1998), 30–112. Rabbinic statements on the accusation of blasphemy can be found also in Tobias Kriener, *"Glauben an Jesus"—ein Verstoß gegen das zweite Gebot? Die johanneische Christologie und der jüdische Vorwurf des Götzendienstes* (Neukirchen-Vluyn: Neukirchener, 2001), 7–25.

[40] In this respect, the critical view established by J. Louis Martyn, *History and Theology in the Fourth Gospel* (New York: Harper & Row, 1968; 2nd enl. ed., Nashville: Abingdon, 1979; 3rd ed., Louisville: Westminster John Knox, 2003), is correct and should not be watered down.

This is also mirrored in John's narrative. While the Jewish authorities accuse Jesus for unduly usurping divine origin and honors and therefore demand his death, the Gospel claims that he truly *is* from above, that he *is* the Son in unity with the Father (10:30), and even that he *is* God (1:1–2, 18; 20:28; cf. 1 John 5:20). But contrary to his Jewish contemporaries, the evangelist does not consider this a denial of the monotheistic confession.[41] Jesus' divine honors are not in competition with the uniqueness of the one God of Israel and the Scriptures because, according to the Johannine view, the Father has given the Son his unique authority to give life and enact judgment (John 5:22–23, 26). God's love for the Son is said to originate even before the creation of the world (17:24), and therefore John can write that the Father and the Son are "one." It should be noted that the grammatical form used for "one" is neuter, not masculine; thus the oneness of Jesus and the Father is not the oneness of two gods but still maintains a form of biblical monotheism that Larry Hurtado has aptly called "binitarian." Within this tight relationship between the Father and the Son, there is, of course, a slight element of subordination, as the relationship between the Father and the Son cannot be reversed. The Father is indeed greater than Jesus (14:28).[42] But this does not mean that Jesus is only divine or "god-like," as exegetes have claimed[43] in order to avoid an offense against Judaism. When John uses θεός as a designation for Jesus, there is no "reduction" in meaning; in 1 John 5:20, he is even called "the true God," just as the Father is called "the true God" in John 17:3.[44] So, the evangelist and his

[41] Cf. also Thomas Söding, "'Ich und der Vater sind eins' (Joh 10,30): Die johanneische Christologie vor dem Anspruch des Hauptgebotes (Dtn 6.4f)," *ZNW* 93 (2002): 177–99.

[42] Cf. the article by Charles K. Barrett, "'The Father Is Greater than I' (John 14.28): Subordinationist Christology in the New Testament," in idem, *Essays on John* (Philadelphia: Westminster, 1982), 19–36.

[43] See the discussion in Ernst Haenchen, *Johannesevangelium*, ed. Ulrich Busse (Tübingen: Mohr, 1980), 116–18; cf. the ET: idem, *A Commentary on the Gospel of John*, trans. R. W. Funk, Hermeneia (Philadelphia: Fortress, 1984). The strongest reduction of the meaning, due to a distinctive interest in the Jewish–Christian dialogue, is advocated in the commentary by Klaus Wengst, *Das Johannesevangelium*, 2 vols., THKNT 4 (Stuttgart: Kohlhammer, 2000/2001), 46–48.

[44] This is not a conflation between the Logos and God, as John also avoids any conflation between the Father and the Son. "To call the Word 'God' is not to collapse

community would respond to the accusation of unduly claiming divine honors for a mere human with the simple point that he *is* God, and that the Father has bestowed divine authority on him.

We can, therefore, imagine that for the majority of contemporary Jews, including those in the diaspora, the Johannine community and its leaders had abandoned true monotheism and advocated for a heresy, a teaching about—as later authors would call it—"two powers in heaven."[45] Thus, it is quite conceivable that the diaspora synagogue was no longer willing to consider such "heretics" as Jews, even if some of them had Jewish origins and even if the whole community felt its beliefs were still based on the Scriptures. There is no need to ascribe such a rejection to a decision of the rabbis in Palestine, as J. Louis Martyn and others have suggested, but it is quite plausible that diaspora synagogues after 70 CE were in the position to reject such a deviant group from their assemblies, which could bring Jesus followers into considerable legal troubles.[46] Such troubles may be reflected in John's hints at an exclusion from the synagogue that might even cause the death of some Jesus followers (John 16:2-3). We cannot develop these

---

the distinction between 'the Word' and 'God,' as the subsequent distinction between 'Father' and 'Son' makes clear; it is, rather, to use the highest degree of qualitative predication regarding the subject, the Word: the Word has the quality, the reality, even the identity of God" (Marianne Meye Thompson, *John: A Commentary*, NTL [Louisville: Westminster John Knox, 2015], 29).

[45] Cf. the title of the important monograph on rabbinic responses to Christianity and Gnosticism: Alan F. Segal, *Two Powers in Heaven: Early Rabbinic Reports about Christianity and Gnosticism* (Waco: Baylor University Press, 2012 [1977]).

[46] On the factors that could lead to the so-called parting of the ways, cf. Frey, *Glory of the Crucified One,* 66–67; idem, "Temple and Identity in Early Christianity and in the Johannine Community: Reflections on the 'Parting of the Ways'," in *Was 70 CE a Watershed in Jewish History? On Jews and Judaism before and after the Destruction of the Second Temple*, ed. Daniel R. Schwartz and Zeev Weiss, AJEC 78 (Leiden: Brill, 2012), 447–507; idem, "Towards Reconfiguring Our Views on the 'Parting of the Ways': Ephesus as a Test Case," in *John and Judaism: A Contested Relationship in Context*, ed. R. Alan Culpepper and Paul N. Anderson, RBS (Atlanta: SBL, 2017), 221–30. In my view, the political factors, after the destruction of the Second Temple and the Roman imposition of the *fiscus Iudaicus*, a tax to be paid by all Jews, should not be neglected in their effect of triggering a decision about who belonged to the synagogue or the Jewish "ethnos," and who did not. Those factors were possibly more decisive than strictly theological or doctrinal ones.

aspects further here, but it is clear that while contemporary Jews could accuse Johannine Jesus followers of blasphemy, the Johannine community was convinced that the true insight into Jesus' divine dignity was not an unauthorized divinization of a human but part of the teaching received from the Spirit in post-Easter times (16:13-15).

3. Johannine High Christology and the "Lower Predications"

The statements of high Christology—composed of the predications θεός, "the Son," "the Logos," and also Jesus' ἐγώ εἰμι sayings—are the key to the Christology of the Gospel. These elements provide the frame that determines the understanding of the whole and from which all the other christological predications have to be interpreted.

This is an important methodological decision: all the scholarly attempts to interpret Johannine Christology historically and in its theological substance from one of the lower christological predications, such as Messiah,[47] prophet,[48] or the motif of the messenger,[49] cannot do justice to the Johannine concept. The scholarly confidence that we might be able to historically reconstruct an early Johannine (and still basically Jewish) "sending," prophet, or Messiah Christology[50] has been decisively

[47] Thus Georg Richter, *Studien zum Johannesevangelium*, ed. Josef Hainz, BU 13 (Regensburg: Pustet, 1977), who suggests a Jewish Christian *Grundschrift* in which the community gives an apologetic defense of Jesus' Messiahship after the exclusion of its Jewish members from the synagogue. Jesus is a prophet like Moses (according to Deut 18:15-16), a human, selected from his people to be the Messiah, but not from a divine origin (cf. idem, *Studien*, 355). Thus, in the closure of the suggested *Grundschrift* (John 20:30-31a), the title "Son of God" is still missing. This is thought to be only an addition by the evangelist. For further criticism, cf. Frey, *Die johanneische Eschatologie*, vol. 1: *Ihre Probleme im Spiegel der Forschung seit Reimarus*, WUNT 97 (Tübingen: Mohr Siebeck, 1997), 287–94.

[48] Cf. also Wayne A. Meeks, *The Prophet-King: Moses Traditions and the Johannine Christology*, NovTSup 14 (Leiden: Brill, 1967); and Peder Borgen, *Bread from Heaven: An Exegetical Study of the Conception of Manna in the Gospel of John and the Writings of Philo*, NovTSup 10 (Leiden: Brill, 1965).

[49] Cf. Jan-Adolf Bühner, *Der Gesandte und sein Weg im 4. Evangelium: Die kultur- und religionsgeschichtlichen Grundlagen der johanneischen Sendungschristologie sowie ihre theologiegeschichtliche Entwicklung*, WUNT 2/2 (Tübingen: Mohr, 1977).

[50] As in the authors mentioned in the two previous footnotes, specifically Bühner and Meeks.

questioned. Thus, there is no real possibility to get to an earlier Johannine source or layer, a Jewish Christian *Grundschrift*[51] or a "Gospel of Signs,"[52] by just subtracting the traits of John's high Christology. With the questioning and the collapse of those theories of various pre-Johannine (or early Johannine) sources, layers, or editions of the Gospel,[53] the widely established patterns of community development[54] have lost their textual basis. Therefore, John's Christology can no longer be explained from such an alleged development from an earlier Johannine lower level to the high level of the evangelist (or even further on, to the redactional level, or the Epistles). Rather, it should be interpreted within the given context, and within the framework of the θεός predication.

That is not to say that the other christological titles and predications are not unimportant. They show that the evangelist is aware of a wide variety of messianic traditions which he adopts in parts of his narrative and integrates into his comprehensive high Christology. Already the opening of the narrative after the prologue provides a considerable range of christological predications attributed to Jesus: "the stronger one" (1:26-27), the Lamb of God (v. 29), the one who baptizes in the Spirit (v. 33), God's chosen one (v. 34),[55] the Messiah (v. 41), the

[51] Thus Richter, *Studien zum Johannesevangelium*.

[52] Thus the suggestion by Robert T. Fortna, *The Gospel of Signs: A Reconstruction of the Narrative Source Underlying the Fourth Gospel*, SNTSMS (Cambridge: Cambridge University Press, 1970); idem, *The Fourth Gospel and Its Predecessor* (Edinburgh: T&T Clark, 1988); and also Urban C. von Wahlde, *The Earliest Version of John's Gospel: Recovering the Gospel of Signs* (Wilmington, Del.: Michael Glazier, 1989).

[53] The idea of two successive editions of the Gospel, influentially suggested by Raymond E. Brown (*The Gospel according to John*, AB 29 [New York: Doubleday, 1966], 1:xxxv–xxxvi) has been adopted by numerous North American scholars, including Robert T. Fortna. It has recently been developed into a very detailed three-stage pattern in the commentary by Urban C. von Wahlde, *The Gospel and Letters of John*, 3 vols. (Grand Rapids: Eerdmans, 2010). There, von Wahlde distinguishes verse by verse and word by word between a first, a second, and ultimately a third edition of John (see *Gospel and Letters of John*, 1:150–54), but these detailed suggestions are hypothetical and should be considered to be a learned kind of "science fiction."

[54] Cf. Martyn, *History and Theology*; Raymond E. Brown, *The Community of the Beloved Disciple: The Loves and Hates of an Individual Church in New Testament Times* (New York: Paulist Press, 1979). See above, pp. 4–8.

[55] In my view the reading ἐκλεκτὸς θεοῦ is the *lectio difficilior* over against "Son of God."

king of Israel (v. 49), the Son of God (v. 49), and the Son of Man (v. 51). From the beginning of the narrative, Jesus is linked with almost all the known christological predications, and when the "true Israelite" Nathanael calls him "Son of God" and "king of Israel" (1:49), Jesus obviously is presented as the Messiah of Israel who is to come according to contemporary Jewish expectation. There is no messianic secret in John, but Jesus' dignity is openly declared from the very beginning, revealed in his acts or "signs" (2:11), and confessed by his followers throughout the Gospel, from Nathanael (1:49) to Thomas (20:28).

Moreover, the readers are already informed from the prologue about Jesus' divine identity. This enables them to draw on a deeper "knowledge" than we can presuppose for the various characters (e.g., disciples and opponents) within the Johannine narrative. According to the prologue, Jesus is the eternal Logos who is God (1:1, 18), the one in whom the divine glory is present (v. 14), and the only-begotten one (vv. 14, 18) who makes known the invisible Father (v. 18). From here, readers can even perceive whether the characters within the text of the Gospel narrative come close to the insights presented in the prologue, whether they still stay behind that knowledge or even stumble about with inappropriate expectations. This technique, the interplay between the knowledge of the readers and the views uttered by the narrative figures, is an important factor for the readers' perception of "meaning" and, thus, for the communication of meaning throughout the narrative.

Before Jesus' first appearance, John (the Baptist) rejects the most common messianic categories of messiah, Elijah, or "the prophet," and with his triple "I am not" negation (οὐκ εἰμί, 1:20–21),[56] he subtly prepares for Jesus' "I am" (ἐγώ εἰμι), which becomes so characteristic for Jesus' self-revelation in John's Gospel. Jesus truly is what the Baptizer denies himself to be, and, of course, he is much more.

But the Baptizer's negative testimony also shows that John indeed adopts and utilizes the whole range of contemporary Jewish messianic expectations:[57] the royal Davidic messiah, the prophetic figure of the returning Elijah, and the eschatological figure of "the prophet" like

[56] The third instance is shortened to a simple "no."

[57] See Richard Bauckham, "Messianism according to the Gospel of John," in *Challenging Perspectives on the Gospel of John*, ed. J. Lierman, WUNT 2/219 (Tübingen:

Moses as announced in the Torah (Deut 18:15-18). In his rejection of any proper messianic function, John the Baptist, as depicted in John's Gospel, points to another one who is to come, namely, Jesus. With the presentation of the three diverse lines of messianic expectation, the author of the Fourth Gospel obviously wants to address the totality of contemporary Jewish expectations, which Jesus is claimed to fulfill and even surpass in his divine authority.

3.1 Elijah

This is quite clear for the expectation of the return of the prophet *Elijah*, which is mentioned in numerous Jewish texts that are based on Malachi 4:5-6 (= 3:23-24 LXX) and the earlier account of Elijah's rapture (2 Kgs 2).[58] In contrast with the Synoptic Gospels, neither John the Baptist (Mark 9:11-13; Matt 11:14; 17:10-12) nor Jesus is positively linked with the expectation of the coming Elijah. Instead, the Baptist openly rejects such an identification, and quite appropriately. John's portrayal of the Baptist is not shaped according to prophetic traits but is thoroughly changed from the image of a prophet of doom and repentance to that of a first witness to Jesus' identity and saving function.

3.2 The Prophet

Things are more complicated with the second predication rejected by the Baptizer, the figure of *the prophet*. In John 1:21, the predication probably

Mohr Siebeck, 2006), 34–68, who rightly demonstrates that John draws on Palestinian Jewish traditions (34–35).

[58] This expectation prominently stands at the end of the Hebrew canon of the prophets. Postbiblical texts that adopt the expectation are the praise of the fathers in Ben Sira (Sir 48:10-11); Ps.-Philo's Liber antiquitatum biblicarum (48.1); a small exegetical fragment from Qumran (4Q558) where Mal 3:23 is quoted; and also the Targumim and rabbinic texts. In 4Q521 2 III, 2, the conversion of the fathers toward their sons (Mal 3:24a) is mentioned. Cf. also Justin, *Dial.* 8.4 and 49.1. On the reception of Elijah in the NT, see the thorough monograph by Markus Öhler, *Elia im Neuen Testament: Untersuchungen zur Bedeutung des alttestamentlichen Propheten im frühen Christentum*, BZNW 88 (Berlin: de Gruyter, 1997); concerning the Jewish expectation, cf. in particular pp. 16–22; cf. also Bauckham, "Messianism according to the Gospel of John," 36–37.

refers to the expectation of an eschatological figure, developed from Deuteronomy 18:15-18,[59] and such an identity is appropriately denied by the Baptizer. But Jesus himself is actually called a prophet in several passages of the Gospel. The Samaritan woman calls the Judean stranger "a prophet" when he talks to her about her life and situation (John 4:19), and so she asks him for religious instruction. But in the same context, the term is later excelled by "the Messiah" (4:25-26, 29) and "the Savior of the world" (4:42), so that it is clear that Jesus' function as a prophet is only a step on the way toward his more ample revelation to the woman and her village. Similarly, after the healing of the man born blind, the initial confession "he is a prophet" (9:17) is later outperformed by "he is from God" (v. 39) and by the title "Son of Man" (vv. 35-37). After the feeding of the multitude, when the Galileans say "that this must be the prophet who is to come into the world" (6:14), they seek to make him their king. However, their idea is immediately disqualified. Instead, Jesus disappears to a mountain and later accuses them of only filling their belly and not really seeing the sign (v. 26). So, the identification of Jesus with a prophet or even "the prophet" (thus referring to the expectation based on Deut 18) is presented as a part of an intra-Jewish debate (7:40, 52) but is ultimately classified as a misunderstanding or at least an insufficient view of Jesus' real identity.

3.3 The Messiah

The predication *Messiah* and its translation Χριστός is much more crucial since Ἰησοῦς Χριστός is the core confession of Jesus followers from the very beginning. Already during his earthly ministry, some of his followers considered Jesus a messianic figure (within the plurality of messianic conceptions in contemporary Judaism[60]) on account of his

[59] The expectation is attested in 1 Macc 4:41-50; 14:41 and in a number of texts from Qumran (e.g., 4QTest 5–8; 1QS IX, 11); it was also prominent in Samaritan eschatology. Another notable effect of the prophetic expectation were the so-called sign prophets (per Josephus' designation), who rose as charismatic leaders in a certain analogy to the Moses tradition, causing popular movements (cf. Bauckham, "Messianism according to the Gospel of John," 42–49). In Acts 3:22, Jesus himself is identified as a prophet like Moses.

[60] On the variety of messianic traditions in general, see John J. Collins, *The Scepter and the Star: The Messiahs of the Dead Sea Scrolls and Other Ancient Literature* (New

healings or his teaching, and after he was sentenced to death with the charge of being a messianic pretender his earliest followers in the post-Easter period consistently called him Χριστός ("the Messiah").[61] But whereas Χριστός was soon used like a part of his name without a particular consideration of the wider messianic background, John is the only Gospel author who presents the Greek transcription of the Aramaic technical term *mešiḥā* (Μεσσίας) and even translates that term for his readers first with "the Anointed One" (John 1:41) and with Χριστός (4:25). Obviously, the evangelist wants to point to the Palestinian Jewish background of the term and to the related expectations.

The predication is also clearly rejected by the Baptizer in his initial questioning in John 1:20, where the suggestion of his possible messiahship is mentioned first and most prominently. But unlike the terms Elijah or "the prophet" this title is attributed to Jesus without any constraint. While the Baptizer is "not the Christ" (1:20), Jesus *is* "the Messiah" or Christ. Thus, the first disciples claim to have found "the Messiah" (v. 41), which is then explained by the phrase "of whom Moses in the Law and also the Prophets wrote" (v. 45). Jesus actually *is* the Messiah, as is explicitly proclaimed by Jesus himself when he answers the expectation of the Samaritan woman (speaking in Judean terms)—"I know that the Messiah comes"—with an expression of self-revelation: "I am he, that is speaking to you" (4:26).

John also adopts aspects of intra-Jewish debates about the messiah, his provenance (1:47; 7:41-42), or hidden origin (7:27), the "signs"

York: Doubleday, 1995); William Horbury, *Jewish Messianism and the Cult of Christ* (London: SCM Press, 1998); and Gerbern S. Oegema, *The Anointed and His People*, JSPSup 27 (Sheffield: Sheffield Academic, 1998). On the Qumran library in particular, see Johannes Zimmermann, *Messianische Texte aus Qumran*, WUNT 2/104 (Tübingen: Mohr Siebeck, 1998).

[61] Hengel, "Jesus the Messiah of Israel," 1–7 shows that the very early pre-Pauline confession Χριστὸς ἀπέθανεν (cf. Rom 5:8; 14:9, 15; 1 Cor 8:11; 15:3; Gal 2:21) can only be explained in such a way that the death of Jesus was connected from the very beginning with his messiahship during his ministry or at least with his condemnation as a messianic pretender; cf. also idem, "Jesus as Messianic Teacher of Wisdom." See also Jörg Frey, "Der historische Jesus und der Christus der Evangelien," in *Von Jesus zur neutestamentlichen Theologie: Kleine Schriften II*, ed. Benjamin Schliesser, WUNT 368 (Tübingen: Mohr Siebeck, 2016), 29–84; idem, "Continuity and Discontinuity between 'Jesus' and 'Christ'."

he is expected to perform (7:31), or the idea that he should stay forever (12:34). In so doing, he confirms his familiarity with a wide variety of Jewish ideas and discourses. But in those debates, as presented in the Gospel, the messianic knowledge of the Jews does not lead to a positive confession; instead, Jesus' contemporaries stumble at his provenance from Nazareth (7:42), his earthly parents (6:42), and the idea of his departure (12:34). Thus, the evangelist actually casts some doubts on at least some messianic beliefs of the Jewish tradition as they are understood by Jesus' contemporaries. It is clear, therefore, that John's christological concept goes far beyond what could have been known or said about the messiah: there is some modification in the fulfillment.

In John 12:27, Martha's confession links the terms Χριστός and "Son of God," and the same connection is presented in the closure of the book in 20:31: readers should believe in Jesus as the Χριστός and the "Son of God," and the combination might imply a certain climax. Although the idea of a "son of God" is closely linked with the messiah in Jewish tradition, and the title can be derived from various biblical and early Jewish traditions,[62] the double expression suggests that the aim of the Gospel is not simply to lead Jewish readers to belief in Jesus as the Messiah but moreover to deepen their view of the Christ Jesus in terms of a "higher" christological dignity.[63] Although it is never denied that Jesus *is* the Messiah or, in other terms, the "king of Israel" (1:49) or also the "king of the Jews" (19:19–22), the Gospel leads to a deepened understanding of Jesus' identity which is expressed by "higher" christological titles than "Messiah" or "Christ."

3.4 The Sending Motif

Before turning to those "higher" predications, we have to reflect on the *sending motif*, which has often been included among the "lower"

[62] Cf. Martin Hengel, *The Son of God* (Philadelphia: Fortress, 1983).

[63] The meaning of the purpose statement in John 20:30–31 cannot be determined from the text-critically uncertain verbal form ἵνα πιστεύ[σ]ητε. Even if the aorist were original, this would not necessarily mean that the purpose of the work is to lead unbelieving readers to initial faith in Jesus (as the Messiah). The whole design of the Gospel with its explaining and interpreting remarks points to the view that the Gospel aims at deepening the faith of readers who already know the Jesus story (e.g., from Mark).

christological predications: Jesus is the one sent by the Father, and he reveals the Father who has sent him. This structure is behind some of the "synoptic" sayings in John. For example, it appears in John 13:20: "Whoever receives the one whom I send receives me; and whoever receives me receives him who sent me." In John, the motif characterizes the relationship between the Father and the Son and, analogously, the relationship between Jesus and his disciples or apostles (cf. 13:16 and 20:22-23).

In New Testament scholarship, the sending motif has long been accounted for by reference to a gnostic redeemer myth.[64] But since such an explanation is too anachronistic and since a redeemer myth of that type cannot be found before the rise of Manichaeism, scholars have pointed to the cultural and legal phenomenon of commissioning, which can be traced from the ancient Orient down to the rabbinic period.[65] According to those cultural and legal conventions, a messenger acts by the authority of the one who sent him, but in this authority he is totally dependent on the sender and also obliged to act according to his commission.

But this does not mean that the motif is to be interpreted as an element of a subordinationist "lower" Christology.[66] John does not merely point to a human messenger or prophet but to the one being sent from the Father, from the heavenly realm, into the world. Thus, Jesus represents God's divine authority, and as he testifies to what he has seen and heard above (John 3:11, 32), he is the unique revealer of the Father. Thus, the sending motif is actually an expression of Jesus' authorization, and, for this reason, it cannot be contrasted with the

[64] This is most prominently present in Rudolf Bultmann's commentary, which draws on the research by Richard Reitzenstein; cf. Jörg Frey, "Auf der Suche nach dem Kontext des vierten Evangeliums," in *Kontexte des Johannesevangeliums*, ed. Jörg Frey and Udo Schnelle, WUNT 175 (Tübingen: Mohr Siebeck, 2004), 3–46 (15–20); idem, *Die johanneische Eschatologie*, 1:133–40.

[65] Bühner, *Der Gesandte und sein Weg*; cf. Karl-Heinrich Rengstorf, "ἀποστέλλω κ.τ.λ," *TDNT* 1:398–447.

[66] Bühner considered the sending Christology the most original stratum of Johannine Christology, but he could only arrive at such a view by excluding the prologue from his investigation. When the prologue is adequately considered, the sending motif is presented in a very different framework.

"higher" christological titles but must be interpreted within the Johannine framework of the high Christology presented in the prologue and in the other high christological predications.

3.5 The Predications "Son of God" and the "Son"

The sending motif is closely connected to the use of the terms *Son of God* and the particularly Johannine usage of *the Son*. Since the notion of Jesus as God's Son is firmly embedded in the prominent sending formulas, we find that the Johannine and Pauline traditions share a common strand: God has sent "his Son" (John 3:17) or even "his only begotten Son" (1 John 4:9) for the purpose of salvation and life.[67]

In accordance with the earlier tradition in Paul and in Mark, the Fourth Gospel calls Jesus "God's Son" or "the Son of God." The term is introduced in John 1:49 together with "king of Israel" as an interpretation and heightening of the traditional title "Messiah" (1:41). This term is also similarly linked with "Messiah" in 11:27 and 20:31.[68] In 3:16 and 3:18 it is also linked with μονογενής (cf. 1:14, 18), which emphasizes the uniqueness of Jesus' Sonship: his relationship with God as his Father is strictly distinguished from the relationship of the disciples and the "children of God" (τέκνα θεοῦ) with God as their Father, which is only mediated through Jesus and his singular Sonship.[69] And, of course, Jesus' uniqueness is also claimed in contrast with the numerous other figures considered "sons of God," divine, or "saviors" within the pagan world.[70]

[67] For the background of these sending formulas in Paul and pre-Pauline theology, see Gal 4:4 and Rom 8:3.

[68] On the traditional links between messiah and son of God, see 2 Sam 7:14; Ps 2:7; 89:26–27; 4QMidrEschat[a] III, 10–12; 4 Ezra 7:28–29; 13:32, 37, 52; 14:9; and 1 En. 105:2. These passages confirm that "'the Son of God' could have been used as a messianic title" (thus Bauckham, "Messianism according to the Gospel of John," 58).

[69] The "sonship" or "daughtership" of the disciples is not mentioned in John before Easter day (John 20:17), and in this passage the clear distinction between the relation between Jesus and his Father and the relation between the disciples and God as their Father is clearly maintained. On the problems, see the monograph by Frances Back, *Gott als Vater der Jünger im Johannesevangelium*, WUNT 2/336 (Tübingen: Mohr Siebeck, 2012).

[70] Although the rivalry with the claims of the Roman Empire and pagan cults is presented more implicitly than explicitly, the contradiction between the veneration

Thus, the predication "Son of God" fundamentally distinguishes Jesus from all other humans and assigns him to the side of God. Therefore, the Jews interpret his claim to be God's Son as a crime worthy of receiving the punishment of death (John 19:7), whereas the Johannine Jesus in his bold exegesis of Psalm 82 uses the biblical address to Israel "I said, 'You are Gods!'" (Ps 82:6) to legitimize his claim as "God's Son" (John 10:36). In John, God's Son is already understood as a divine being, and therefore the belief in "the Christ, the Son of God" (20:31) is more than just the belief in Jesus as the Messiah: it is a fully valid expression of John's view of Jesus Christ as a divine being.[71]

Thus, there is no semantic difference in John between the terms "the Son of God" (John 1:49; 3:18; 5:25; 10:36; 11:4, 27; 19:7; 20:31) and the absolute and shortened form of the predication "the Son." In 3:17 "the Son" is introduced as the continuation of the term "his only-begotten Son" (3:18);[72] and in 3:35, the unique relationship between the loving Father and the Son is presented as the ultimate source of Jesus' eschatological authority. Consistently, the Son is determined by his relationship with the Father: he is loved by the Father (3:35; 5:20; 10:17; 15:9; 17:23-24, 26), both work together in unity (5:21-22), and the Father is visible in the Son (14:9) for the Son is in the Father and the Father is in the Son (10:38; 14:11).[73] In the farewell prayer, the Father-Son motif is ultimately linked with the sending motif. Here, in the concluding dialogue between the Son and the Father who has sent him and to whom the Son will now return, the unity between the two (17:21) comes to its climactic expression, and we can see how the Fourth Evangelist understands "the Son." Although he adopts "Son of God" as a traditional

---

of Jesus as Son of God and Savior and the claims of other sons of God (or *divi filii*) and so-called saviors was clearly perceptible for contemporary readers. Jesus' kingdom is, indeed, not from this world, but the loyalty to this kingship certainly relativizes or questions any further loyalty to other powers, particularly including those claiming divine honors or salvific qualities.

[71] Cf. also John 5:25; 10:36; 11:4; 19:7; 1 John 1:3, 7; 3:8, 23; 4:10, 15; 5:5, 10-11.

[72] Cf. also 1 John 5:12 and 5:13.

[73] Cf. Rudolf Schnackenburg, "'Der Vater, der mich gesandt hat': Zur johanneischen Christologie," in *Anfänge der Christologie*, Festschrift Ferdinand Hahn, ed. Cilliers Breytenbach and Henning Paulsen (Göttingen: Vandenhoeck & Ruprecht, 1987), 275–92 (286).

predication, one linked with messianic traditions, the term has now become much more: in his unity with the Father (10:30) the "Son" is himself "God."

3.6 The Son of Man

This is also confirmed by the use of the *Son of Man* title,[74] which is especially connected with the heavenly dimension and Jesus' heavenly origin. Whereas in the Synoptics the term is used as an enigmatic term with a variety of notions,[75] the Johannine usage is somewhat more consistent. The term is introduced in the climax of the opening chapter in John 1:51 where it is used in a subtle transformation of the Jacob-Bethel episode:[76] the Son of Man (which readers will understand as the earthly Jesus) is presented as the "house of God" (Gen 28:19), the place of the divine presence on earth upon which the angels ascend and descend. In John 3:13 and 6:62, the ideas of Jesus' heavenly origin and his descent and ascent are linked with the title, and in other passages it is linked, in Johannine terms, with the idea

[74] See the discussion on the background and character of the predication in John in the monographs by Robert Rhea, *The Johannine Son of Man*, ATANT 76 (Zürich: Theologischer Verlag, 1990); Delbert Burkett, *The Son of Man in the Gospel of John*, JSNTSup 56 (Sheffield: JSOT Press, 1991); Markus Sass, *Der Menschensohn im Evangelium nach Johannes*, TANZ 35 (Tübingen: Francke, 2000); Benjamins Reynolds, *The Apocalyptic Son of Man in the Gospel of John*, WUNT 2/249 (Tübingen: Mohr Siebeck, 2008); cf. also the important contribution by Francis Moloney, "The Johannine Son of Man Revisited," in *Theology and Christology in the Fourth Gospel*, ed. Gilbert van Belle, Jan G. van der Watt, and Petrus Maritz, BETL 184 (Leuven: Peeters, 2005), 177–202.

[75] There are basically passages in which the term just seems to replace an "I," thus, for example, in the saying about the Sabbath (Mark 2:28) or in the sayings about Jesus' impending passion (Mark 8:31; 9:31; 10:33 par.), while in others, it refers to an eschatological figure who is yet to come and will enact a final judgment (e.g., Mark 14:61 and Matt 25:31). Scholars are further divided as to whether and in which cases both notions are fused,and Jesus is identified with the coming Son of Man. Above all, there is the difficult question of whether (or in which passages) the term might originate with the earthly Jesus and in which cases it is attributed to him by the later tradition or the synoptic redactions. All these issues cannot be discussed in the present context.

[76] On the interpretation of the episode in the Jewish tradition, see Brown, *Gospel according to John*, 1:90–91; and Craig S. Keener, *The Gospel of John: A Commentary* (Grand Rapids: Hendrickson, 2003), 1:489–91.

of his "exaltation" (3:14; 8:28; 12:34) and "glorification" (12:23; 13:31-32). Although the saying in John 3:14, which is a reference to the Old Testament episode of the uplifted serpent (Num 21:4-9), may be a variation of the synoptic announcements of suffering,[77] the connection of the title "Son of Man" with the verb ὑψοῦν differs from Mark's sayings about Jesus' suffering and deliverance (Mark 8:31; 9:31) and points indirectly to his exaltation to the Father beyond his exaltation on the cross (cf. John 12:32). In John 3:13 and 6:62, the title is particularly associated with Jesus' heavenly origin. Finally, the title appears in conjunction with the motif of Jesus' authorization. In John 5:27, the view that God has given to Jesus the authority to have life in himself, or even to give life, and also to enact the judgment is explained by an allusion to Daniel 7:14 (LXX and Theodotion), "for he is (the) Son of Man."[78] Here, the apocalyptic background of the title and its reference to a heavenly figure is most clearly stressed. As the "Son of Man," Jesus is the representative of the Father in whom humans not only encounter God's eschatological agent but even God himself. Thus, in John, the title is an expression of high Christology, linked with the titles "Son," "Logos," and "God."

We see, therefore, that the high christological expressions that frame the Gospel (John 1:1; 20:28)—Jesus as the divine, primordial Logos, the Word through whom the world has been created (1:3, 10), and even "God" (1:1, 18; 20:28)—provide the framework within which all the other predications, both the higher and the lower ones, have to be interpreted.[79] It is the perspective from which the narrative episodes of Jesus' ministry are also to be read.

[77] This is particularly suggested by the δεῖ in connection with the title "Son of Man," cf. Mark 8:31.

[78] This is the only passage in John where the article in the christological title ὁ υἱὸς τοῦ ἀνθρώπου is missing. The indeterminate υἱὸς τοῦ ἀνθρώπου exactly matches the Greek in Dan 7:13 LXX or Theodotion. This is a good argument for the assumption that, at least in the present context of Jesus' authorization for communicating life and enacting judgment, the title is deliberately connected with the tradition of Dan 7.

[79] Despite such a high christological framework, we should not forget that Jesus' true humanity is nowhere questioned in John.

4. The Presentation of Jesus' Divine Authority in Johannine Narratives and Discourses

Jesus' divine identity and authority are not only presented in the christological titles and predications but also in the Johannine narratives and in Jesus' discourses.

Among John's narratives, the "signs" episodes in particular are where Jesus is said to have "revealed his glory" (John 2:11). For this purpose, the Johannine "miracle stories" are characteristically shaped with a distinctive modification of the literary genre of miracle stories[80] toward a multilayered form of narration, "enriched" by interspersed references to a deeper dimension of the event or to its meaning within the whole of the Gospel. In all the Johannine miracle narratives, we can discover a structure in which—apart from the narration of the miracle—certain textual elements refer to other passages in the Gospel. These references open up symbolic aspects of meaning and direct the reader to the full significance of the Christ event and to the salvation effected by Jesus' death and resurrection.[81] In the first Cana episode (2:1-11), for example, these pointers include the hint of the "third day" (v. 1); the enigmatic mention of the "hour" of Jesus (v. 4); the (unnecessary) allusion to the purification practice of "the Jews" (v. 6); and at the end the statement that the bridegroom (or, rather, Jesus?) has not acted like "every human" (v. 10).[82] In the second sign episode in John 4,

[80] Cf. Jörg Frey, "From the *Sēmeia* Narratives to the Gospel as a Significant Narrative: On Genre-Bending in the Johannine Miracle Stories," in *The Fourth Gospel as Genre Mosaic*, ed. Kasper Bro Larsen, Studia Aarhusia Neotestamentica 3 (Göttingen: Vandenhoeck & Ruprecht, 2015), 209–32, with reference to Harold W. Attridge, "Genre Bending in the Fourth Gospel," *JBL* 121 (2002): 3–21. For a comprehensive discussion of the Johannine miracle stories, cf. *Kompendium der frühchristlichen Wundererzählungen*, vol. 1: *Die Wunder Jesu*, ed. Ruben Zimmermann (Gütersloh: Gütersloher Verlagshaus, 2013), in particular the introduction to the Johannine semeia stories by Uta Poplutz, "Hinführung," 659–68.

[81] Cf. in particular Christian Welck, *Erzählte Zeichen: Die Wundergeschichten des Johannesevangeliums literarisch untersucht: Mit einem Ausblick auf Joh 21*, WUNT 2/69 (Tübingen: Mohr Siebeck, 1994); see also Frey, "From the *Sēmeia* Narratives to the Gospel."

[82] On this, see the detailed demonstration in Welck, *Erzählte Zeichen*, 135–38; see also Frey, "From the *Sēmeia* Narratives to the Gospel," 217–22; and—for an extensive interpretation—Jörg Frey, "Das prototypische Zeichen (Joh 2,1–11)," in *The Opening of*

the stress on the phrase "Your son lives!" (4:50; cf. v. 51, 53) and the reference to the "hour" (v. 53) of the healing point the reader beyond the individual narrative and link the event narrated to the events of Jesus' "hour" in which not only physical but eternal life is constituted.[83] Thus, the Johannine semeia episodes are significant for Jesus' whole salvific work; they are exemplary tales of the salvation that comes through Jesus, not merely reports of some past events of his earthly activity.

The typically Johannine design helps to establish the connection between what is narrated with "what is signified" and thus precisely makes the narrated event, or rather the narration itself, a "sign."[84] In the reading of each individual sign narrative, readers are directed to the whole of the Christ event and to the salvation that is based on his cross and resurrection. Due to this characteristic literary technique, the Johannine sign narratives can function not only to produce admiration of Jesus' miraculous power[85] but moreover to awaken faith in Jesus' true nature as the Son of God and divine giver of life (cf. John 20:30-31). As the true significance and dignity of Jesus could only be perceived in a post-Easter time through the "remembrance" of the Spirit, it is clear that only from this perspective can Jesus' deeds be narrated and understood as a revelation of his true glory. Consequently, the glory revealed in Jesus' signs is not a splendor visible to physical eyes or a perception that was already accessible to Jesus' contemporaries. It is, rather, the glory that was bestowed on Jesus in "his hour" and disclosed

---

John's Narrative (John 1:19-2:22): Historical, Literary, and Theological Readings from the Colloquium Ioanneum in Ephesus, ed. R. Alan Culpepper and Jörg Frey, WUNT 385 (Tübingen: Mohr Siebeck, 2017), 165–216.

[83] Cf. Welck, *Erzählte Zeichen,* 140–48.

[84] According to Welck, *Erzählte Zeichen,* 288–93, the sign is, strictly speaking, not the past event or episode narrated in John but rather the sign for the reader, the "written sign" (cf. John 20:30), that is, the Johannine text in its particular narrative design and with the hints to the meaning of the narrated events as deliberately inserted by the evangelist. It is the text that has the power to draw readers to a certain insight.

[85] Such an admiration or a "belief" merely triggered by the impressive signs is criticized as insufficient, most explicitly in John 2:23-25, but also in John 6 where the Galileans want to make Jesus a king because of the feeding of the multitude. But when the reader is told that Jesus withdraws to a mountain (v. 15) and later states that the crowd did not see a sign (v. 26), the reaction of the crowd is presented as wrong or at least insufficient.

to his disciples only later through the remembrance of the Spirit that caused this insight into Jesus' true dignity, thus authoring a christological development in the post-Easter period.

4.1 Jesus' Divine Authority and Identity as the Light of the World (John 9)

A good example of this is the extensive narrated dialogue of the healing of the man born blind in John 9:1-41. This is the episode which was J. Louis Martyn's chief paradigm in his interpretation of John as a "two-level drama" and in relating the Gospel narrative to the process of the "parting of the ways" between the synagogue and the Johannine community.[86]

The extensive episode goes far beyond the short narration of the miracle in the first verses (9:1-7). It is well structured in seven scenes,[87] wherein the themes addressed already in the first verses are discussed in various groups. It would be odd to explain this expertly crafted text from a totally speculative reconstruction of the miracle account in a hypothetical "signs source" or from an even earlier and shorter miracle story.[88] Not only the interpretive dialogues but already the brief

[86] Cf. Frey, "From the *Sēmeia* Narratives to the Gospel," 222–25; and idem, "Sehen oder Nicht-Sehen? (Die Heilung des blind Geborenen)—Joh 9,1–41," in Zimmerman, ed., *Kompendium der frühchristlichen Wundererzählungen*, 1:725–41. Cf. also Mattias Rein, *Die Heilung des Blindgeborenen (Joh 9): Tradition und Redaktion*, WUNT 2/73 (Tübingen: Mohr Siebeck, 1995); and Michael Labahn, "'Blinded by the Light': Blindheit und Licht in Joh 9 im Spiel von Variation und Wiederholung zwischen Erzählung und Metapher," in *Repetitions and Variations in the Fourth Gospel: Style, Text, Interpretation*, ed. G. van Belle, M. Labahn, and P. Maritz, BETL 223 (Leuven: Peeters, 2009), 453–504.

[87] Cf. Rein, *Die Heilung des Blindgeborenen*, 170–72: (1) the healing story (vv. 1-7), (2) which is followed by a discussion with the neighbors (vv. 8-12); (3) an initial questioning by the Pharisees (vv. 13-17); (4) an interlude with the Pharisees questioning his parents (vv. 18-23); (5) a subsequent questioning by the Pharisees/*Ioudaioi* (vv. 24-34); (6) the new encounter of the healed man with Jesus (vv. 35-38); and, finally, (7) a scene with Jesus and some of the Pharisees (vv. 39-41).

[88] Cf. Frey, "Sehen oder Nicht-Sehen?" 737–38; and the extensive discussion in Rein, *Die Heilung des Blindgeborenen*. Although the evangelist was probably aware of stories about the healings of blind men from the synoptic tradition, we cannot be sure that he drew on a particular *Vorlage* for the composition of John 9.

narration of the miracle itself are shaped by distinctively Johannine elements: in contrast with the synoptic healings of the blind, this man is blind from birth, making this miracle greater than those in all the parallels. Jesus does not answer a request from the blind man or from others but takes the initiative when he "sees" the man enter (v. 1). Finally, the miracle is not performed openly but only discovered and discussed in retrospect when the blind man comes back from washing himself in the pool, testifying to various groups about his healing and the one who caused it.

In the subsequent dialogues and debates, the man comes to increasingly clearer confessions of faith, calling Jesus first a prophet (9:17), then saying he comes "from God" (v. 33), and, finally, after the introduction of the term "the Son of Man" (v. 35), he even worships him (v. 38). In the course of this trial, he presents himself as a disciple of Jesus (vv. 27–28) and is, consequently, expelled from the synagogue of the disciples of Moses (v. 34). In the end, Jesus pronounces his verdict about the Pharisees who have been blinded by the light in their encounter with the light (v. 39), whereas the blind man had come to receive both physical and spiritual light. So, the themes of the story are sin and belief and the works of Jesus who, as the "light of the world" (v. 5), gives light to the blind and blinds those who claim to see or to know. Thus, the episode functions as an illustration of Jesus' earlier self-predication as "the light of the world" (8:12). It is embedded in a symbolic framework in which washing oneself in the pool or the "one being sent"[89] becomes an image for purification by Jesus, or the purification from sins. Similarly, healing from blindness is a symbol for the spiritual process of coming

[89] The striking translation or rather interpretation of the place name Σιλωάμ (John 9:7; cf. שִׁלֹּחַ = *Shiloah*, Isa 8:6; and Σιλωά in Josephus, *J.W.* 5.140, 145) with the term "sent" or "the one who is sent" (ὃ ἑρμηνεύεται ἀπεσταλμένος) introduces a symbolic meaning, as the "one being sent" is linked with the sending motif in the Gospel. Although the term ἀπεσταλμένος is otherwise used with regard to the Baptizer (John 1:6; 3:28), whereas the sending of Jesus is regularly expressed by use of the verb πέμπω (ὁ πέμψας με, 5:37; 6:44; 7:28; 8:16, 18, 26, 29; 12:49; used of the Baptizer in 1:33), the terms are interchangeable in John, and the reference to Jesus in the narrative aside in 9:7 cannot be overlooked. For further symbolic interpretations with regard to Isa 8:6 and the motif of "living water," cf. Hartwig Thyen, *Das Johannesevangelium*, HNT 6 (Tübingen: Mohr Siebeck, 2005), 460–61.

to belief. Seeing and blindness, coming to the light and staying in the darkness, even life and death are presented as the consequences of Jesus' entire sending and ministry (9:39).

The episode is deliberately designed as an exemplary and paradigmatic narrative that cannot be read merely on the level of Jesus' past ministry, nor can it be read as a mere mirroring of the healing of a blind man by a Christian charismatic, as Martyn suggested.[90] The generalization of the narrated event is brought about differently, by means of symbolic overtones, theological themes, and numerous connections with the overall plot of the Gospel. The episode thus serves as a paradigm of the saving "works of God" (9:4) in general. Historically, the description of the Pharisees and their official role and the expulsion from the synagogal community (v. 22) obviously refer to processes that happened to the Johannine community in later times. Likewise, the christological insight expressed in the episode mirrors the high Christology developed in the Johannine community in post-Easter times, and the climactic confession of faith and veneration of Jesus finally point to Jesus' divine authority as should be perceived from the Johannine narration.

4.2 Jesus' Divine Authority in the Lazarus Episode (John 11)

The most impressive demonstration of Jesus' divine life-giving power is the resurrection (or rather revivification[91]) of Lazarus. Here, Jesus' eschatological authority is presented in narrative mode,[92] in the depiction of Jesus performing an act which was traditionally considered the proper

[90] Cf. Martyn, *History and Theology*, 40–45.

[91] In the narrative, it is presupposed that Lazarus, after his resurrection, will die again. Thus, the act merely points to the eschatological resurrection (and also to the resurrection of Jesus), but the difference remains.

[92] Cf. the more extensive interpretation in Jörg Frey, *Die johanneische Eschatologie*, vol. 3: *Die eschatologische Verkündigung in den johanneischen Texten*, WUNT 117 (Tübingen: Mohr Siebeck, 2000), 401–62; see also Otfried Hofius, "Die Auferweckung des Lazarus: Joh 11,1–44 als Zeugnis narrative Christologie," in idem, *Exegetische Studien*, WUNT 223 (Tübingen: Mohr Siebeck, 2008), 28–45; Ruben Zimmermann, "The Narrative Hermeneutics of John 11: Learning with Lazarus How to Understand Death, Life, and Resurrection," in *The Resurrection of Jesus in the Gospel of John*, ed.

work of God himself (Deut 32:39; 1 Sam 2:6 LXX; etc.).[93] The problem was already in view in John 5, where Jesus claims the Father has authorized him to enact his eschatological works of judging and giving life (John 5:21-22, 26-27).[94] His properly divine authority and life-giving power is now openly demonstrated in the resurrection of Lazarus, and the consequences of this pivotal manifestation of Jesus' authority are clear: the Jewish leaders under the advice of Caiaphas sentence him to death (11:47-53),[95] not because of his provocative act in the temple area, as it is presented in Mark (Mark 11:15-19), but because of the demonstration of his divine authority, ultimately in the resurrection of Lazarus. According to the Johannine narrative, Jesus has to die because he acts like God, which is considered by the Jewish leaders as an undue usurpation of divine honors. Despite the perspective of the Jewish leaders, the Johannine view communicated to the readers argues that Jesus truly has divine dignity, and that the Father has given him the authority to enact his eschatological works.

In this last "miracle" or semeia narrative in the Gospel, the Johannine interpretation of the act is not presented in subsequent discourses and dialogues (as in John 5, 6, and 9), but in the ἐγώ εἰμι saying at the center of the pericope, even before the miracle is narrated (11:25-26): Jesus *is* the resurrection and the life, even in the context of physical death.[96] This is the densest expression of the claim that, in Jesus, God

---

Craig R. Koester and Reimund Bieringer, WUNT 222 (Tübingen: Mohr Siebeck, 2008), 75–101.

[93] See the extensive discussion in Frey, *Die johanneische Eschatologie*, 3:357–63.

[94] Cf. Frey, *Die johanneische Eschatologie*, 3:363–69.

[95] Accordingly, the inquiry by Hannas (John 18:12-23) does not lead to a sentence of death, nor does the very brief scene of Jesus' presentation before Caiaphas (18:24) add anything substantial to what is narrated before. The data rather suggest that John has used the synoptic scene of the trial before the Sanhedrin and the high priest (Mark 14:53-65) and inserted that scene, with characteristic changes, into John 11.

[96] The saying shows that the present-oriented eschatology of the Gospel and the idea of eternal life as a present possession of the believers does not preclude that they will suffer physical death. There is no reason to speculate about a hope for physical immortality in the Johannine community or to assume that physical death was irrelevant for the evangelist or his readers. The gift of eternal life does not lead to a spiritualizing view of the irrelevance of bodily life but implies the continuation of the relationship with God based on faith in Jesus, even in the case of physical death and

in his creative, life-giving power has become present. The present-oriented eschatology is articulated here as a consequence of Christology: the resurrection of the dead and the last judgment, which were traditionally expected at the end time, are now present in Jesus and—in the post-Easter period—in his word.

The whole Lazarus episode shows elements of characteristically Johannine design, as does the narration of the miracle in the climactic final scene: it is Jesus who calls the dead man from the grave, as is promised in John 5:28 concerning the Son of Man, and he also commands that he be freed of his graveclothes (11:44).[97] He acts in his divine authority and thus in silent company with the Father who answers his desires even before a prayer is pronounced.[98] Therefore, the miracle excels any of the other biblical revivification stories, those of the Old Testament (1 Kgs 17:17-24; 2 Kgs 4:18-37) and also those of the Synoptics (Mark 5:21-43 par.; Luke 7:11-17) and Acts (Acts 9:36-42; 20:9-10): The deceased did not die just now, but four days ago (John 11:17, 39). There is no longer any spark of life left in him, and there can be no uncertainty about the reality of his death. He is already buried and the grave is closed. Unlike in other resurrection stories, Jesus does not touch the deceased but simply calls him from the distance to come out. Jesus calls back to life a corpse that stinks, that is,

---

beyond physical death. This can be linked with the sayings about the resurrection "on the last day" (John 6:39, 40, 44, 54). See the argument in Frey, *Die johanneische Eschatologie*, 3:391–400.

[97] Cf. similarly John 18:8. The mention of the graveclothes and the napkin also links the story with John 20, where the disciples find the tomb well arranged. They conclude that Jesus has stripped off the clothes and the napkin (vv. 6-7), with the implication that he rose by his own power of life (cf. 10:18). This is an important aspect of Johannine Christology: as a divine being, Jesus was not merely resurrected by God, but rose from the dead by the authority given to him. The belief the disciples arrive at on the Easter day is, therefore, not only that Jesus has risen from the dead, but that he has the divine power to overcome death. The mention of the graveclothes and the napkin in John 11:44 and 20:6-7 is a subtle literary device to communicate this to the readers.

[98] John 11:41-42 shows that Jesus, strictly speaking, does not need to pray. Public prayer is only for the information of the crowd, and Jesus merely thanks the Father that he has already been answered, whereas the previous inner dialogue between the Son and the Father is only presupposed but not expressed.

one that is already in the process of decay so that, even in the view of ancient readers, there was no hope of return left.[99] And, most significantly, he does not pray to God like the prophets but gives a command by his proper divine authority, and the dead hears his voice and comes out (cf. 5:28-29). Thus, the narrative is a prominent example of John's technique of increasing the synoptic miracles and modifying the genre of miracle or resurrection stories in accordance with his christological intention to present Jesus as God.

In the case of the dramatically well-structured pericope, all our attempts to get back to an earlier form of the narrative must remain completely speculative.[100] It would be odd, therefore, to interpret the episode designed as the culmination point of Jesus' earthly ministry from the hypothetical assumption of a shorter and more elementary resurrection or healing story without the dialogues and theologically meaningful verses. But, in consequence, the historical reference of the narrative becomes even more unattainable and ultimately remains in the dust. In view of the fact that the names of the narrative figures, Mary, Martha, and Lazarus, can be found in Luke, where Mary and Martha act in similar roles (Luke 10:38-42), and Lazarus is the central figure in a parable (16:19-31), it is almost certain these figures belong to earlier tradition. However, there the three are not yet

[99] Scholars have referred to mostly later Jewish traditions, according to which the soul returns to the body for three days before it definitively leaves it, so that after the three days there is definitely no hope for return. While we cannot ascertain that such traditions are presupposed here, the episode was soon interpreted in the sense that the mention of the fourth day brings out this particular dimension of the miracle (thus Melito of Sardis, homily on the Pascha 570). For discussion, cf. Frey, *Die johanneische Eschatologie*, vol. 2: *Das johanneische Zeitverständnis*, WUNT 110 (Tübingen: Mohr Siebeck, 1998), 199–200.

[100] Scholars who advocate for a pre-Johannine signs source have suggested that an earlier and simpler form of the miracle narrative was part of that source, whereas all the dialogue or explicative verses were attributed to the evangelist or a later redaction. But those exegetical patterns have been decisively questioned in the last three decades, and the existence of a source that underlies the whole Johannine narrative can no longer be assumed. See most clearly Gilbert van Belle, *The Signs Source in the Fourth Gospel: Historical Survey and Critical Evaluation of the Semeia Hypothesis*, BETL 116 (Leuven: Peeters, 1994); and Schnelle, *Antidocetic Christology*; cf. also Frey, *Die johanneische Eschatologie*, 3:405–7.

assembled into a family. Accordingly, we should even reckon with the possibility that the evangelist created the composition of the Bethany stories, the raising of Lazarus, and the anointing by Mary, as a palimpsest based on texts of Mark[101] and Luke.[102] The plots fit so well with each other: In Luke 16, the rich man asks for the poor Lazarus to return to life to warn his brothers, but then he is told that even if Lazarus could return, they wouldn't believe him and repent (vv. 26-31). The narration of John 11:1–12:19 develops just that option: Lazarus returns to the living, humans come to see him (12:9), but the Jewish leaders do not believe. Instead, they put to death Jesus who revitalized him from the dead.

But be that as it may, the present text is the most impressive narrative expression of John's high Christology. And in its textual pragmatics it seems to push readers to a correction of their christological presuppositions and to deepen the views of the identity and function of Jesus. Several aspects are important here.

a) When the sisters of Lazarus call Jesus to come and heal their sick friend, they express confidence in him as a healer. When they later blame him with the accusation that if he had been present their brother would not have died (John 11:21, 32), their positive but insufficient view of Jesus' real identity and function is openly demonstrated. In their view, Jesus could have healed his friend if he were present, but once Lazarus has died, all hope is gone. The sisters apparently consider Jesus a human healer, rather than the divine life giver, and his physical absence seems to be a particular problem for them. This is in accordance with the problems referred to in John's farewell discourses where Jesus' departure (13:33, 36; 16:7), that is, his absence and invisibility (14:18, 20; 16:10, 16-19), in the post-Easter period seems to be the main problem of the addressees. For this reason, the author tries to convince them that Jesus' departure was necessary (16:7) and that,

[101] The scene of Jesus' anointing by an unknown woman from Bethany (Mark 14:3-9) underlies the Johannine anointing narrative (John 12:1-11), but now the unknown woman is identified with one of the two sisters, Mary from Bethany.

[102] Thus the suggestion by Hartwig Thyen, "Die Erzählung von den Bethanischen Geschwistern (Joh 11,1–12,19) als 'Palimpsest' über synoptischen Texten," in *The Four Gospels 1992*, Festschrift Frans Neirynck, ed. F. van Segbroeck, 3 vols., BETL 100 (Leuven: Peeters, 1992), 3:2021–50; idem, *Johannesevangelium*, 537–38.

even in his "absence," he actively supports his followers.[103] Martha and Mary's complaint is, therefore, related to the fears and hopes of the community of addressees, so that the whole episode can be read as an interaction with their christological and eschatological beliefs.

b) Martha's hope for the resurrection on "that day" (11:24) is directly corrected by Jesus' "I am" saying (vv. 25-26) as it crudely underestimates his divine authority and life-giving power in the present. Without denying the eschatological resurrection of the dead, the narrative strongly confirms the idea that, in the presence of Jesus (or, later, his word), his life-giving power is present and that divine, eternal life is communicated to all those who believe in him.

c) The narrative may frustrate readers because Jesus does not immediately come to see his ill friend when he is clearly informed about his illness (11:3). Instead, it seems as if Jesus waits until Lazarus dies (v. 6) for the sole purpose of performing a greater deed later. Psychologically, such an act is not conceivable or reconcilable with a loving intention of Jesus for his friends or followers. So we are prompted to look for a literary interpretation of the scheme of "suggestion, negative response, and exceeding positive action," which is used here and similarly in several other passages within John's Gospel.[104] The Johannine text deliberately frustrates the reader's expectations and works with that frustration in order to "shape the implied reader's response," that is, "to clarify, to modify, and to deepen the Christological expectations of the implied reader, bringing them into harmony with those of the implied author."[105] This process also communicates a deeper understanding of

[103] On the purpose of the farewell discourses, cf. the thorough discussion in Frey, *Die johanneische Eschatologie*, 3:119–34.

[104] This can be especially seen in Jesus' rejection of his mother's hint in John 2:3-5, which is, nevertheless, followed by a miracle; it is also seen in the rejection of the royal servant in 4:48, which is also followed by a positive action, the healing of his son. Furthermore, a similar structure is found in John 7, where Jesus' brothers urge him to go to Jerusalem, which is at first rejected, only to be fulfilled shortly thereafter when Jesus does precisely what the brothers had suggested. Cf. the articles by Charles H. Giblin, "Suggestion, Negative Response, and Positive Action in St. John's Portrayal of Jesus (John 2,1–11; 4,46–54; 7,2–14; 11,1–44)," *NTS* 26 (1979/1980): 197–211; and Adele Reinhartz, "Great Expectations: A Reader-Oriented Approach to Johannine Christology and Eschatology," *LT* 3 (1989): 61–76. See also Frey, *Die johanneische Eschatologie*, 1:327–29.

[105] Thus Reinhartz, "Great Expectations," 66.

the authority and identity of Jesus, who is not merely a prophet or healer but the divine prince of life.

d) One final aspect is important. Within the episode, there is also an increasing perception of the motifs of death and life. For instance, when learning about Lazarus' illness, Jesus' statement sounds almost cynical; nevertheless, it marks the program of the whole episode: "This illness does not lead to death, rather it is for God's glory, so that the Son of God may be glorified through it" (11:4). While the reality of Lazarus' death is expressed with growing clarity,[106] Jesus' power over life is also presented with increasing potency.[107] But even more than this, during the episode the idea is established that Jesus, on his way to raise Lazarus, also approaches his own death (v. 16), which is decided upon after his mighty deed. On the other hand, he is "the resurrection" only as the risen one, and thus he calls out Lazarus as a prolepsis and—in some manner—also a consequence of his own death and resurrection. The eternal life he gives is ultimately rooted in laying down his own life "for the sake of the people," (vv. 51-52). Thus, the narration of the miracle, or even the narrated miracle itself, is based on Jesus' whole salvific ministry. The resurrection of Lazarus is an illustration of the life given to those who believe in him (11:25-26; 5:24-25) and is, eschatologically speaking, a foreshadowing of the resurrection expected in the event of physical death (6:39, 40, 44, 54).[108]

4.3 Jesus' Divine Authority in the Johannine Discourses: The ἐγώ εἰμι Sayings

John's high Christology is further expressed in the discourses of the Johannine Jesus, which are also presented in the light of the events of his crucifixion and resurrection. We should keep in mind that all the Johannine discourses of Jesus, in their present form, were shaped and articulated in the post-Easter period, and there are even a number

[106] Verse 11: he has fallen asleep; v. 14: he has died; v. 17: he is already four days in the grave when Jesus arrives; v. 39: he stinks.

[107] Verse 11: Jesus will awake him; v. 24: Lazarus will be resurrected on the last day; vv. 25-26: Jesus himself is the resurrection; vv. 43-44: Lazarus is called out from the grave and is freed from the bandages.

[108] Cf. Frey, *Die johanneische Eschatologie*, 3:457–62.

of linguistic features that demonstrate the retrospective view on his whole ministry, including the events of his "hour." This is most striking in the Johannine farewell discourses where Jesus, even before his death and resurrection, uses Greek aorist or perfect forms to say that he has already been glorified (John 13:31-32), that he has conquered the world (16:33), or, in an imperfect, that he was with his disciples (17:12) but now is no more in the world (v. 11).[109] With these verbs, Jesus apparently looks back at events that are, in the flow of the narrative, still to come, events such as his glorification (13:31), his victory (16:33), or his departure from the world (17:11). Thus, the post-Easter perspective of the community of addressees intrudes into the narrative quite obviously, appearing in the words and discourses of Jesus and representing a developed Christology that shapes the whole Gospel.

Most distinctively, Jesus' divine authority is expressed in the ἐγώ εἰμι sayings, which are characteristic for the preaching of the Johannine Jesus. In John, the ἐγώ εἰμι formula is used both "absolutely"[110] and in connection with metaphorical predications such as bread, light, shepherd, and vine,[111] as well as in related forms.[112] The various forms are interconnected[113] and must be interpreted as a coherent language device that distinctively occurs in the words of Jesus.[114] In its linguistic form, the phrase adopts the formula of divine revelation from the Scriptures, אֲנִי הוּא ("I am He") or אֲנִי יְהוָה ("I am Yahweh"), rendered in the

[109] Occasionally, such retrospective forms can also be found in other Johannine discourses; cf. John 3:13, where Jesus' ascent to the Father is referred to in a Greek perfect. See Frey, *Die johanneische Eschatologie*, 3:252–54.

[110] 6:20; 8:24, 28, 58; 13:19; 18:5, 6, 8.

[111] 6:35, 41, 48, 51; 8:12 (cf. 9:5); 10:7, 9, 11, 14; 11:25; 14:6; 15:1, 5.

[112] 4:26; 8:18, 23; 9:5; inverted in 7:34, 36; 12:26; 14:3; 17:24. Additionally, the "I am" formula is prepared for by the Baptizer's negative "I am not . . ." in 1:19-21, and the deictic variants ("this is" / "you are") in 1:30, 33-34, 49; 4:19 before the "I am" of Jesus is encountered for the first time in 4:26.

[113] Cf. David M. Ball, *"I Am" in John's Gospel: Literary Function, Background and Theological Implications,* JSNTSup 124 (Sheffield: Sheffield Academic, 1996); and the important articles by Hartwig Thyen, "Ich bin das Licht der Welt: Das Ich- und Ich-Bin-Sagen Jesu im Johannesevangelium," *JAC* 35 (1992): 19–42; and idem, "Ich-bin-Worte," *RAC* 17 (1995): 147–213.

[114] The only exception is the self-identification of the healed man in John 9:9.

LXX by the expression ἐγώ εἰμι.[115] Thus, Jesus speaks with the words of God's revelation at the burning bush (Exod 3:14) or of the divine self-presentations in Ezekiel and Deutero-Isaiah. There is no better means to present Jesus as the incarnate Word of God than having him speak out the divine self-presentation of the "revelation formula."

The use of the formula is already anticipated in the opening of John's narrative by the negative "I am not" in the words of the Baptizer (1:20-21) and by confessions of the type "you are" uttered by Nathanael (v. 49) and the Samaritan woman (4:19). In the encounter with her, Jesus identifies himself as the Messiah, using the "I am" formula for the first time (v. 26: "I am (he), the one who is speaking to you"). In its absolute form, the formula is used in Jesus' epiphany in the storm in 6:20 when he comforts the disciples by saying ἐγώ εἰμι—"It is I. Do not be afraid." In this pericope, the phrase could be adopted from Mark's version of the story (Mark 6:20), but while the formula has no programmatic function in the Synoptics, John develops it into a programmatic device for presenting Jesus' divine authority.

When the formula is used absolutely, the issue is not a mere recognition[116] but the comforting or terrifying insight that in Jesus God himself is encountered in his saving or judging action. This is most openly demonstrated when, in the scene of Jesus' arrest, after the repeated ἐγώ εἰμι, the armed band of Jewish and Roman soldiers draws back and falls to the ground before Jesus. The grotesqueness of this "involuntary veneration" demonstrates the divine power of Jesus' words. This is also

[115] In addition to the works of Thyen, "Ich bin das Licht der Welt" and idem, "Ich-bin-Worte," see the thorough study by Catrin H. Williams, *I Am He: The Interpretation of Ani Hu in Jewish and Early Christian Literature,* WUNT 2/113 (Tübingen: Mohr Siebeck, 2000) for a background on these sayings.

[116] In his influential commentary, Rudolf Bultmann (*Das Evangelium des Johannes,* 20th ed. [Göttingen: Vandenhoeck & Ruprecht, 1985 (1941)], 167–68, n. 2) separated the absolute "I am" sayings from those with metaphorical predications and interpreted most of the latter in the context of his hermeneutic as "recognition formulas," that is, expressions in which no new content is revealed, but which merely express the fulfillment in Jesus of what was previously hoped. In this way, the "I am" sayings were interpreted too one-sidedly in the context of Bultmann's interpretive interests and in the context of his understanding of revelation and faith. If one takes into account the linguistic interlinking of these statements with the absolute "I am" sayings, this interpretation can no longer be maintained. See Thyen, "Ich bin das Licht der Welt," 36–37.

confirmed by a brief explanation following Jesus' self-presentation as "the light of the world" (8:12). In 8:16, the formula is unfolded in an almost exegetical manner: "I am not alone but I and the Father who sent me." In Jesus' "I am"—also in its metaphorically expanded form—the unity of the Father and the Son (10:30) comes to its densest expression: Jesus speaks not merely with his own authority but with divine authority. The metaphorical "I am" sayings, in which the revelation formula is connected with easily accessible metaphors that draw on biblical motifs (bread, light, shepherd, wine),[117] can be regarded as kernel sayings of the Johannine discourses of Jesus. As such, they are the most distinctive expressions of the christological self-revelation of the Johannine Jesus and of the high Christology of the Fourth Gospel.

4.4 Divinity in Paradoxical Narration: The Johannine Passion Story

Jesus' divinity is not only presented in his signs and discourses but also, in a paradoxical manner, in his "hour," that is, his trial and crucifixion. Jesus' death (and resurrection) are given the utmost weight in the Johannine presentation, and it seems that John's ultimate intention is that his readers do not stumble on Jesus' departure and death, but rightly see him as the glorified crucified one in the light of Easter.[118]

John's particular interest in the interpretation of the death of Jesus is already evident from the sheer amount of space he devotes to the passion narrative, including the farewell discourses which are unparalleled in the Synoptics. But the second part of the Gospel, which C. H. Dodd called the "book of the passion," is not the only part of John's Gospel occupied by those events. There is also a dense web of anticipatory interpretations from the very beginning of the Gospel which provides the reader with hermeneutical categories in advance. Narrative prolepses about Jesus' betrayal and death, such as the mention of the "Lamb of God" in 1:29, the explanation that Jesus actually spoke about the destruction and resurrection of the "temple of his body"

[117] See Thyen, "Ich bin das Licht der Welt," 231–50.

[118] See the extensive argument in Frey, "Die *theologia crucifixi* des Johannesevangeliums"; idem, *Glory of the Crucified One*, 172–76.

in 2:22, and the allusion to the lifting up of the serpent in 3:14, as well as explanatory asides, can be found in almost every chapter. Thus, the evangelist conveys the categories of the soteriological interpretation of Jesus' death and introduces the distinctive categories of "exaltation" and "glorification" that seem to be totally unfitting to the event of a crucifixion, but constitute the paradoxical interpretation of the events of Jesus' "hour": so the serpent episode is taken as a visual prefiguring of the "uplifting" of the Son of Man, and in 12:23 Jesus proclaims, "The hour has come for the Son of Man to be glorified." Unlike the suggestion of some scholars, this cannot be understood as a euphemistic downplaying of the cruelty of Jesus' death. It is, instead, an interpretation taken from the Scriptures where it is said that God's servant will be "lifted up and greatly glorified" (Isa 52:13 LXX). For John, the deeper, true understanding of Jesus' passion and death is based on the Scriptures and mediated by the teaching of the post-Easter Spirit.

This is also adopted in John's design of the passion story.[119] From the very beginning, the story is designed according to the idea that Jesus consciously and willfully enters his passion (John 13:1-3; 18:4). He is not the victim of vicious intrigues. Rather, in every act of his passion, he is the active participant, acting in unity with the Father. Therefore, the idea of escaping the "hour" (12:27) or not drinking the "cup" of death (18:11) is strictly rejected,[120] and Jesus' last word cannot be the cry of godforsakenness (Mark 15:34) but only the triumph of fulfillment (John 19:30).

Thus, Jesus commissions Judas to act (13:26-27), and he delivers himself into the hands of the soldiers to obtain freedom for his disciples (v. 8). When he is interrogated by Annas (vv. 20, 23) and Pilate (v. 34; 19:11), he responds in a self-confident and majestic manner. As

[119] Concerning the theological motifs in John's passion story, see the thorough monograph by Manfred Lang, *Johannes und die Synoptiker. Eine redaktionsgeschichtliche Analyse von Joh 18–20 vor dem markinischen und lukanischen Hintergrund*, FRLANT 182 (Göttingen: Vandenhoeck & Ruprecht, 1999), 308–32.

[120] On the critical reception and rejection of Mark's Gethsemane episode, see Frey, "Das vierte Evangelium auf dem Hintergrund der älteren Evangelientradition: Zum Problem: Johannes und die Synoptiker," in idem, *Die Herrlichkeit des Gekreuzigten: Studien zu den Johanneischen Schriften I*, ed. J. Schlegel, WUNT 307 (Tübingen: Mohr Siebeck, 2013), 265–71; see also below, p. 73–75.

a culprit, he renders a guilty verdict against his own judge (19:11), he actively carries his cross (v. 17), brings about the fulfillment of Scripture (vv. 28-29), and even dies by actively giving up or delivering his spirit (v. 30). All these acts are narrated in deliberate contrast to Mark's narrative, and the differences are due not to a different Johannine source but to a different theological intention.

This can be seen even more clearly from the theological elements of the Johannine passion account. In the encounter with Pilate, Jesus professes his otherworldly kingship (18:36-37), and from the cross he is universally proclaimed king (19:19-23). His kingship differs from the political claims he was accused of. In that respect, he is not guilty, as Pilate declares repeatedly. Yet the readers should notice that, in paradoxical reversal, he *is* the true king, and we can even assemble elements of an enthronement ritual:[121] he proclaims his kingship (18:36); is vested and crowned (19:2); is presented to the crowd (v. 14), which reacts with a negative acclamation ("crucify," v. 15); is "uplifted" and enthroned on the cross (v. 16); and has placed over him a proclamation written in all languages (v. 19). These elements in John's narrative design contribute to a paradoxical counterimage. While Jesus is actually crucified, he is spiritually enthroned as the true king, and his kingdom is the realization of God's kingdom (cf. 3:3, 5).

The paradox is obvious. Jesus was put to death because he made himself (or, rather, *was*) God's Son (19:7), and in his death he is uplifted and enthroned to reign as the true king. The narrative design of John's passion account aims at suggesting such a change of perspective to its readers so that they are able to recognize the divine glory even and particularly in the crucified one. The Gospel as a whole, in its narrative and theological design, is shaped to evoke that perspective in its readers, to deepen their view of Jesus and to foster a true understanding of his death and departure according to John's advanced spiritual insight.

[121] Cf. Frey, *Die johanneische Eschatologie*, 3:271–75; idem, "From the 'Kingdom of God' to 'Eternal Life': The Transformation of Theological Language in the Fourth Gospel," in *John, Jesus, and History*, vol. 3: *Glimpses of Jesus through the Johannine Lens*, ed. Paul N. Anderson, Felix Just, and Tom Thatcher, ECL 18 (Atlanta: SBL, 2016), 439–58 (455–57).

5. The Theological Aim of the Gospel: True Understanding

Where does such an insight come from? How did it evolve? Which circumstances could contribute to the unique Johannine view of Jesus' divine authority and his true kingship?

Two groundbreaking approaches of North American scholarship wrestled with these questions and looked for explanations in relation to the "parting of the ways" between the Johannine community and synagogal Judaism. According to J. Louis Martyn's suggestion,[122] the full elaboration of John's high Christology could be imagined only as a consequence of the distancing from the synagogue (and thus as a tendentially "un-Jewish" element). But this does not do justice to the conviction of the Johannine evangelist that, in his high Christology, the truth of the oneness of the biblical God is not endangered. For John, the Father and the Son are still one God, not two. And this monotheistic, "binitarian" unity is circumscribed by the neuter ἕν, not the masculine. Raymond Brown alternatively reckoned hypothetically with the influence of "heterodox" (temple-critical) Jewish and Samaritan groups[123] that triggered the christological development that ultimately resulted in the split from the "orthodoxy" of the synagogue. But if we are unable to reconstruct the earlier stages of Johannine Christology while it was still within a Jewish synagogal context, such a speculation is unfounded.

In my view, the "Christian" impulse should not be underestimated here. If the Johannine view did not develop within the context of a "sectarian" segregation but in open discussion with other early Christian views, especially the Gospel of Mark, Johannine Christology can only be understood as expressing the consequences of its view that, as the Messiah, Jesus brings eschatological salvation and eternal life. Such an explanation from the mainstream of the gospel tradition is more plausible than the reference to heterodox forms of Judaism or to pagan influences.

Of course, John was not the first to voice the conviction that the earthly Jesus should be seen in closest relation to God, although it is

122 Martyn, *History and Theology*, 125–43.

123 Brown, *Community of the Beloved Disciple*, 36–47.

expressed in a particularly pointed form here. Already in Mark, Jesus has the authority to forgive sins (Mark 2:7), and already in Paul Jesus could be presented as a messenger from the divine realm (Phil 2:6) and mentioned on the same level with the one God (1 Cor 8:6). All these expressions could appear offensive or even blasphemous to contemporary Jews, although none of these convictions necessarily meant a definitive separation from the relatively pluralistic world of contemporary Judaism.

It is most likely that the precise development can no longer be reconstructed in detail. But the theological reason given in John's Gospel should be taken seriously, as it constitutes the self-conception of the Johannine community. According to the Fourth Gospel, it is the Spirit-Paraclete who guided the disciples in the post-Easter period to their deeper insights, thus authoring the image of Johannine Christology. The process is described as the remembrance of the Jesus story in light of the Scriptures (John 16:13-15; 14:26). Passages such as Isaiah 52:13 LXX, where the terms of "lifting up/exalting" and "glorifying" are linked and both related to the suffering servant of God, might have been central in communicating the categories, but ultimately the Johannine understanding of Christ's significance is a result of the thorough reconsideration of the view that eschatological salvation is based on the death and resurrection of Jesus and mediated through belief in him. If the eschatological relevance of Jesus is radically conceived, it is simply unavoidable to focus on his authority and identity and to describe it not just in functional and ontological terms, but even in divine categories.

From the eschatological relevance of Jesus (or of the reaction of humans to his appearance), it appears necessary to ask about the ultimate reason for such a significance, or even about the ultimate reason for the salvation that is located in Jesus' unity with the Father (John 10:30) and in the primordial will of God and his love for his creatures (3:16).

6. Johannine High Christology as a Challenge for Contemporary Theology

Therefore, John presents Christology as theology and theology as Christology. This is a challenge not only for ancient readers but also for modern theological interpretation. What does it mean to call Jesus "God" in the context of contemporary thought about superpowers, superstars, and fictional superheroes? And what does it mean to see the true God in Christ, the glorified crucified one? How does this affect our traditional and modern categories and values? There is not space to develop these issues here, so I have to limit myself to mentioning just a twofold challenge to our concepts of God and to Christology.

First, the challenge is to identify an appropriate Christian concept of God.[124] If the crucified one is ultimately God, the Father is not untouched by the death of his Son. Or phrased differently, the living God does not stay on the side of the immortal but embraces human death and all the depths of human history. Thus, through the death of the Son of God, the image of God "the Father" is significantly reconstituted and structurally changed. If this is the biblical God, there is a marked contrast with all the ideas of philosophical theology.

Furthermore, God—that is, emphatically, the biblical God—is now freshly and ultimately defined by his exclusive relationship to the "Son," who makes God known (John 1:18) both in his ministry and in the way he "images" him, so that the one who "sees" Jesus "sees" the Father (14:7, 9). Thus, the invisible God, who cannot be represented by any image, has in Christ—and *ever since* the history of Christ—an "image," which is the only means through which God's true nature can be known.

The hermeneutical challenge can also be expressed with regard to Christology: What does it mean to call Jesus "God" in a post-ontological era? How can we ensure that this does not question his true humanity? Can we just repeat, or should we rephrase, the Christology of Christ's "two natures"?

In my view, we cannot deny that the evangelist had a view of Jesus as ontologically different from all humans.[125] But he was also aware that Jesus' true glory could not be perceived with the physical eyes of

[124] Cf. Frey, *Glory of the Crucified One*, 333–44.

[125] This was rejected by Rudolf Bultmann, but mostly due to hermeneutical considerations or with regard to contemporary philosophical reflection. Therefore, he could only phrase Christology as soteriology, that is, with Christ's function for human existence in view.

his contemporaries, but was only revealed to the disciples in the post-Easter period in which the understanding of the cross as "glorification" was developed.

This implies that, in his narrative depiction of the Jesus story, the evangelist was hermeneutically aware that he did not simply draw a picture of the Jesus of history "as he was," but shaped the memory of the Jesus story under the presupposition of the paschal light and of the teaching of the Spirit. This means that the glory which overflows the path of the earthly Jesus was perceived and inserted in retrospect. The glory revealed in Jesus' signs is actually the glory revealed by the narrative text written in the light of post-Easter insights. Even more so, the idea of a primordial glory of Jesus (17:5) and of his "incarnation" are the ultimate consequences of the Easter revelation, rather than the presupposition of Jesus' earthly ministry.

Christian dogmatics has quickly adopted the logical and temporal priority of preexistence and incarnation, but historically and, as I assume, also in the awareness of the Johannine author, the priority is in the Easter experiences and the post-Easter Spirit that inspired the remembrance of the earthly Jesus and ultimately reshaped his image in the Gospel narrative. This is the only interpretation that can make sure that Jesus' humanity is not endangered by his depiction as divine.

Therefore, an ontological understanding of the divinity of Jesus seems to be unwarranted, even though the evangelist probably shared it. This being conceded, a functional understanding of Jesus' divine authority and identity is still a valuable hermeneutical option. Jesus is God, as he is the only one in whom eschatological life is granted. He can be characterized as divine since it is in his ministry and narrated history that the invisible God is made known—in relation with us humans—as everlasting love.

2

THE QUEST FOR THE JESUS OF HISTORY

Historical Tradition in the Fourth Gospel

Is the Fourth Gospel history, or is it theology? Or is it a combination of both? And if it is a combination, how are the two dimensions intertwined? On the basis of the considerations about John's focus on Christology, presented in the previous chapter, we might conclude that it is predominantly interested in theology and that its historical value, therefore, is questionable, if not even mostly fictional. But the Gospel states clearly that it narrates the story of Jesus of Nazareth, his ministry and death, as a "factual," not fictional, story, and that the "history" narrated is foundational for the theological meaning conveyed.

In this chapter, I will address the difficulties of the quest for historical traditions or even the historical Jesus in John. To begin, we will briefly look at the history of research and what has been called the dehistoricization of John in modern scholarship.[1] Then, we will consider more recent attempts to reintroduce the quest for history in

[1] See Paul N. Anderson, *The Fourth Gospel and the Quest for Jesus: Modern Foundations Reconsidered*, LNTS 321 (New York: T&T Clark, 2006), 43–74, who correspondingly speaks about the "De-Johannification of Jesus" (74–97); see also Robert Kysar, "The Dehistoricizing of the Gospel of John," in *John, Jesus, and History*, vol. 1: *Critical Appraisals of Critical Views*, ed. Paul. N. Anderson, Felix Just, and Tom Thatcher, SBL Symposium Series 44 (Atlanta: SBL, 2007), 75–102; Jack Verheyden, "The De-Johannification of Jesus: The Revisionist Contribution of Some Nineteenth-Century German Scholarship," in idem, 109–20; and Mark Allan Powell, "The De-Johannification of Jesus: The Twentieth Century and Beyond," in idem, 121–32.

Johannine interpretation and their methodological problems before we can have a closer look at some examples of historically valid traditions or information in John. Here we can analyze how the evangelist adopts and reshapes his traditions due to his narrative and theological interests in order to create his own story of Jesus and to design it in a manner that brings to expression the christological insights at which he arrived.

1. The Dehistoricization of the Fourth Gospel in New Testament Scholarship

Modern critical scholarship has largely abandoned the search for the Jesus of history in John and thus dismissed John from the quest for the historical Jesus.

Although this double statement merely marks the critical "consensus" established by scholars such as Albert Schweitzer, Adolf Jülicher, or William Wrede[2] at the beginning of the twentieth century,[3] some fundamental observations go back to the very earliest scholarly discussion about the Gospels.

At the end of the second century, Clement of Alexandria noted that, after the other three evangelists had recorded the "bodily things" (σωματικά) about Jesus, John composed his work as a "spiritual gospel" (πνευματικὸν εὐαγγέλιον, *Hyp.* 6).[4] This observation not only established a longstanding tradition of spiritualizing many "bodily" details in John; more fundamentally, Clement's remark is an early reaction to the problem that would inevitably arise due to the existence of the four-Gospel collection: the problem of differences among the four Gospels, especially the Synoptics and John, with respect to content and arrangement,

[2] Adolf Jülicher, *Einleitung in das Neue Testament* (Tübingen: Mohr Siebeck, 1894), with numerous subsequent editions; William Wrede, *Charakter und Tendenz des Johannesevangeliums* (Tübingen: Mohr, 1903); Albert Schweitzer, *Die Geschichte der Leben-Jesu-Forschung* (Göttingen: Vandenhoeck & Ruprecht, 1913), ET: *The Quest of the Historical Jesus: First Complete Edition*, trans. W. Montgomery, J. R. Coates, S. Cupitt, and J. Bowden (London: SCM Press, 2000).

[3] See Jörg Frey, *Die johanneische Eschatologie*, vol. 1: *Ihre Probleme im Spiegel der Forschung seit Reimarus*, WUNT 97 (Tübingen: Mohr Siebeck, 1997), 38–39.

[4] According to Eusebius, *Hist. eccl.* 6.14.7. See Jörg Frey, *The Glory of the Crucified One: Christology and Theology in the Gospel of John*, trans. W. Coppins and C. Heilig, BMSEC 6 (Waco: Baylor University Press, 2018), 199–200.

chronology and topography, and also numerous narrative and linguistic details. While some authors in the ancient church, such as Origen[5] and Theodore of Mopsuestia,[6] openly noted the difficulties (e.g., the chronology of Jesus' ministry or the cleansing of the temple), the majority either preferred John's "eyewitness" testimony or attempted to harmonize the accounts. The latter of these two options was adopted by Augustine in his work *De consensu evangelistarum*,[7] and it was this method of harmonization that dominated interpretative practice up until the rise of modernity.

The persuasive power of harmonization only faded away when, with the rise of critical historical thinking, interpreters claimed the liberty to see the evangelists as human individuals, which led to a new acknowledgment of their proper interests and perspectives.[8] In this framework, the differences among the canonical Gospels were openly addressed,[9] harmonistic views were increasingly rejected,[10] and the traditional attribution of the Fourth Gospel to an apostolic eyewitness

[5] Origen (*Comm Jo.* 10.2) already observed that a precise comparison of the Gospels led either to the general disputation of their reliability, to the adherence to only one of them, or to seeking—as was his own practice—the truth no longer in the letters alone. For more on how the early church handled the disagreements between the Gospels, cf. Helmut Merkel, *Die Widerspüche zwischen den Evangelien: Ihre polemische und apologetische Behandlung in der Alten Kirche bis Augustin*, WUNT 13 (Tübingen: Mohr, 1971).

[6] See his commentary on John, which is now available in English: Theodore of Mopsuestia, *Commentary on the Gospel of John*, ed. Joel C. Elowsky, Ancient Christian Texts (Downers Grove, Ill.: InterVarsity, 2010).

[7] On Augustine and his legacy, see Francis Watson, *Gospel Writing: A Canonical Perspective* (Grand Rapids: Eerdmans, 2013), 13–61.

[8] Thus, in 1778, Gotthold Ephraim Lessing, "Neue Hypothese über die Evangelisten als bloß menschliche Geschichtsschreiber betrachtet," in *G. E. Lessings Werke*, ed. P. Rilla, (München: Aufbau, 1976), 7:614–35.

[9] On the works of Reimarus and their effects, see Henk J. de Jonge, "The Loss of Faith in the Historicity of the Gospels," in *John and the Synoptics*, ed. Adalbert Denaux, BETL 101 (Leuven: Peeters, 1992), 409–21.

[10] This was done for literary and aesthetic reasons by Johann Gottfried Herder in his exposition of John, "Von Gottes Sohn, der Welt Heiland, nach Johannis Evangelium: Nebst einer Regel der Zusammenstimmung unserer Evangelien aus ihrer Entstehung und Ordnung," in *Sämmtliche Werke*, ed. B. Suphan, vol. 19 (Berlin: Weidemann, 1880), 253–424: "Was sich nicht vereinigen läßt, stehe einzeln da, jeder Evangelist mit seinem Verdienst. Mensch, Stier, Löwe und Adler, sie wollen zusammengehn und den Trhon der Herrlichkeit tragen, nicht aber in Eine Gestalt, in Ein

was questioned.[11] But whereas the two-source hypothesis came to be a widely accepted literary solution to the Synoptic problem by the mid-nineteenth century,[12] Johannine issues remained a thorny thicket for interpreters. Therefore, the images of the historical Jesus in the nineteenth century were still crafted from a combination of synoptic materials and Johannine ingredients.[13] The "spiritual" Jesus of the Johannine discourses, detached from the ballast of the Palestinian soil, appeared more attractive and acceptable to interpreters in the nineteenth century than the apocalyptic Jesus of the Synoptics predicting his own eschatological parousia "on the clouds."[14]

Most influential for the emerging critical view of John was Ferdinand Christian Baur's idealistic reading of John within his Hegelian construction of early Christian history. Baur considered John's presentation of the history of Jesus merely "a free elaboration of the basic conceptions expressed in the Prologue to the Gospel."[15] Although his very late dating

---

Diateßaron coalisirt seyn. . . . Vier Evangelisten sind, nd jedem bleibe sein Zweck, seine Gesichtsfarbe, seine Zeit, sein Ort" (416).

[11] The apostolic authorship of John was most thoroughly questioned by Carolus Theophilus Bretschneider, *Probabilia de evangelii et epistolarum Joannis, Apostoli, indole et origine eruditorum iudidiis modeste subiecit* (Leipzig: Stein, 1820); see also the earlier work of Edward Evanson, *The Dissonance of the Four Generally Received Evangelists, and the Evidence of Their Respective Authority Examined* (Ipswich: George Jermyn, 1792). Cf. Jörg Frey, "Auf der Suche nach dem Kontext des vierten Evangeliums," in idem, *Die Herrlichkeit des Gekreuzigten. Studien zu den Johanneischen Schriften I*, ed. J. Schlegel, WUNT 307 (Tübingen: Mohr Siebeck, 2013), 45–87 (52–53).

[12] The two-document hypothesis (which has been the majority solution of the Synoptic problem up until now) was firmly established by Heinrich-Julius Holtzmann, *Die synoptischen Evangelien, ihr Ursprung und geschichtlicher Charakter* (Leipzig: Engelmann, 1863).

[13] See Albert Schweitzer, *Geschichte der Leben-Jesu-Forschung*, 9th ed. (Tübingen: Mohr, 1984), 226.

[14] The issue of eschatology in particular triggered modern Gospel criticism, which can be seen most prominently in the posthumously edited fragments by the oriental scholar Hermann Samuel Reimarus in the late eighteenth century, in the attempt at a Hegelian "synthesis" by Ferdinand Christian Baur in the nineteenth century, and also in the existentialist "redefinition" of eschatology by Rudolf Bultmann in the twentieth century. See the extensive survey in Frey, *Die johanneiche Eschatologie*, 1:10–11 (on Reimarus), 33–36 (on Baur), and 85–119 (on Bultmann).

[15] Ferdinand Christian Baur, "Über die Composition und den Charakter des Johannesevangeliums," *ThJ* 3 (1844): 1–191, 397–475, 615–700 (474); see Jörg Frey,

of the Gospel and the Epistles to around 170 CE was not accepted by the majority of his followers, his influence definitely established the insight that the Fourth Gospel was not an eyewitness testimony and that the Johannine discourses of Jesus were freely composed, thus attesting to a thorough transformation of the Jesus tradition.[16] Toward the end of the nineteenth century, the leading scholars had arrived at a consensus that the Gospel was a kind of "theological allegory"[17] and was therefore virtually invalid for reconstructing the history of Jesus.[18] Historically valid information about Jesus could only be taken from Mark, the Sayings Source, and other synoptic materials, but not from John. The most important achievement for Jesus research by the turn of the twentieth century was, therefore, that the image of the earthly Jesus could now be portrayed without the spiritualizing elements of the Fourth Gospel.[19] This was influentially articulated by Albert Schweitzer, whose "consequently eschatological" interpretation of Jesus[20] set the stage for the History of

---

"Ferdinand Christian Baur and the Interpretation of John," in *Ferdinand Christian Baur and the History of Early Christianity*, ed. Martin Bauspiess, Christof Landmesser, and David Lincicium, trans. R. F. Brown and P. C. Hodgson (Oxford: Oxford University Press, 2017), 206–35 (220).

[16] Cf. Frey, *Die johanneische Eschatologie*, 1:37–38.

[17] Thus Alfred Loisy, *Le quatrième évangile* (Paris: Picard, 1903), 75, who goes further, saying, "a work of learned speculation which formally has nothing in common with the preaching of the historical Christ."

[18] See, e.g., Adolf Jülicher, *Einleitung in das Neue Testament*, 1st ed. (Tübingen: Mohr 1894): John is "eine philosophische Dichtung mit religiöser Tendenz aus der dritten christlichen Generation . . . für die Geschichte des Christus im Fleisch . . . fast ohne Wert." The Gospel shows how "der vielleicht grösste Denker der damaligen Christenheit sich den Erdenwandel des Heilands vorstellte . . . die Wahrheit naiv mit der Wirklichkeit identificierend."

[19] The interpretation in liberal Protestant theology of the late nineteenth century had always been "spiritualizing" to some degree, as Jesus' teaching was reconstructed with some Johannine elements. Thus, the kingdom appeared more present, rather than strictly eschatological, and more internal, rather than strictly "otherworldly." In this respect Schweitzer was revolutionary with his "consequently eschatological" view of Jesus and his teaching of the kingdom.

[20] On this movement, inaugurated by Johannes Weiss and efficiently propagated by Albert Schweitzer's brilliant history of "Life-of-Jesus-Research," see *History of New Testament Research From Jonathan Edwards to Rudolf Bultmann*. The first edition from 1906 was translated into English as *The Quest for the Historical Jesus: A Critical Study of Its Progress from Reimarus to Wrede*, trans. W. Montgomery (London: A&C Black,

Religions School and also for Rudolf Bultmann and his followers. In marked contrast to the eschatology of Jesus, John was now considered the most clearly noneschatological,[21] "mystical" Gospel.[22]

However, two issues were still unresolved at the beginning of the twentieth century: the relationship between John and the Synoptics and the question of John's sources. Both these issues are related to the question of whether John draws on separate narrative sources, or rather on the Synoptics (primarily Mark), as its principal source—albeit in a very selective and original manner—and thus directly affect the question of the historical source value of the Fourth Gospel.

2. The Issue of John's Sources and Dependence on Mark

Obviously, the question of John's historical value is strongly linked with the question of its sources. If the Gospel is rather late and not authored by an eyewitness, it has to be asked whether it draws on earlier (written or oral) sources that can contain valid information about earlier periods of the Jesus movement or even the history of the earthly Jesus himself.

It is no coincidence, therefore, that the very first attempts of Johannine source criticism were strongly motivated by the expectation of discovering an additional source for the history or the teaching of Jesus.

1910); the revised and updated second edition, *Geschichte der Leben-Jesu-Forschung*, was translated as *The Quest of the Historical Jesus: First Complete Edition*, trans. W. Montgomery, J. R. Coates, S. Cupitt, and J. Bowden (London: SCM Press, 2000). On Schweitzer's "thoroughgoing eschatology," see Wendell Willis, "The Discovery of the Eschatological Kingdom: Johannes Weiss and Albert Schweitzer," in *The Kingdom of God in 20th Century Interpretation*, ed. Wendell Willis (Peabody, Mass.: Hendrickson, 1987), 1–14.

[21] Or, to use Bultmann's term, "non-apocalyptic." Only by means of a thorough redefinition of the term "eschatology" could Bultmann consider the work of the evangelist to be the clearest expression of the "eschatological awareness" in early Christian thought. Cf. Jörg Frey, "Johannine Christology and Eschatology," in *Beyond Bultmann. Reckoning a New Testament Theology*, ed. Bruce W. Longenecker and Mikeal C. Parsons (Waco: Baylor University Press, 2014), 101–32; idem, *Die johanneische Eschatologie*, 1:86–118.

[22] See Frey, *Die johanneische Eschatologie*, 1:43–47. For Schweitzer, the only possible relation with Jesus after the failure of the apocalyptic eschatological expectations could be a mystic one. This is also mirrored in his work on Paul, *Die Mystik des Apostels Paulus* (Tübingen: Mohr, 1930), which had a considerable impact on more recent Pauline research in the so-called New Perspective on Paul.

When, in 1886, Hans-Hinrich Wendt[23] tried to reconstruct a source of Jesus' discourses which he thought originated from the Apostle John, without the objectionable miraculous narratives, his suggestion was guided by the desire for a source of Jesus' teaching that was philosophically more acceptable than the synoptic accounts and could not be so easily dismissed on the basis of miracle accounts.[24] When his contemporary Julius Wellhausen suggested an original *Grundschrift* (basic document) of the Gospel in 1908 that contained a chronological framework of only one year and lacked the lengthy Johannine discourses, his search was likewise guided by an interest in recovering an additional narrative source about Jesus that could supplement Mark's framework of Jesus' ministry, but that did not contain the long and repetitious dogmatic discourses Wellhausen could not consider a source for the teaching of Jesus the Jew.[25]

Although Rudolf Bultmann was uninterested in the quest for the historical Jesus for strictly theological reasons, his view of John's sources[26] could point to trajectories of Johannine tradition from an originally Semitic milieu. He assumed that John's discourses and also the hymn behind the Johannine prologue could have originated in gnosticising Baptizer circles in the Transjordan region, a milieu that could be considered more original than that of the synoptic traditions.[27]

[23] Hans Hinrich Wendt, *Die Lehre Jesu*, 2 vols. (Göttingen: Vandenhoeck & Ruprecht, 1886); he further developed this in some later works. In *Die Lehre*, Wendt built upon some of the earlier, more speculative suggestions by Alexander Schweizer and Christian Hermann Weisse. See Frey, *Die johanneische Eschatologie*, 1:51–53.

[24] Cf. also Gilbert van Belle, *The Signs Source in the Fourth Gospel: Historical Survey and Critical Evaluation of the Semeia Hypothesis*, BETL 116 (Leuven: Peeters, 1994), 11–12.

[25] See Julius Wellhausen, *Das Evangelium Johannis* (Berlin: Reimer, 1908). On Wellhausen's introduction of the method of *Literarkritik* (redaction criticism) into Johannine scholarship, see Frey, *Die johanneische Eschatologie*, 1:53–66. On Wellhausen's Gospel criticism, see Baird, *History of New Testament Research*, 2:151–56; on his image of Jesus, see Hans-Dieter Betz, "Wellhausen's Dictum 'Jesus was not a Christian, but a Jew' in Light of Present Scholarship," *ST* 45 (1991): 83–110.

[26] On Bultmann's source theory, see the thorough work of D. Moody Smith, *The Composition and Order of the Fourth Gospel: Bultmann's Literary Theory* (New Haven, Conn.: Yale University Press, 1965); see also Frey, *Die johanneische Eschatologie*, 1:119–42.

[27] In Bultmann's view, the evangelist himself was a former disciple of the Baptizer from a gnosticizing group that venerated the Baptizer, who was then converted to Jesus. Accordingly, Bultmann assumed that the evangelist had taken sources—in particular gnostic revelatory discourses and an original Logos hymn—originally related

But Bultmann's source theory, especially his revelatory discourses, and his assumption of a gnostic background of the Gospel or its author did not find general acceptance, even within his school. Somewhat later, after the first Qumran discoveries, other scholars boldly claimed that the parallels from the Dead Sea Scrolls supported not only a Palestinian Jewish background for the Johannine materials or the author of the Gospel,[28] but also a greater historical source value for the Fourth Gospel.[29] But apart from the fact that the scrolls fostered a stronger perception of the Jewish elements in John,[30] those claims regarding the background of the evangelist or the historical source value of John were soon judged to be overstated.[31]

Roughly at the same time, during World War II, there was a remarkable change in scholarship regarding the issue of John's dependence on or independence from the Synoptics. Earlier scholarship from

---

to a mythic redeemer figure or to the Baptizer and only secondarily related to Jesus and integrated into the Fourth Gospel. While the assumption of a pre-Johannine Logos hymn (in various versions) found numerous supporters, the revelatory discourses as reconstructed by Bultmann were only accepted by few of his disciples. See Frey, *Die johanneische Eschatologie*, 1:127–29.

[28] Thus Karl Georg Kuhn, "Die in Palästina gefundenen hebräischen Texte und das Neue Testament," *ZTK* 47 (1950): 192–211, who claimed that the "native soil" of John's Gospel had been found in the nonorthodox, or (as he thought) gnostic, Palestinian Jewish milieu of the Dead Sea Scrolls (209–10). Cf. similar bold claims later in James H. Charlesworth, "The Dead Sea Scrolls and the Gospel according to John," in *Exploring the Gospel of John*, Festschrift D. Moody Smith (Louisville: Westminster John Knox, 1996), 69–97, who speculates about "the vivid memory of an Essene who had become a Christian" (88).

[29] Thus in particular William F. Albright, "Recent Discoveries in Palestine and the Gospel of St. John," in *The Background of the New Testament and Its Eschatology*, Festschrift C. H. Dodd (Cambridge: Cambridge University Press, 1956), 153–71 (esp. 170–71); and Frank Moore Cross, *The Ancient Library of Qumran and Modern Biblical Studies* (London: Duckworth, 1958), 161–62: "John preserves authentic historical material which first took form in an Aramaic or Hebrew milieu where Essene currents still ran strong."

[30] For a recent discussion, see Jörg Frey, "Recent Perspectives on Johannine Dualism and Its Background," in *Text, Thought, and Practice in Qumran and Early Christianity*, ed. Ruth A. Clements and Daniel R. Schwartz, STDJ 84 (Leiden: Brill, 2009), 127–57.

[31] For a more balanced view, see Richard J. Bauckham, "Qumran and the Fourth Gospel: Is There a Connection?" in *The Scrolls and the Scriptures: Qumran Fifty Years After*, ed. Stanley E. Porter and Craig A. Evans, JSPSup 26 (Sheffield: Sheffield Academic Press, 1997), 267–79; and Frey, "Recent Perspectives on Johannine Dualism," 127–57.

Baur[32] to Theodor Zahn[33] and Hans Windisch,[34] and also Benjamin Wisner Bacon[35] or Burnett H. Streeter in the Anglo-Saxon world,[36] had considered John to be dependent particularly on Mark, so that the question could only be whether John wanted to supplement or to replace the Synoptics.[37] The turn of the tide came about with a small but influential book written in the wake of World War II by the young Cambridge clergyman Percifal Gardner-Smith.[38] Mostly in debate with Bacon, Gardner-Smith emphasized the differences between Mark and John while only superficially looking at their commonalities, and from those differences he postulated (though did not demonstrate) John's independence.[39] The new perspective appeared revolutionary, and its rhetoric appealed

[32] See Ferdinand Christian Baur, *Kritische Untersuchungen über die kanonischen Evangelien* (Tübingen: Fues, 1847), 239–80; see further Heinrich Julius Holtzmann, "Das schriftstellerische Verhältnis des Johannes zu den Synoptikern," *ZWT* 12 (1869): 62–85, 155–78, 446–56.

[33] Theodor Zahn, *Einleitung in das Neue Testament*, 2nd ed., 2 vols. (Leipzig: Deichert, 1900), 2:500–529.

[34] Hans Windisch, *Johannes und die Synoptiker: Wollte der vierte Evangelist die älteren Evangelien ergänzen oder ersetzen?* UNT 12 (Leipzig: Hinrichs, 1926).

[35] Benjamin W. Bacon, *The Fourth Gospel in Research and Debate* (New York: Moffat, Yard & Co., 1910), 368; on Bacon's scholarship, see Baird, *History of New Testament Research*, 2:299–305.

[36] Burnett H. Streeter, *The Four Gospels: A Study of Origins Treating of the Manuscript Tradition, Authorship, and Dates* (London: Macmillan, 1924); on Streeter, see Baird, *History of New Testament Research*, 2:265–66.

[37] Thus the leading question in Windisch, *Johannes und die Synoptiker.*

[38] P. Gardner-Smith, *Saint John and the Synoptic Gospels* (Cambridge: Cambridge University Press, 1938); cf. D. Moody Smith, *John among the Gospels: The Relationship in Twentieth-Century Research* (Minneapolis: Fortress, 1992), 37–44; and the thorough critical analysis of the argument and the reception of the book by Joseph Verheyden, "P. Gardner-Smith and the 'Turn of the Tide,'" in *John and the Synoptics*, ed. A. Denaux, BETL 101 (Leuven: Peeters, 1992), 423–52.

[39] See the criticism by Ismo Dunderberg, *Johannes und die Synaoptiker*, Annales Academiae Scientiarum Fennicae / Dissertationes humanarum litterarum 69 (Helsinki: Akateeminen Kirjakauppa, 1994), 23; and Verheyden, "P. Gardner-Smith," who summarizes the argument in the book as follows: "The similarities are considered insufficient evidence for literary dependence, and then the dissimilarities are enumerated and judged as incapable of reasonable explanation on the basis of the hypothesis" (427); "Gardner-Smith's analysis of the Synoptic-like pericopes reads almost as a collection of anti-dependence slogans" (429).

to many scholars. The positive reception of the book by British scholars W. F. Howard and especially C. H. Dodd,[40] and the compatibility of the independence hypothesis with the views of Bultmann and his school,[41] achieved a temporary breakthrough for the view of John's independence in British[42] and German[43] scholarship. In North America, the idea of an independent development or trajectory of the Johannine tradition and of a proper Johannine signs source (or even signs gospel) became the majority view, shared by a diverse range of scholars such as Helmut Koester and James Robinson,[44] Raymond E. Brown,[45] J. Louis Martyn,[46] Robert T. Fortna,[47] Wayne A. Meeks,[48] and D. Moody Smith.[49]

[40] Wilbert F. Howard, *Christianity according to St. John* (London: Duckworth, 1943), 17, n. 2; see already the reference by C. H. Dodd, *History and the Gospel* (London: Nisbet, 1938), 80, n. 2; later idem, *The Interpretation of the Fourth Gospel* (Cambridge: Cambridge University Press, 1953), 449, n. 2; and idem, *Historical Tradition in the Fourth Gospel* (Cambridge: Cambridge University Press, 1963), 8, n. 2.

[41] The view of John's independence was more compatible with the hypothesis that the roots of Johannine tradition lay in the milieu of early Baptizer circles as well as with the assumption of distinctive pre-Johannine sources for the miracles and the passion narrative.

[42] It should be noted also that the father of the hypothesis of the literary priority of John, John A. T. Robinson, was strongly inspired by Gardner-Smith; see John A. T. Robinson, "The New Look on the Fourth Gospel," in *Studia Evangelica 1*, ed. Kurt Aland et al. (Berlin: Akademie-Verlag, 1959), 338–50 (340).

[43] See, e.g., the positive reception in the first account of Johannine research after World War II by Ernst Haenchen, "Aus der Literatur zum Johannesevangelium 1929–1956," *TRev* 23 (1955): 295–335 (303).

[44] Cf. James M. Robinson, "The Johannine Trajectory," in Helmut Koester and James M. Robinson, *Trajectories through Early Christianity* (Philadelphia: Fortress, 1971), 232–68; Helmut Koester, *Ancient Christian Gospels: Their History and Development* (Philadelphia: Trinity, 1990), 250–51.

[45] Raymond E. Brown, *The Gospel according to John*, vol. 1, AB 29 (New York: Doubleday, 1966), xlvii.

[46] J. Louis Martyn, *History and Theology in the Fourth Gospel*, 3rd ed. (Louisville: Westminster John Knox), 31, n. 5.

[47] Robert T. Fortna, *The Gospel of Signs: A Reconstruction of the Narrative Source Underlying the Fourth Gospel*, SNTSMS (Cambridge: Cambridge University Press, 1970).

[48] Wayne A. Meeks, "The Man from Heaven in Johannine Sectarianism," *JBL* 91 (1972): 44–72.

[49] See Smith, *John among the Gospels*; furthermore idem, "Jesus Tradition," in *Handbook for the Study of the Historical Jesus*, ed. Tom Holmén and Stanley E. Porter, 4 vols. (Leiden: Brill, 2010), 3:1997–2039 (2038).

Of course, there were always dissenting voices. Most prominent among them were C. K. Barrett, in his magisterial commentary from 1955,[50] and Bultmann's younger colleague in Marburg, Werner Georg Kümmel,[51] who still favored the idea of John's dependence on Mark. But it was not until the 1980s, when a large number of scholars began to question the various reconstructions of pre-Johannine sources, that the view of the independence or even "priority"[52] of the Fourth Gospel and its traditions lost its plausibility.[53] Criticism of the assumptions of pre-Johannine sources had been nourished from the influence of linguistic and narrative studies, the perception of the stylistic coherence of the Fourth Gospel,[54] and, not least, from the diversity of the various alleged sources and the often-recognized circularity of the argument of the source critics.[55] With the destruction of the signs-source theory by Gilbert van Belle and others,[56] and the questioning of the idea of a separate

[50] Charles Kingsley Barrett, *The Gospel according to St. John: An Introduction with Commentary and Notes on the Greek Text* (London: SPCK, 1955), 34–45.

[51] Werner Georg Kümmel, *Einleitung in das Neue Testament* (Heidelberg: Quelle & Meyer, 1963), 137.

[52] Thus the scholars who suggested an early dating: John A. T. Robinson, *The Priority of John* (London: SCM, 1985); and Klaus Berger, *Im Anfang war Johannes: Datierung und Theologie des vierten Evangeliums* (Stuttgart: Quell, 1997).

[53] For more details, cf. Jörg Frey, "Das vierte Evangelium auf dem Hintergrund der älteren Evangelientradition: Zum Problem: Johannes und die Synoptiker," in *Die Herrlichkeit des Gekreuzigten: Studien zu den johanneischen Schriften I*, ed. Juliane Schlegel, WUNT 307 (Tübingen: Mohr Siebeck, 2013), 239–94 (255–60).

[54] See Eugen Ruckstuhl and Peter Dschulnigg, *Stilkritik und Verfasserfrage im Johannesevangeliums: Die johanneischen Sprachmerkmale auf dem Hintergrund des Neuen Testaments und des zeitgenössischen hellenistischen Schrifttums*, NTOA 17 (Freiburg Schweiz: Universitätsverlag; Göttingen: Vandenhoeck & Ruprecht, 1991); and the falsification of the Fortna hypothesis in Eugen Ruckstuhl, "Sprache und Stil im johanneischen Schrifttum," in idem, *Die literarische Einheit des Johannesevangeliums*, enl. new ed., NTOA 17 (Freiburg Schweiz: Universitätsverlag; Göttingen: Vandenhoeck & Ruprecht, 1987), 304–31; see also Frey, *Die johanneische Eschatologie*, 1:429–45.

[55] See the thorough criticism of the source theories of Georg Richter and Jürgen Becker in Frey, *Die johanneische Eschatologie*, 1:273–97.

[56] Van Belle, *Signs Source in the Fourth Gospel*; Frans Neirynck, "The Signs Source in the Fourth Gospel: A Critique of the Hypothesis," in *Evangelica II: 1982–1991: Collected Essays*, ed. F. van Segbroeck, BETL 94 (Leuven: Leuven University Press, 1991), 651–77; cf. also Udo Schnelle, *Antidocetic Christology in the Gospel of John: An Investigation of the Place of the Fourth Gospel in the Johannine School*, trans. Linda M. Maloney (Minneapolis:

source in the passion narrative,[57] scholars such as Frans Neirynck and Maurits Sabbe,[58] Martin Hengel,[59] Udo Schnelle,[60] Hartwig Thyen,[61]

Fortress, 1992); Daniel Marguerat, "La 'source des signes' existe-t-elle?" in *La communauté johannique et son histoire*, ed. Jean-Daniel Kaestli et al. (Geneva: Cerf, 1990), 60–93.

[57] Cf. the convincing monograph by Manfred Lang, *Johannes und die Synoptiker: Eine redaktionsgeschichtliche Analyse von Joh 18-20 vor dem markinischen und lukanischen Hintergrund*, FRLANT 182 (Göttingen: Vandenhoeck & Ruprecht, 1999), who shows that the Johannine passion narrative can be completely explained from Mark and, in some passages, Luke, when the Johannine perspective of interpretation is considered. There are, of course, still dissenting views, thus, e.g., Jürgen Becker, *Das Evangelium nach Johannes*, vol. 2: *Kapitel 11–21*, 3rd ed., ÖTK 4/2 (Gütersloh: Gütersloher Verlagshaus, 1991), 634–38; and, more recently, the reconstruction by Frank Schleritt, *Der vorjohanneische Passionsbericht: Eine historisch-kritische und theologische Untersuchung zu Joh 2,13–22; 11,47–14,31 und 18,1–20,29*, BZNW 154 (Berlin: de Gruyter, 2007).

[58] See Frans Neirynck, "John and the Synoptics," in *Evangelica: Gospel Studies—Étude d'Évangile*, ed. F. van Segbroeck, BETL 60 (Leuven: Peeters, 1982), 365–400; idem, "John and the Synoptics: The Empty Tomb Stories," in *Evangelica II*, 571–99; idem, "The Anonymous Disciple in John 1," in *Evangelica II*, 617–49; idem, "The Signs Source in the Fourth Gospel: A Critique of the Hypothesis," in *Evangelica II*, 651–77; idem, "John 4:46–54: Signs Source or Synoptic Gospels," in *Evangelica II*, 679–87; idem, "John 5:1–18 and the Gospel of Mark: A Response to Peder Borgen," in *Evangelica II*, 699–711; Maurits Sabbe, "The Arrest of Jesus in Jn 18,1–11 and Its Relation to the Synoptic Gospels," in *L'Évangile de Jean: Sources, redaction, théologie*, ed. Marinus de Jonge, BETL 44 (Gembloux: Duculot; Leuven: Leuven University Press, 1977), 203–34; idem, "The Anointing of Jesus in Jn 12,1–8 and Its Synoptic Parallels," in *The Four Gospels 1992*, Festschrift Frans Neirynck, ed. F. van Segbroeck, 3 vols., BETL 100 (Leuven: University Press, 1992), 3:2051–82; idem, "The Trial of Jesus before Pilate in John and Its Relation to the Synoptic Gospels," in *John and the Synoptics*, ed. Adalbert Denaux, BETL 101 (Leuven: Peeters, 1992), 341–85. See also the report by Michael Labahn and Manfred Lang, "Johannes und die Synoptiker: Positionen und Impulse seit 1990," in *Kontexte des Johannesevangeliums*, ed. Jörg Frey and Udo Schnelle, WUNT 175 (Tübingen: Mohr Siebeck, 2004), 443–515 (450–51).

[59] Martin Hengel, *Die johanneische Frage: Ein Lösungsversuch, mit einem Beitrag zur Apokalypse von J. Frey*, WUNT 67 (Tübingen: Mohr Siebeck, 1993), 208–9; idem, *The Johannine Question* (London: SCM Press, 1989), 75.

[60] Udo Schnelle, "Johannes und die Synoptiker," in *The Four Gospels 1992*, 2:1799–814; idem, *Einleitung in das Neue Testament*, 8th ed. (Göttingen: Vandenhoeck & Ruprecht, 2013), 577–81.

[61] Hartwig Thyen, "Johannes und die Synoptiker," in *John and the Synoptics*, ed. Adalbert Denaux, BETL 101 (Leuven: Peeters, 1992), 81–107; idem, "Die Erzählung von den Bethanischen Geschwistern (Joh 11,1–12,19) als 'Palimpsest' über synoptischen Texten," in *The Four Gospels 1992*, 3:2021–50, with the all-too daring hypothesis that the Johannine text plays with all three synoptic Gospels.

and Richard Bauckham[62] reestablished the view that John draws on a knowledge of synoptic traditions and texts, not only in its latest redactional layer, the appended chapter 21, but even in the work of the evangelist. This implies that John adopts and modifies the gospel genre originally created by the author of Mark rather than independently inventing it a second time.[63] It also implies that John's narrative framework is basically built upon the synoptic framework,[64] supplemented with additional community traditions. Of course, the type of dependence in view here differs from the dependence that exists between Mark and Matthew or Luke. But this is only appropriate in view of the fact that the author of the Fourth Gospel takes an eclectic approach, deliberately shaping his materials (cf. John 20:30-31).[65]

Even more provoking is Richard Bauckham's substantial case for the idea that the Fourth Gospel not only draws on Mark but also addresses readers who know Mark's Gospel, providing them with both supplementary material[66] and a deeper theological interpretation of the traditional gospel story.

In my view, these arguments, which are largely in agreement with the theories of the period before Gardner-Smith, are widely convincing. A number of narrative sequences in John are best explained by

[62] Richard J. Bauckham, "John for Readers of Mark," in *The Gospels for All Christians*, ed. Richard J. Bauckham (Grand Rapids: Eerdmans, 1998), 147–71.

[63] Cf. Schnelle, "Johannes und die Synoptiker," 1801–2; idem, *Einleitung in das Neue Testament*, 580; Frey, "Das vierte Evangelium," 264.

[64] An important compositional argument are the common narrative sequences in Mark 6–8 and John 6, and in the Passion narrative, see Schnelle, "Johannes und die Synoptiker," 1805–13; idem, *Einleitung in das Neue Testament*, 578; see extensively Ian D. Mackay, *John's Relationship with Mark: An Analysis of John 6 in the Light of Mark 6–8*, WUNT 2/182 (Tübingen: Mohr Siebeck, 2004).

[65] Advocates for the independence of John (or the evangelist) had often conceded that a harmonization of the Johannine tradition with Synoptic tradition happened in the post-Johannine redaction, e.g., in John 21, whereas the Johannine community prior to that redactional stage was said to be unaware of Synoptic materials.

[66] Bauckham, "John for Readers of Mark," 170, argues that John does not only supplement but also complements Mark's story, whereas reversely Mark can also be read as complementing John's story. This is true with respect to chronological issues and the identification of narrative figures such as Mary from Bethany as the woman anointing Jesus (John 11:2) or Caiaphas as the high priest in office (11:49). The critical corrections, however, should not be underestimated.

the Fourth Evangelist's knowledge of Mark,[67] and many details in common episodes and sayings are also better explained from a direct influence of Mark than from more complicated assumptions about common oral traditions,[68] Johannine adoption of pre-synoptic material, pre-Johannine adoption of pre-synoptic material,[69] or a harmonization merely on the level of a late Johannine redaction,[70] while still considering the evangelist unaware of the synoptic tradition.[71] Many of the constructions of the supporters of Johannine independence simply lack historical plausibility.[72] Distinctive differences such as the Johannine silence about Jesus' baptism and the installation of the Eucharist, or the Johannine design of the passion narrative with its difference regarding the last words of Jesus, can also be understood as a critical adoption or

[67] Thus in particular the sequence in John 6, with the feeding of the multitude (John 6:1-15 // Mark 6:32-44), the appearance on the sea (John 6:16-21 // Mark 6:45-52), the crossing of the sea (John 6:22-25 // Mark 6:53-54), the demand for a sign (John 6:26 // Mark 8:11-13), and Peter's confession (John 6:66-71 // Mark 8:27-30), and also the sequence of the passion narrative (see Schnelle, *Einleitung in das Neue Testament*, 577).

[68] Thus Jürgen Becker, *Das Evangelium nach Johannes*, vol 1: *Kapitel 1–10*, 3rd ed., ÖTK 4/1 (Gütersloh: Gütersloher Verlagshaus, 1991), 45.

[69] Thus, e.g., Anton Dauer, *Die Passionsgeschichte im Johannesevangelium*, SANT 30 (München: Kösel, 1972), 121, 164, etc.

[70] Thus Bultmann's remarks on John 21 in his commentary, as well as other interpreters reckoning with an "ecclesiastical redaction" of John.

[71] The methodological problem has rarely been considered that independence or ignorance of synoptic materials is much more difficult to prove than a certain kind of reception. See Frey, "Das vierte Evangelium," 258.

[72] This is especially true when we have to consider that early Christian groups, including the Johannine communities, were not encapsulated sectarian groups but in exchange with the world around them and, of course, also with other Jesus followers. See the considerations by Richard J. Bauckham, "For Whom Were Gospels Written," in Bauckham, *The Gospels for All Christians*, 9–48. For further discussion, cf. Craig L. Blomberg, "The Gospels for Specific Communities *and* All Christians," in *The Audience of the Gospels: The Origins and Function of the Gospels in Early Christianity*, ed. Edward W. Klink III, LNTS 353 (London: T&T Clark, 2010), 111–33; Richard J. Bauckham, "Is There Patristic Counter-Evidence? A Response to Margaret Mitchell," in Klink, *Audience of the Gospels*, 68–110; and Martin Hengel, *Die vier Evangelien und das eine Evangelium von Jesus Christus*, WUNT 224 (Tübingen: Mohr Siebeck, 2008), 184–96.

correction of Mark,[73] from the perspective of Johannine Christology and theology.

To illustrate this point, I will mention the most telling and, in my view, the most compelling example.[74] The episode about Jesus' prayer in Gethsemane (Mark 14:32-42) is not narrated in the Johannine passion narrative. But was it really unknown to the evangelist or his readers? There are several passages scattered throughout the Gospel in which the motifs of that story (e.g., Jesus being troubled, the prayer to be rescued or spared from death, "drinking the cup," "the hour," and the coming of the adversary) are adopted, albeit in a significantly different manner.

a) At the end of the first part of the farewell discourse, the quote in John 14:31, "Arise, let us go from here" (ἐγείρεσθε, ἄγωμεν ἐντεῦθεν), clearly adopts the end of the Gethsemane narrative of Mark 14:42, "Arise, let us go, the one who delivers me is at hand" (ἐγείρεσθε, ἄγωμεν· ἰδού, ὁ παραδιδούς με ἤγγικεν), which provides a transition to the episode of Jesus' arrest. In John, however, there are three more chapters of farewell discourses until the story of Jesus' arrest is narrated in 18:1-11. In addition to the quotation[75] of the two final words of Mark's Gethsemane episode, there is the motif of the adversary approaching, which is presented in the immediately preceding verse, albeit with the difference that John refers not to Judas but to the "ruler of the world" (14:30b), who is about to encounter Jesus in his death.

b) Whereas the single brief quotation in John 14:31 could not prove dependence on Mark, the existence of two more passages adopting motifs from the Gethsemane story strengthen the case. In 12:27-28, just after the proclamation of Jesus' "hour" (v. 23), Jesus says, "Now my soul is troubled. And what should I say—'Father, save me from this hour?' No, it is for this reason that I have come to this hour. Father, glorify your

[73] Interestingly, John 3:24 hints at a detail from the synoptic account of John's imprisonment "as though it were something already known to the readers/hearers and as though a chronological point were at issue" (Bauckham, "John for Readers of Mark," 153).

[74] Frey, "Das vierte Evangelium," 265–71.

[75] It is disputed, however, whether the exact correspondence of two subsequent words can be considered a quotation, but in this case several other motifs strengthen the argument: (1) the motif of the coming adversary in the immediate context of John 14:30b and (2) the narrative continuation in 18:1.

name." Here we can find the motif of Jesus being troubled (Mark 14:34; cf. Ps 41/42 LXX); the motif of the "hour," mentioned twice in Mark's Gethsemane episode (Mark 14:35, 41); and the idea of a prayer of Jesus to be rescued from "this hour," which corresponds to Mark not only in its content but even in the formal fact that both contain quoted speech. The significant difference between the two passages is that John explicitly rejects the prayer as it is uttered in Mark's Gethsemane scene. The verbatim quote of Jesus' prayer in John 12:28 refers to a divine commissioning or necessity, which is the reason John feels it necessary to openly reject the idea of a prayer to escape the "hour."

c) Later, in the context of Jesus' arrest, which follows the Gethsemane scene in Mark, Jesus rebuffs the disciples' attempt to defend him with the sword, arguing, "The cup which the Father has given Me, shall I not drink it?" (John 18:11). Again, the motif of "drinking the cup" is adopted, together with Jesus' voluntary acceptance of his destiny as commissioned by the Father, so that the argument confirms the reversal of Jesus' prayer in Gethsemane.

The references to the motifs of Mark's Gethsemane pericope in three different and quite dispersed contexts can only be explained by the assumption that the evangelist knew Mark's story, but instead of retelling it, he adopted its central motifs and provided a correction or even rejection in accordance with his own christological insights. In John's view, Jesus could not have really tried to escape the cup of his death, and therefore he explicitly rejected the prayer recorded in Mark. Likewise, in John's christological view, Jesus could not have felt really forsaken by God, and therefore his last word on the cross is not the lament of the righteous sufferer from Psalm 22 (as in Mark 15:34) but is deliberately changed into a cry of triumph and fulfillment (John 19:30).

The manner in which John presents the motifs of the Gethsemane episode is significant. While the episode is not narrated, one of its motifs—the "hour"—is not only adopted but extensively used as a programmatic keyword for the events surrounding Jesus' death.[76] Furthermore, other motifs are used in various combinations in three different and unconnected contexts (chapters 12, 14, and 18). The

[76] On the motif of Jesus' hour in John, see Frey, *Die johanneische Eschatologie*, 2:216–21.

relatively insignificant end of Mark's pericope ("Arise, let's go!") is verbally reproduced, but the main content of the episode, Jesus' prayer to be spared from the hour, is explicitly rejected and replaced by a different request more in agreement with John's Christology. The use of the motifs in various combinations in three different parts of the Gospel can only be explained as a Johannine reception of the episode, not conversely. Furthermore, the procedure cannot be explained from the mere use of traditions as a quarry for the evangelist's own narrative, but instead deserves to be considered as an explicit interaction with the ideas John rejected in Jesus' words within 12:27–28 and 18:11—that is, an open criticism of Mark's story.

This is only conceivable if the implied readers were aware of this prayer of Jesus, meaning that they had knowledge of the synoptic material, including the narrative of Jesus' passion, which is explicitly criticized by the Johannine Jesus—or rather by the evangelist who brings his words to expression. At least here, John addresses readers (or hearers) of Mark's story, and he uses that story to present his own christological viewpoint, according to which Jesus deliberately enters his "hour" and "drinks the cup" given to him by the Father (in other words, he accepts death in unity with the Father and as fulfillment of his mission, as John 19:30 confirms).

Without providing further examples here, we can conclude that the Fourth Gospel presupposes a knowledge of the synoptic corpus and is best understood as a selective and critical reinterpretation of the earlier Jesus tradition, in particular Mark (possibly including elements from Luke).[77] In light of the example presented above, the idea that John wrote his gospel in complete ignorance of or independence from the synoptic materials can no longer be maintained.

The consequences of this conclusion for Johannine source criticism are clear: if a knowledge of Mark's narrative underlies the Johannine narrative, it is impossible to prove the existence of other continuous narrative sources behind John's Gospel, either for John's miracles or for the passion account. Of course, it is also impossible to exclude the knowledge or existence of other narrative sources. They can, at best,

[77] Cf. Schnelle, *Einleitung in das Neue Testament*, 580–81; and Hengel, *The Johannine Question*, 75.

be hypothetically assumed, but not demonstrated. If one here applies the theory of Occam's razor, that is, if the explanation with the fewest additional assumptions is to be preferred, the best option is to reckon with Mark as the most basic source, which is then used quite freely. For the narrative episodes unattested in Mark, we can then assume (and in some points also demonstrate) that the evangelist draws on discrete narrative traditions[78] and sayings,[79] most probably transmitted and shaped by the Johannine community and its language. But the selectiveness and creativity of the evangelist should not be underestimated. His free and creative use of all his sources—the Scriptures and the earlier Jesus tradition—differs from the Synoptics and makes John unique among the Gospels. Since we cannot assume that the evangelist completely integrated his sources into his gospel, any attempt to reconstruct John's sources accurately and completely can only be considered "science fiction."[80]

The issue of John's historical source value, however, is not facilitated by this conclusion. On the contrary, John's dependence on Mark seems to strengthen the dehistorization of John: if the differences between John and Mark are largely to be explained by the theological intentions of the evangelist, it is rather unlikely that they can contribute alternative data for reconstructing the history of Jesus or of the earlier community. If John knows Mark or even writes for readers of Mark, the Johannine narration is at an even greater distance from the historical origins of the Jesus tradition.

However, the Fourth Gospel is neither a myth, nor a mere allegory, nor—as Hartwig Thyen has boldly phrased it—a "palimpsest" overwriting

[78] This has been demonstrated with regard to the miracle stories by Michael Labahn, *Jesus als Lebensspender: Untersuchungen zu einer Geschichte der johanneischen Traditionen anhand ihrer Wundergeschichten*, BZNW 9 (Berlin: de Gruyter, 1999).

[79] On the traditional sayings behind the Johannine discourses, see the extensive study by Michael Theobald, *Herrenworte im Johannesevangelium*, HBS 34 (Freiburg im Breisgau: Herder, 2002).

[80] Thus, the methodological chances of source criticism are very limited. The image of an evangelist compiling various sources into his gospel writing, as was presented in Bultmann's commentary, lacks any historical plausibility. See Frey, *Die johanneische Eschatologie*, 1:141–42.

the Synoptics.[81] It is a factual narrative[82] that claims to tell the story of the earthly Jesus, analogous to the Synoptics and in deliberate adoption of the genre originally "invented" by Mark; it is a narrative about the ministry and death of the earthly Jesus, from his encounter with John the Baptist until his resurrection appearances, located in a particular region, at clearly defined places, and at a precisely marked time.

But how can the evangelist maintain this claim while at the same time so freely reshaping the Jesus story? How can he claim to present the better story when he provides "alternative facts" by rejecting or altering earlier traditions? These questions touch on not only historical but fundamentally theological issues.

Therefore, a responsible interpretation cannot neglect historical questions. It must confront John with the different views of Mark, the other Synoptics, and their sources, and it must ask about the source value of John's narrative and about the historical traditions behind the Fourth Gospel. It may be true that some questions can no longer be answered or that the outline of historical events or contexts fades in the dust of the tradition process. But forgoing the historical questions, as is popular in some modern reading strategies,[83] would be an improper and insufficient answer to the claims of the text.

[81] Thus Thyen, "Die Erzählung von den Bethanischen Geschwistern (Joh 11, 1–12,19)."

[82] On the characterization of the Johannine narrative "within the framework of narratology, factuality, and fiction," see Susanne Luther, "From Bethlehem, according to the Promise, or Rather from Nazareth? Narrative and History in John's Gospel," *Early Christianity* 8 (2017): 9–29 (18–23), where John's narrative is classified as a "factual text with fictionalizing literary strategies" (21). For the terms "fictional" and "factunal" as used in narratological theory, see G. Genette, "Fictional Narrative, Factual Narrative," *Poetics Today* 11 (1990): 755–74. See also the interdisciplinary discussion in *Wirklichkeitserzählungen: Felder, Formen und Funktionen nicht-literarischen Erzählens*, ed. Christian Klein and Matias Martinez (Stuttgart: Metzler, 2009).

[83] There is no doubt that the synchronic and narrative reading of the text has fostered a great number of observations and enabled a much more adequate understanding of the whole, but disregarding the historical questions would only be water on the mills of either fundamentalism or categorical skepticism, both of which are inappropriate in view of the text. In light of these challenges, a sound philological and historical method is indispensable.

3. The Quest for History in John: Methodological Problems in Recent Approaches

But how can we ask about historical tradition in the Fourth Gospel? How can we determine the historical source value of the elements of the Johannine text? For decades, the pioneering work of C. H. Dodd on "Historical Tradition in the Fourth Gospel" was the only note-worthy study on the related problems, and although Dodd assumed John's independence from the Synoptics, his work is valuable even for scholars who are convinced that John knew at least Mark's Gospel.[84] Only in the past two decades has there been a number of attempts to revitalize interest in the historical issues and to restore a more positive view of John's historical source value.

In the present framework, we cannot present and discuss all these attempts in detail. Instead, we will have a closer look at some methodological problems that can be found in various attempts of what we could call "rehistoricizing" the Fourth Gospel.

Some of these approaches are still driven by the conviction that the Fourth Gospel is authored by an apostolic eyewitness[85] who

[84] Dodd, *Historical Tradition.* For the subsequent discussion, cf. the survey by Don A. Carson, "Historical Tradition in the Fourth Gospel: After Dodd, What?" in *Gospel Perspectives*, vol. 2: *Studies of History and Tradition in the Four Gospels*, ed. R. T. France and David Wenham (Sheffield: JSOT Press, 1981), 83–145. More recently, see Francis J. Moloney, "The Fourth Gospel and the Jesus of History," *NTS* 46 (2000): 42–58; Craig A. Evans, "The Historical Reliability of John's Gospel: From What Perspective Should it be Assessed?" in *The Gospel of John and Christian Theology*, ed. Richard J. Bauckham and C. Moser (Grand Rapids: Eerdmans, 2008), 91–119; James H. Charlesworth, "The Historical Jesus in the Fourth Gospel: A Paradigm Shift?" *JSHJ* 8 (2010): 3–46. For a more recent comprehensive analysis, see D. Moody Smith, "Jesus Tradition in the Gospel of John," in Holmén and Porter, *Handbook for the Study of the Historical Jesus*, 3:1997–2039; and Jörg Frey, "Johannesevangelium," in *Jesus Handbuch*, ed. Jens Schröter and Christine Jacobi (Tübingen: Mohr Siebeck, 2017), 137–45.

[85] Thus, e.g., Don A. Carson, *The Gospel according to John* (Leicester: InterVarsity; Grand Rapids: Eerdmans, 1991), 40–81; Craig L. Blomberg, "The Historical Reliability of John: Rushing in Where Angels Fear to Tread?" in *Jesus in Johannine Tradition*, ed. Robert T. Fortna and Tom Thatcher (Louisville: Westminster John Knox, 2001), 71–82; idem, *The Historical Reliability of John's Gospel: Issues and Commentary* (Downers Grove, Ill.: InterVarsity, 2002); Andreas J. Koestenberger, "Early Doubts of the Apostolic Authorship of the Fourth Gospel in the History of Modern Biblical Criticism,"

could claim firsthand knowledge. We cannot discuss the numerous problems with this traditional claim here,[86] but even if the author were an eyewitness of Jesus' whole ministry, this would not necessarily support the view that the historical reference of his work is more reliable than the other Gospels. Therefore, the traditional view of Johannine authorship, which some conservative scholars (Roman Catholic[87] or Protestant[88]) feel obliged to defend for various reasons, cannot be a decisive or even helpful argument with regard to John's historical reliability, and scholars who express their views from such a perspective may be in greater danger of underestimating

---

in idem, *Studies on John and Gender: A Decade of Scholarship*, Studies in Biblical Literature 38 (New York: Peter Lang, 2001), 17–47; idem, *John*, BECNT (Grand Rapids: Baker, 2004).

[86] I have presented the problems of the traditional view on Johannine authorship in Frey, "Das Corpus Johanneum und die Apokalypse des Johannes: Die Johanneslegende, die Probleme der johanneischen Verfasserschaft und die Frage der Pseudonymität der Apokalypse," in *Poetik und Intertextualität der Apokalypse*, ed. S. Alkier, T. Hieke, and T. Nicklas, WUNT 346 (Tübingen: Mohr Siebeck, 2015), 71–133 (see in particular pages 90–103).

[87] Cf. the most learned Roman Catholic commentary of the period before the Second Vatican Council by Marie-Joseph Lagrange, *Évangile selon Saint Jean*, 2nd ed., *EBib* 16 (Paris: Gabalda, 1925). For more recent Roman Catholic scholarship, see Benedikt Schwank, *Evangelium nach Johannes: Erläutert für die Praxis* (St. Ottilien: EOS, 1998); Robert Mercier, *L'Évangile "pour que vous croyez": Le quatrième évangile (selon Saint Jean)* (Montreal: Wilson & Lafleur, 2010).

[88] In addition to the authors mentioned above in n. 85, cf. the "classics" of conservatism, the British adversary of F. C. Baur, Joseph Barber Lightfoot, and the German adversary of Harnack and contemporary liberal theology, Theodor Zahn. See Joseph Barber Lightfoot, *Biblical Essays* (London: Macmillan, 1983), 47–122; idem, *The Gospel of St. John: A Newly Discovered Commentary*, ed. Ben Witherington III and Todd D. Still (Downers Grove, Ill.: IVP Academic, 2015); cf. also Martin Hengel, "Bishop Lightfoot and the Tübingen School on the Gospel of John and the Second Century," *Durham University Journal: Supplement* (1992): 23–51 (repr. in Lightfoot, *The Gospel of St. John*, 326–59); Geoffrey L. Treloar, *Lightfoot the Historian: The Nature and Role of History in the Life and Thought of J. B. Lightfoot (1828–1889) as Churchman and Scholar*, WUNT 2/103 (Tübingen: Mohr Siebeck, 1998). For Zahn's scholarship, see his very learned introduction to the NT and his commentary on John: Theodor Zahn, *Einleitung in das Neue Testament*, 3rd ed., 2 vols. (Leipzig: Deichert, 1906); idem, *Das Evangelium des Johannes*, repr. of the 5th/6th edition (Wuppertal: Brockhaus, 1983 [1921]).

the theological intentions and the authorial creativity of the Gospel author.[89]

But the "rehistorization" of John has also been advocated by scholars who do not presuppose the Johannine author tradition. Richard Bauckham, who attributes the Gospel to the Presbyter John mentioned by Papias[90] (who could be at most an eyewitness of the last days of Jesus), points to historiographical features in John and concludes that the evangelist had a more distinctive historical interest than previously thought.[91] A wider discussion has been hosted by the SBL group John, Jesus, and History, stimulated by Paul Anderson's energetic plea for a reconsideration of John's historical source value. The project has produced a monograph by Anderson and three collections of detailed studies,[92] thereby providing an important stimulus for scholarship, especially since the range of contributors does not only include supporters of the general tendency of the project[93] but

[89] See also Frey, *Glory of the Crucified One*, 28–30.

[90] Richard J. Bauckham, "The Beloved Disciple as an Ideal Author," *JSNT* 39 (1993): 21–44, repr. in idem, *The Testimony of the Beloved Disciple: Narrative, History, and Theology in the Gospel of John* (Grand Rapids: Eerdmans, 2007), 73–91; idem, "Papias and Polykrates on the Origins of the Fourth Gospel," *JTS* 33 (1993): 24–69. Thus also extensively Hengel, *Die johanneische Frage*, 75–113, 219–224, and 275–325.

[91] Richard J. Bauckham, "Historiographical Characteristics of the Gospel of John," *NTS* 53 (2007): 17–36, repr. in idem, *Testimony of the Beloved Disciple*, 93–112.

[92] Paul N. Anderson, *The Fourth Gospel and the Quest for Jesus: Modern Foundations Reconsidered*, Library of New Testament Studies (London: T&T Clark, 2006; 2nd ed., 2007); Anderson, Just, and Thatcher, eds., *John, Jesus and History*, vol. 1; *John, Jesus, and History*, vol. 2: *Aspects of Historicity in the Fourth Gospel*, ed. Paul N. Anderson, Felix Just, and Tom Thatcher, ECL 12 (Atlanta: SBL, 2009); *John, Jesus, and History*, vol. 3: *Glimpses of Jesus through the Johannine Lens*, ed. Paul N. Anderson, Felix Just, S.J., and Tom Thatcher, ELC 18 (Atlanta: SBL, 2016).

[93] See, e.g., the rather critical views by a number of Johannine specialists such as Gilbert van Belle and Sydney Palmer, "John's Literary Unity and the Problem of Historicity," in Anderson, Just, and Thatcher, *John, Jesus, and History*, 1:217–28; John Painter, "Memory Holds the Key: The Transformation of Memory in the Interface of History and Theology in John," in idem, 229–45; Jean Zumstein, "Story, Plot, and History in the Johannine Passion Narrative," in Anderson, Just, and Thatcher, *John, Jesus, and History*, 3:109–18; Annette Merz, "Response to the Essays in Part 2," in idem, 299–317; Michael Theobald, "Johannine Dominical Sayings as Metatexts of Synoptic Sayings of Jesus: Reflections on a New Category within Reception History," in idem,

also critical voices. Within those volumes, a number of programmatic statements of the endeavor, as well as some of the contributions, raise various methodological questions.

In the present context, we will focus on those methodological issues and impasses that should be avoided in order to arrive at valuable conclusions.

3.1 The "Historicizing Approach" and the Neglect of the Author's Perspective

The first impasse is rooted in what I have elsewhere called the "historicizing approach."[94] In this way of reading John, advocated by great conservative scholars such as Zahn and Westcott[95] but also by some contemporary evangelical commentators,[96] John is primarily read as information about the time and history of the earthly Jesus. All the textual elements are related to the level of the time and history of Jesus and his contemporaries, while interferences from later periods or from the perspective of the Johannine author and his addressees are ignored or largely denied.

To be sure, this is one of the classical approaches of reading John. It was applied already in antiquity, without being contrasted with the predominant "theological" reading, and it was also practiced by reformers such as John Calvin.[97] This approach seems in accordance with the fact that John apparently claims to narrate the story of the earthly Jesus, as it happened, authenticated by the "beloved disciple," that is, an eyewitness (at least of Jesus' passion) "who wrote these things"

383–406; and Jörg Frey, "From the 'Kingdom of God' to 'Eternal Life': The Transformation of Theological Language in the Fourth Gospel," in idem, 439–48.

94 See Frey, *Glory of the Crucified One*, 7–11.

95 See Brooke Foss Westcott, *The Gospel according to St. John: The Greek Text with Introduction and Notes*, 2 vols. (London: Murray. 1908); and Zahn, *Das Evangelium des Johannes*.

96 Thus Leon Morris, *The Gospel according to John* (Grand Rapids: Eerdmans, 1995); Carson, *Gospel according to John*; Andreas J. Köstenberger, *John*, BECNT (Grand Rapids: Baker Academic, 2004); and also Blomberg, *Historical Reliability of John's Gospel.*

97 See the edition of the Latin text in Johannes Calvin, *In Evangelium secundum Johannem Commentarius*, ed. Helmut Feld, 2 vols., Ioannis Calvini opera omnia denuo recognita, ser. 2, vol. 11/1–2 (Geneva, 1997–1998).

(John 21:24). As long as scholars could take for granted the Johannine authorship tradition and leave aside or harmonize the differences between John and the Synoptics, the "historicizing approach" largely remained unquestioned.

But a closer look at the way interpreters try to explain certain textual data and the differences from the Synoptics reveals the insufficiencies of the approach.

To illustrate the exegetical effects of this approach, we can have a brief look at the Nicodemus dialogue in which Jesus talks about being born "through water and spirit" as an initiation into the kingdom of God (John 3:5). In Christian tradition, these words have predominately been linked with Christian baptism, as it is quite natural for readers who know baptism as the initiation rite of the Christian community. Historicizing authors argue, however, that Jesus' words to Nicodemus cannot point to Christian baptism. After all, Nicodemus, a Pharisee contemporary with Jesus, would not have understood such a reference at this time.[98] Instead, those authors suggest a reference to either Jewish purification rites or John's practice of baptism, which Nicodemus, as a historical figure, could have known.[99] Other suggestions rely on remote sources about ancient Jewish medical concepts of human procreation wherein "water" is a euphemism for human semen or for the

[98] Richard J. Bauckham (*Gospel of Glory: Major Themes in Johannine Theology* [Grand Rapids: Baker Academic, 2015], 82), expresses the criterion in this way: "A plausible interpretation must make sense in its narrative context, which is John's conversation with Nicodemus, a Pharisaic member of the Jewish ruling council, in Jerusalem at an early stage of Jesus' earthly ministry." At least, Bauckham does not want this criterion to be confused "with the assumption that the narrative is a historical report of a conversation that actually took place" (82). The question is, however, whether an interpretation has to make sense for us as historically informed readers with a detailed source-based knowledge about Pharisees and Jerusalem and the possible intellectual background of a figure like Nicodemus, or whether it had to make sense for the addressees of John with little or no firsthand knowledge about the historical situation in Jerusalem at the time of Jesus and without a historically reflected conception of the thought world of a Jewish leader at that time. For them, a blending of the horizons, in particular with regard to "the Jews" or Jewish leaders, without a critical historical distinction is much more expected, and this is also confirmed by the image of "the Jews" in other passages of the Gospel.

[99] See the references in Bauckham, *Gospel of Glory*, 85.

process of physical birth.[100] Others emphasize that in the Johannine context the focus is on the spiritual birth, so the mention of water is of reduced relevance.[101] But apart from the inadequacies of those suggestions with regard to their use of Jewish sources, they altogether dismiss the dimension which was apparently quite obvious for Christian readers at the end of the first century: that this is a reference to the water rite they knew as the initiation into the realm of Jesus, namely baptism.[102] Even if it is true that a plausible interpretation has to make sense in its narrative context, which is the conversation between Jesus and Nicodemus, we have to ask whether we can really limit the Johannine meaning to what a Jerusalem Jew at the time of Jesus—according to our historical knowledge—could have understood. For a Christian reader at the end of the first century, other things might have been plausible, as the Fourth Gospel shows in connection with other figures such as Caiaphas and Pilate who utter truths they could not have uttered as historical persons in their historical context. If John lets Caiaphas speak out the truth about the sacrificial character of Jesus' death and Pilate testifies to his innocence, this does not make sense in their historical setting. But for John's readers, it is a testimony to the truth about Jesus. In the same way, we must consider how the

[100] See the references in Bauckham, *Gospel of Glory*, 86–87.

[101] Such a tendency can also be found in Bauckham's own suggestion (*Gospel of Glory*, 89–90) that the phrase should be understood as "the womb-water that is Spirit" so that Jesus' saying can be rephrased as follows: "To enter the kingdom of God, one must be born not from the womb-water of a human mother, but from the womb-water that is Spirit." Such a reading is, as Bauckham points out, easily understandable from scriptural passages about a spiritual restoration through the Spirit from on high (Isa 32:15 LXX; Ezek 26:17; Hos 1:10). However, the syntax of John 3:5 does not suggest that the reader should relate water to a natural birth in the past while spirit (with the additional metaphor of water as womb water) is related to a spiritual birth yet to come. Thus, Bauckham's attempt at solving the problem without primary reference to baptism is likewise unconvincing. As he admits that there is a "secondary reference to baptism in 3:5," and, as early readers such as Justin Martyr (*1 Apol.* 61.3–5) have perceived, we have to ask whether this could not be the primary reference for the Johannine readers as well.

[102] Those readings would even require the assumption that for the Johannine community, or—if Bauckham's view about the wider audience of the Gospel is correct—the wider circle of readers envisaged by John, baptism (as Christian baptism or baptism in the name of Jesus) was unknown.

Johannine readers would have received and understood the Nicodemus narrative, and when we do so it is clear that the Christian initiation rite of baptism certainly made sense to them.

From here, the impasse of the historicizing approach is quite obvious: it takes seriously the fact that the Fourth Gospel wants to tell the story of the earthly Jesus, a story precisely located in space and time, but it dismisses the other fact that the Johannine story is written from the later perspective of its author, his community, and his time, and that it presupposes later developments, problems, and insights that have influenced the narration and the theological language. In its eagerness to ascertain historical events and real words of the earthly Jesus, this approach neglects that the Fourth Gospel is written from the perspective of its author, and that this also includes the narration of events and the phrasing of Jesus' words, which may have been shaped from the later experiences of the community and from the theological insights of the author.

3.2 Explanations and Psychological Suggestions from beyond the Text

Another impasse linked with the historicizing approach lies in the attempt of interpreters to explain the plausibility of the narrated sequence of events or of the Johannine dialogues by introducing explanations from beyond the text or from their own psychological reasoning.

When handling the literary aporia of John 14:31, where Jesus prompts the disciples to leave but continues talking for three more chapters until the group actually goes to the garden beyond the Kedron valley (18:1), Zahn conjectures that Jesus spoke the words of John 15–17 "no longer while reclining at the table but while standing or perhaps while walking."[103] Westcott even speculates that Jesus may have spoken the words about the vine as he passed the temple gate with the golden vine in the company of the disciples.[104] Both interpreters insert "events"

[103] Zahn, *Das Evangelium des Johannes*, 576. Cf., more recently, also Blomberg, *Historical Reliability of John's Gospel*, 205.

[104] Westcott, *Gospel according to St. John*, 2:187, 197.

that are not at all supported by the text in order to make the sequence of *textual* units plausible as a sequence of *historical* events, but leave other possible explanations of the textual problems unconsidered. To mention a more recent author well aware of the discussions about the literary problem of John 14:31, Ben Witherington III explains that the material of John 13–17 might have been delivered on two sequential evenings of the Passover festival before it was then formed into the Johannine discourses.[105] This is just another historicizing speculation inserted into the text in order to maintain its literary unity, but that is also completely unsupported by the text.

With such conjectures, a historicizing approach creates possibilities or, at best, plausibilities, which are no more than imaginings or speculations of the respective interpreter. Such explanations are obsolete as soon as one perceives and acknowledges the freedom and independence of the Gospel author in the selection and shaping of his material.

Of course, we know from narratology that readers are expected to fill the gaps and blank spaces in the story with their own imagination, and we can study this at large in the church fathers as well as in many modern interpretations. But the plausibility created here is not that of historical accuracy but rather that of the creative imagination of the individual reader.

It is certainly inspiring to speculate about the gaps in the dialogue between Jesus and the Samaritan woman[106] and why Jesus switches between levels of meaning, but this does not create an argument that the dialogue happened just as it is presented in the text. An even more instructive example is the narrative of the wine miracle at Cana (John 2:1-11). Here interpreters have always speculated about the numerous details

[105] Ben Witherington III, *John's Wisdom: A Commentary on the Fourth Gospel* (Louisville: Westminster John Knox, 1995), 231.

[106] For example, scholars have often tried to explain why the woman comes to the well not in the morning or evening, as is customary, but at high noon, and then conjectured that she had a devastating reputation so that she had to avoid meeting other people (thus Morris, *Gospel according to John*, 228). But this is unwarranted by the text, especially because the woman later actually informs and calls the people from her village (John 4:28-30). Apparently, the aside in 4:6 deserves a different, probably symbolic explanation and is not just meant to be part of an accurate historical account.

that are not explained:[107] Why were Jesus' mother and family invited? Why did the wine run out so early? And what was the reason for Jesus' harsh rejection of his mother's suggestion when he nevertheless acts afterward by performing the miracle she requested? As is already present in the works of some of the church fathers, modern historicizing commentators such as Godet[108] and Zahn infer psychological explanations to create plausibility for the sequence of events and the dialogues. So, it is suggested that Jesus' mother was a relative of the bridegroom's family.[109] Or that, because Nathanael was from Cana, he managed to get the group invited.[110] Interpreters say that Jesus' disciples drank too much so that the wine ran out on the first day.[111] Others even suggest that Mary could not expect a miracle because Jesus had not yet performed miracles, therefore she might just have asked Jesus and his friends to go to the grocer and buy more wine.[112] The grotesquery of such explanations is obvious.

Likewise, with regard to Jesus' rejection of his mother, it is suggested that Jesus tells her that he is now grown up and does not need such a maternal hint. Another suggestion is that Mary was guilty because she was ignorant of Jesus' divine knowledge when she informed him of the situation.[113] All these introjections from daily psychology or from dogmatic considerations are *not* part of the text but imaginative fictions

[107] See the overview of the history of interpretation in Jörg Frey, "Das prototypische Zeichen (Joh 2,1–11)," in *The Opening of John's Narrative (John 1:19–2:22): Historical, Literary, and Theological Readings from the Colloquium Ioanneum in Ephesus*, ed. R. Alan Culpepper and Jörg Frey, WUNT 385 (Tübingen: Mohr Siebeck, 2017), 165–216 (188–94).

[108] Frédéric Godet, *Kommentar zu dem Evangelium des Johannes*, 4th ed., 2 vols. (Hannover: Meyer, 1903).

[109] Fridrich Lücke, *Commentar über das Evangelium des Johannes*, 3rd. ed., 2 vols. (Bonn: Weber, 1840/1843), 1:468; and Alfred Wikenhauser, *Das Evangelium nach Johannes*, RNT 4 (Regensburg: Pustet, 1948), 73.

[110] Thus Lagrange, *Évangile selon Saint Jean*, 51.

[111] Thus Zahn, *Evangelium des Johannes*, 150.

[112] Zahn, *Evangelium des Johannes*, 150; Bernhard Weiss, *Das Johannes-Evangelium*, 9th ed., KEK 2 (Göttingen: Vandenhoeck & Ruprecht, 1902), 91.

[113] Thus Gregory of Nyssa in a homily; cf. Adolf Smitmans, *Das Weinwunder zu Kana: Die Auslegung von Jo 2,1–11 bei den Vätern und heute*, BGBE 6 (Tübingen: Mohr Siebeck, 1966), 106.

filling the narrative lacunae in order to create a logical or psychological credibility while distracting the reader's attention from the actual narrative devices. For sure, the narrative logic of the text works even with those gaps, but this is part of the narrative or literary design and not an invitation to uncover historical credibility.

As soon as one perceives the freedom of the Fourth Evangelist in selecting and shaping his material from a retrospective and theological or didactic viewpoint, the historicizing approach must be considered inappropriate. It neglects the fact that the Johannine narrative is written from the narrative and theological perspective of the evangelist, which includes the experiences of the communities up to his time and not least the theological insights gained by the teaching of the Spirit in the post-Easter era. Therefore, the Johannine narrative is deliberately *interpreted* history and not an account merely following the ideal of telling it "as it actually was."[114] Looking for historical tradition in John, therefore, demands taking into consideration John's post-Easter perspective and his distinctive Christology, which shapes his whole narration of Jesus' ministry.

3.3 Harmonization and "Interlocking" between John and the Synoptics

The problems of historical accuracy are most obvious where John and the Synoptics contradict each other. These difficulties—for example, in the presentation of the cleansing of the temple (John 2:13-22; Mark 11:15-17 par.) or in the narration of the beginning of Jesus' ministry (John 1:19–2:11; Mark 1:14-45; cf. John 3:24)—were noticed early on by the church fathers. Origen remarks that a precise comparison of the Gospels could lead either to the general disputation of their historical reliability, or to the decision for only one of them, if the interpretation does not seek the truth on a higher, spiritual level (as Origen ultimately does; *Comm. Jo.* 10.2).

[114] Cf. the dictum by the German historian and theorist of historicism Leopold von Ranke, who attributes to historiography not the task to cope with the past or to teach for the future but simply to tell "wie es eigentlich gewesen" (*Sämmtliche Werke*, vols. 33/34 of *Geschichten der romanischen und germanischen Völker von 1494 bis 1514*, 2nd ed. [Leipzig: Duncker & Humblot, 1874], vi).

Traditional interpretation, based on the assumption of John's apostolic authorship, often preferred John over the Synoptics, not only in chronology but also with regard to the more spiritual design of Jesus' words. But for authors looking for the utmost historical reliability in John *and* the Synoptics, there seem to be no limits to harmonization.

The most discussed paradigm is the cleansing of the temple.[115] In Mark, the event is located at the end of Jesus' ministry, in the context of his only journey to Jerusalem, to the Passover of his death. In John, however, the episode is narrated at the beginning of Jesus' ministry within the context of his first journey to Jerusalem for a Passover, which is unmentioned in Mark. This first journey in John functions as a programmatic episode that foreshadows Jesus' conflict with the Jews in Jerusalem. Whereas in Mark this episode is the occasion for Jesus' arrest, the only reaction in John is a dispute with "the Jews" about Jesus' legacy, in which Jesus utters a logion about the destruction and rebuilding of the temple (John 2:20). This logion is misunderstood by the Jews as a reference to the physical temple but is related to Jesus' body (that is, his death and resurrection) by the evangelist. Here, unlike the Synoptics (cf. Mark 13:1-2; 14:57-58 par.), the temple logion is directly linked with the temple incident. There are further differences: In the Johannine scene, Jesus acts more violently using a whip, expels both oxen and sheep, and hints at other scriptural passages than those quoted in the synoptic account. Due to these differences scholars have suggested that the Johannine account is independent of the Synoptics.[116] But in view of

[115] On the historical interpretation of the temple incident and its meaning in John, see Jean Zumstein, "Johannes 2:13–22 im Plot und in der Theologie des vierten Evangeliums," in Culpepper and Frey, *The Opening of John's Narrative (John 1:19–2:22)*, 275–88; Frey, "Temple and Identity in Early Christianity and in the Johannine Community: Reflections on the 'Parting of the Ways'," in *Was 70 CE a Watershed in Jewish History? On Jews and Judaism before and after the Destruction of the Second Temple*, ed. Daniel R. Schwartz and Zeev Weiss, AJEC 78 (Leiden: Brill, 2012), 447–507 (452–53, 468–69). See further Johanna Rahner, *"Er sprach aber vom Tempel seines Leibes."* BBB 117 (Bodenheim: Philo, 1998).

[116] Thus recently James F. McGrath, "'Destroy This Temple': Issues of History in John 2:13–22," in Anderson, Just, and Thatcher, *John, Jesus, and History*, 3:35–44. Cf. also the discussion in Michael Theobald, "Stellt die johanneische Erzählung von der sogenannten 'Tempelreinigung' Jesu (Joh 2,13–22) eine Relecture ihrer synoptischen Parallelen dar? Kontroverse in der Forschung, nicht im Text," in *Kontroverse Stimmen*

the example presented above, we should instead reckon with a knowledge of the synoptic traditions and an awareness of the distinctives on the side of the Johannine author and some of his intended readers.

However, the decisive question is when Jesus performed such an act in the temple, and what its meaning was for his ministry and death. Did it happen at the end of his ministry, in the context of the Passover of his death, as the Synoptics claim? Or did Jesus perform the cleansing as a prophetic act at its beginning? Or did he cleanse the Jerusalem temple twice, once at the outset and then again at the end of his ministry?[117] Zahn, who relates both accounts to the one single event in the life of Jesus, historically prefers the Johannine dating of the event at the beginning of his ministry,[118] whereas some modern apologists such as Morris, Carson, Köstenberger, and Blomberg still reckon with the possibility that there were actually two different cleansings during the ministry of Jesus.[119] These scholars adopt this "solution" even though

---

im Kanon, ed. Martin Ebner et al., Quaestiones Disputatae 279 (Freiburg im Breisgau: Herder, 2016), 228–60.

[117] Such a harmonistic solution was chosen by many commentators in church history. See the survey by François-Marie Braun, "L'expulsion des vendeurs du temple," *RB* 38 (1929): 178–200.

[118] Zahn, *Das Evangelium des Johannes*, 178–79. Although in Zahn's view Matthew was still the earliest of the synoptic Gospels, he considered that Gospel more thematically oriented than John, so he could give John the chronological priority here. Other interpreters prefer the Johannine placement, such as R. J. Campbell, "Evidence for the Historicity of the Fourth Gospel in John 2:13–22," in *Studia Evangelica*, vol. 7, ed. Elizabeth A. Livingstone (Berlin: Academie Verlag, 1982), 101–20; and Robinson, *Priority of John*, 127–31, with the argument that the forty-six years of construction time fit quite well from the beginning of the temple project in 19 BCE until the year 27 CE. The Johannine account is also preferred by McGrath, "'Destroy This Temple'," 39, with the argument that the combination of temple action and temple logion (as a saying of Jesus) is probably more original than the separated presentation of the two, as in Mark.

[119] Morris, *Gospel according to John*, 167; Carson, *Gospel according to John*, 177; Köstenberger, *Gospel according to John*, 111 (this position is already present in his early work; see *Encountering John: The Gospel in Historical, Literary, and Theological Perspective* [Grand Rapids: Baker, 1999], 76–78); Blomberg, *Historical Reliability of John's Gospel*, 89–90. Cf., most recently, Allan Chapple, "Jesus' Intervention in the Temple: Once or Twice?" *JETS* 58 (2015): 545–69, who naively concludes from the differences between the accounts that there were two separate such events in the life of Jesus.

none of the canonical Gospels actually supports such a possibility: it is simply a harmonizing combination of passages from different texts. In support of such a solution, Blomberg states that the two texts "do not contradict each other at any point and can be combined to form a plausible harmonious whole."[120]

In their apologetic interest, these interpreters even try to avoid the decision of whether John or the Synoptics are more accurate, but instead point to a vague so-called interlocking between them. This means that the story of either tradition is supplemented and explained by information from the other tradition.[121] Thus Blomberg, in his book on the "historical reliability" of John, provides a conjecture about the reason for Jesus' final journey to Jerusalem in the Synoptics on the basis of the Johannine story of Lazarus: Lazarus' illness explains why the synoptic Jesus goes to Jerusalem for his final Passover.[122] Furthermore, the false charges against Jesus, wherein he is accused of threatening to destroy the temple (Mark 14:58-59), are explained by John 2:19 where the temple logion is presented as a prophetic saying of Jesus himself. For Blomberg, the Johannine saying, read as a historically accurate prediction of Jesus, can even explain its use by the false witnesses in the synoptic trial scene[123]—although it is questionable, then, why their witness is called false if Jesus had really predicted the rebuilding of the temple.

Such harmonizing explanations obviously originate in the desire to maintain that John and the Synoptics are "simultaneously credible,"[124] but they abandon the methodological principle that each writing has to be interpreted in its own context. Instead, they supplement each Gospel with "historical" information from the complementary texts. Such an interpretation can do without any concern about sources or literary relations between the Gospels but merely

[120] Blomberg, *The Historical Reliability of the Fourth Gospel*, 90; see already Paul Trudinger, "The Cleansing of the Temple: St. John's Independent, Subtle Reflections," *ExpTim* 108 (1997): 329–30.

[121] Morris, *Gospel according to John*, 40–63; Carson, *Gospel according to John*, 52–55; Blomberg, *Historical Reliability of John's Gospel*, 53–4.

[122] Blomberg, *Historical Reliability of John's Gospel*, 53.

[123] Blomberg, *Historical Reliability of John's Gospel*, 53.

[124] Blomberg, *Historical Reliability of John's Gospel*, 85.

takes both the Synoptics and the Fourth Gospel as supplementary sources of information about the Jesus of history. The argument for John's independence from the Synoptics further supports a view that both traditions might draw on diverse oral traditions so that they can be harmonized or historically interpreted as interlocked testimonies. But in this procedure, historical methodology—not to mention common sense—is sacrificed in favor of the aprioristic principle of defending the alleged historical "truth" of all biblical accounts.

3.4 "Interfluentiality" between the Gospels and Foggy Eclecticism

Similar problems can also be diagnosed in Paul Anderson's attempt to counter the "dehistoricization" of John and the "de-Johannification" of Jesus by reintroducing John into the historical quest for Jesus. When Anderson addresses the problems of the leading critical approaches,[125] he smartly avoids the blunt apologetics of the approaches presented in the preceding section. But the foundation of his argument is similarly problematic. It is a complicated new reconstruction[126] of the relationship among the four Gospels presented under the label "interfluentiality," through which John is ultimately reestablished as a second source for the Jesus story alongside Mark, so that Jesus can now be presented in a "bi-optic perspective."[127]

Somewhat mechanically arguing from the similarities and differences between John and Mark, Anderson suggests early connections between pre-Markan and pre-Johannine traditions, whereby both traditions mutually influence one another.[128] He reckons with a first edition of John briefly after the composition of Mark, in which the

[125] Cf. Anderson, *Fourth Gospel and the Quest for Jesus*, 43–99.

[126] Anderson, *Fourth Gospel and the Quest for Jesus*, 104–12; cf. earlier idem, *The Christology of the Fourth Gospel: Its Unity and Diversity in the Light of John 6*, WUNT 2/78 (Tübingen: Mohr Siebeck, 1996).

[127] Anderson, *Fourth Gospel and the Quest for Jesus*, 127.

[128] Anderson, *Fourth Gospel and the Quest for Jesus*, 106.

author augments, complements, and occasionally corrects Mark.[129] Luke is considered to be later and influenced by John, whereas Matthew, composed in a different "sector" of Christianity, is again corrected by the final edition of John.[130] In this complicated construction, Anderson adopts a number of critical hypotheses that are hard to verify, in particular the view of two editions of John and the idea of a mutual exchange at the level of earlier oral tradition. On the other hand, based on such a construction, Anderson can develop a historical eclecticism that is able to take from each tradition what appears most plausible.

Ultimately, Anderson also accepts the cleansing of the temple as a prophetic sign at the beginning of Jesus' ministry.[131] In Jesus' discourses, Anderson wants to maintain the substantial historical validity of Jesus' "teaching about the way of the Spirit and the reign of truth,"[132] even though it is presented entirely in Johannine language and style. Thus, as in the late nineteenth century, the image of the historical Jesus is freshly "spiritualized" through the influence of Johannine texts. This is possible on the basis of a relatively foggy view of the relationship between Mark and John, expressed by the unclear term "interfluentiality." As far as these considerations stand at the origins of the John, Jesus, and History project, the methodological foundations of this project are too unclear, and Anderson's revisionist agenda might even lead to more arbitrary and methodologically imprecise results.

[129] The assumption, however, provokes questions such as why the first edition of the Gospel might correct Mark's chronology. Anderson (*Fourth Gospel and the Quest for Jesus*, 111) refers to the testimony by Papias (Eusebius, *Hist. eccl.* 3.39.15), who claims that Mark did not present the Jesus story in correct order. However, this can only prove that Papias of Hierapolis considered the order of another gospel, possibly John, more correct than that of Mark; his testimony cannot provide an argument for the view that John is actually more correct in chronological and historical terms.

[130] Anderson, *Fourth Gospel and the Quest for Jesus*, 119–25.

[131] Anderson, *Fourth Gospel and the Quest for Jesus*, 158–61.

[132] Anderson, *Fourth Gospel and the Quest for Jesus*, 171.

3.5 Features of Historiography and the Lack of Criteria for Historical Accuracy

In an interesting attempt at elaborating a historiographical intention of the Johannine author, Richard Bauckham adduces evidence that the Gospel utilizes features of ancient historiography in a density that surpasses even the Synoptics.[133] Bauckham points to the high number of John's exact topographical notes, to the chronological precision with regard to Jewish festivals, and to the data in the passion account, which cannot be explained merely by theological intentions. Of course, Bauckham is well aware that these data are embedded in a theological framework. But from the other side, he is able to argue that ancient historiographers were also selective in their use of material: they would insert narrative asides, employ dialogues and discourses to interpret the narrated events, and even present some eyewitness testimony to establish credibility. Thus, John's narrative techniques are not too far off from those employed by ancient historians.

But attributing John to the ancient genre of "historiography" does not support the claim of historical accuracy or "historicity" of the Johannine account.[134] The textual elements adduced by Bauckham and others are first and foremost part of an authorial strategy of authentication[135] utilized by many ancient authors; they help create a plausible or credible narrative, but cannot prove an accurate historical reference. Although there were different types of historiography in antiquity,[136]

[133] Richard J. Bauckham, "Historiographical Characteristics in the Gospel of John," *NTS* 53 (2007): 17–36.

[134] Cf. Stefan Schreiber, "Die Vita des Königs Jesus: Über die Gattung des Johannesevangeliums," in *Historiographie und Biographie im Neuen Testament und seiner Umwelt*, ed. Thomas Schmeller, NTOA 69 (Göttingen: Vandenhoeck & Ruprecht, 2009), 127–54 (134–35): "Für die heutige historische Frage ist also durch eine Gattungszuweisung als *historia* nichts zu gewinnen" (135).

[135] See the thorough discussion of those strategies in light of more recent theories of history in Susanne Luther, *Die Authentifizierung der Vergangenheit: Literarische Geschichtsdarstellung im Johannesevangelium*, Habilitationsschrift University of Mainz (2018), in preparation for WUNT (Tübigen: Mohr Siebeck, 2019).

[136] For the distinction between "pragmatic" and "pathetic" historiography, see Detlev Dormeyer, "Pragmatische und pathetische Geschichtsschreibung in der

history writing always employed rhetorical and stylistic devices.[137] Lucian's work on history writing,[138] for example, reveals that ancient historiography could often adopt a novelistic character in order to address its audience: "Through narrative construction, historiographical facts are situated within a historiographical narrative, which aims to provide an explanation for past reality and to endow brute facts with meaning."[139] To serve those aims, "the fictional mode of narrative was always part of the comprehension of reality";[140] the fictional elements moreover "do not reduce the truth content, but present reality in a different way—not as mimetic reconstruction or precise representation of past events, but through conscious fictional construction." Thus, in ancient literature, fiction is not generally set against historiography; rather, fictional elements along with narrative and rhetorical strategies "are used to create a certain form of literary historiography, that accepts 'fiction' in the (re)construction of past reality as long as it is adequately employed."[141]

These conclusions are confirmed by modern theorists of narrative and history such as Hayden White, Paul Ricoeur, and Jörn Rüsen,[142]

---

griechischen Historiographie, im Frühjudentum und im Neuen Testament," in Schmeller, *Historiographie und Biographie*, 1–33.

[137] See Luther, "From Bethlehem, according to the Promise," 13–15. See also Knut Backhaus, "Spielräume der Wahrheit. Zur Konstruktivität in der hellenistisch-Geschichtsschreibung," in *Historiographie und fiktionales Erzählen: Zur Konstruktivität in Geschichtstheorie und Exegese*, ed. Knut Backhaus and Gert Häfner, BThS 86 (Neukirchen-Vluyn: Neukirchener, 2007), 1–29.

[138] Lucian, *De historia conscribenda*. See the interpretation of Luther, "From Bethlehem, according to the Promise—or Rather from Nazareth," 14. I do not think that Lucian's text is to be read ironically (as Clare K. Rothschild ["Irony and Truth: The Value of *De Historia Conscribenda* for Understanding Hellenistic and Early Roman Period Historiographical Method," in *Die Apostelgeschichte im Kontext antiker und frühchristlicher Historiographie*, ed. Jörg Frey et al., BZNW 162 (Berlin: de Gruyter, 2009), 277–91] has suggested).

[139] Luther, "From Bethlehem, according to the Promise," 15.

[140] Luther, "From Bethlehem, according to the Promise," 14.

[141] Luther, "From Bethlehem, according to the Promise," 15.

[142] Cf., e.g., Hayden White, *The Content of the Form: Narrative Discourse and Historical Representation* (Baltimore: John Hopkins University Press, 1987); idem, "The Fictions of Factual Representation," in *The Literature of Fact*, ed. Angus Fletcher (New York: Columbia University Press, 1976), 21–44; Paul Ricoeur, *Temps et récit*, 3 vols.

who also emphasize "the constructive and narrative form in which we have access—the only access—to the historical past,"[143] so that any idea of an objective representation of the past is a fiction in itself or, even more, an illusion.

Thus, even if the Fourth Gospel displays numerous historiographical devices and elements of authentication, this cannot prove the claim of a more accurate historical reference. Although place names and information about the time of certain events or other narrative details strongly contribute to anchoring John's story as a factual account in the real world of Jesus, these elements do not necessitate that the information provided is historically accurate information, since they can also be fictional elements introduced with the intention of crafting a credible story.

a) It is true that the Fourth Gospel provides a large number of specific data on places in Jewish Palestine, particularly in Jerusalem,[144] and in many cases the localization of certain events is more precise than in the Synoptics.[145] With these data, the Johannine story is clearly placed within the real world of Jesus and his time, but some of the local notices may also convey symbolic notions, such as the mention of Jerusalem, Judea, and Galilee. They may also serve a literary purpose, such as the aside about Jesus' bread discourse in the synagogue of Capernaum (John 6:59). In numerous cases, it remains an open question how the Gospel author received his information: Did he personally know some places in Jerusalem or does this information come from a literary source,[146] which could ultimately convey local traditions from communities in Galilee or Samaria?[147] In any case, statements of place have more functions than merely embedding the story in a

(Paris: Seuil, 1983–1985); Jörn Rüsen, "Historisches Erzählen," in *Zerbrechende Zeit: Über den Sinn der Geschichte* (Cologne: Böhlau, 2001), 43–105.

143 Luther, "From Bethlehem, according to the Promise," 16, with further references.

144 See the list in Luther, *Authentifizierung der Vergangenheit*, 78, with reference to Urban C. von Wahlde, "Archaeology and John's Gospel," in *Jesus and Archaeology*, ed. James H. Charlesworth (Grand Rapids: Eerdmans, 2006), 523–86 (526–27).

145 Cf. also Bauckham, "Historiographical Characteristics," 99.

146 Advocates of a signs source like to explain the place names in John 2–4 from an itinerary underlying the collection of miracles. See Michael Theobald, *Das Evangelium nach Johannes*, vol. 1, RNT (Regensburg: Pustet, 2007), 279–280.

147 This was the suggestion of Karl Kundsin, *Topologische Überlieferungsstoffe im Johannes-Evangelium*, FRLANT 22 (Göttingen: Vandenhoeck & Ruprecht, 1925).

historical context. They also create plausibility or credibility. And even this may be a fictional device of a well-crafted narration, not a sign of historical accuracy.

b) Things are similar with the numerous references to time in the Fourth Gospel which are also more precise than the synoptic references.[148] These textual elements structure narrative time, for example, with the references to Jewish festivals and the mention of three Passovers. Some of them insert precise temporal references for certain events (e.g., the tenth hour in John 1:39 or the sixth hour in 4:6). But these references also convey symbolic values or contribute to a web of meaningful reference,[149] so they not only contribute to the temporal imagination or embed the Johannine story in a plausible framework of time, but also serve certain theological purposes. Again, the question arises whether the precise temporal location of certain events originates from knowledge or personal memory of the eyewitness, from the use of sources, or even from the fictional activity of the author crafting his meaningful narration. In any case, they cannot be used as a proof of historical or chronological accuracy.

c) An important element of historiographical design is the reference to witnesses or even eyewitnesses, and in what way John's presentation of numerous witnesses for Jesus and, in particular, of the beloved disciple as an eyewitness can be compared with the techniques of ancient historiographers.[150] But although the authentication through the figure of the beloved disciple creates a claim of credibility, it is foremost a construction[151] which cannot be taken as proof of historical accuracy. Furthermore, the Johannine authentication is conspicuously broken in various respects:[152] The beloved disciple remains an anonymous figure whose identity can only be conjectured from the combination of various texts (including the Synoptics[153]), whereas other eyewitnesses (e.g., Jesus' mother, the servants in

[148] Bauckham, "Historiographical Characteristics," 101, writes, "The prevalence of precise chronology in the Gospel of John would have made it look, to competent contemporary readers, more like historiography than the Synoptics."

[149] Potential examples of this can be found in John 4:6, which is a possible reference to the hour of Jesus' death, or the references that constitute the Johannine passion chronology (18:28; 19:14, 31). On the interpretation of the Johannine notices of time, see Frey, *Die johanneische Eschatologie*, 2:173–203.

[150] Bauckham, "Historiographical Characteristics"; idem, *Jesus and the Eyewitnesses: The Gospels as Eyewitness Testimony* (Grand Rapids: Eerdmans, 2008; 2nd ed., 2017).

[151] Thus rightly Luther, *Authentifizierung der Vergangenheit*, 135.

[152] See Luther, *Authentifizierung der Vergangenheit*, 169–71.

[153] The identification of the beloved disciple with John the son of Zebedee is not made in the Johannine text, where the sons of Zebedee are only mentioned in John 21:2. If the beloved disciple is also identified with the unknown disciple called

John 2:6-9, or other disciples) are not used for authentication. Furthermore, some important passages cannot draw on eyewitness testimonies, such as Jesus' dialogues with Nicodemus, the Samaritan woman, or Pilate. Thus, even "the eyewitness account is not merely about a simple observation of events."[154] Instead, it includes "a multifaceted envisioning"[155] and thus authenticates not merely history but also, and perhaps primarily, theology or the truthful interpretation of the narrated story.

The methodological impasses mentioned, the "historicizing" approach to reading, the conjecturing of external historical and psychological explanations, the harmonization with the Synoptics or the vague assumption of a mutual "interfluentiality," and also the reference to features or techniques of ancient historiography cannot yield more clarity about the historical setting of the Fourth Gospel, let alone enhance its "historicity." The approaches suffer from a lack of clarity regarding the sources of John's narrative and also from an underestimation of the author's unique authorial selectivity and liberty, his post-Easter perspective, and his theological aims.

Given these factors at work in the production of the Johannine Gospel, it is far from certain that the author really (let alone *merely*) wanted to narrate things "as they were." Although the Fourth Gospel is neither a myth nor an allegory, it may be similarly mistaken when interpreters want to consider it historiography in the sense of an accurate representation of past events.

4. Methodological Conclusions and Criteria

In order to come to a sound judgment about John's value as a historical source, we must look briefly at some distinctive features of the Fourth

---

together with Andrew in 1:36-39, the identification with John the son of Zebedee is possible, but only on the basis of the list of the first disciples from Mark 1:16-19. The ascription of the Gospel of John to John the son of Zebedee is, therefore, the result of a combination of various passages, a move stimulated but not explicitly supported by the Gospel text. Cf. Frey, "Das Corpus Johanneum," 75–82. See also the variety of suggestions for identification in James H. Charlesworth, *The Beloved Disciple: Whose Witness Validates the Gospel of John?* (Valley Forge: Trinity Press, 1995).

[154] Thus Arthur J. Dewey, "The Eyewitness of History: Visionary Consciousness in the Fourth Gospel," in *Jesus in Johannine Tradition*, ed. Robert T. Fortna and Tom Thatcher (Louisville: Westminster John Knox, 2001), 59–70 (68).

[155] Dewey, "Eyewitness of History," 69.

Gospel and, in particular, its differences from the synoptic tradition. For reasonable and responsible scholarship, these differences call for decisions in terms of historical reference and accuracy.

4.1 An Undeniable Transformation

How can we understand the differences between Mark and John, not only the differences in the selection and arrangement of the material, in the topography and chronology, but also the more remarkable differences in Jesus' language, style, and theological message? As Christopher Tuckett has argued, these differences

> make it very difficult to see both John and the synoptics as equally accurate reflections of the historical Jesus. . . . Most would agree that a focus on the kingdom of God, and extensive use of parables, are the most characteristic aspects of Jesus' teaching. Further, a move from a more theocentric focus of Jesus' teaching (with God and God's kingly rule as central) to a later Christocentric focus (on the importance of the person of Jesus himself) seems easier to envisage than the reverse process. Hence the teaching of the historical Jesus is likely to be more accurately reflected in the synoptic tradition than in John's Gospel.[156]

Just to enter a thought experiment: if we followed authors such as Theodore of Mopsuestia or, at the beginnings of modern criticism, Friedrich Schleiermacher who still historically preferred the testimony of the "beloved disciple,"[157] the reverse question would immediately follow. Why would Mark or Matthew, then, so strongly depart from the allegedly original historical testimony presented by an apostolic eyewitness? Why would the synoptics altogether depart from the

[156] Christopher Tuckett, "Sources and Methods," in *The Cambridge Companion to Jesus*, ed. Markus Bockmuehl (Cambridge: Cambridge University Press, 2001), 121–37 (126–27), quoted by Gilbert van Belle and Sydney Palmer, "John's Literary Unity and the Problem of Historicity," in Anderson, Just, and Thatcher, *John, Jesus, and History*, 1:217–28 (228).

[157] Schleiermacher felt that the writing conveyed the overall impression of authenticity and knowledge of an intimate friend of Jesus. On Schleiermacher's theological *and* historical preference for the Fourth Gospel (and the critical reaction by David Friedrich Strauss), see Frey, *Die johanneische Eschatologie*, 1:23, 31.

language and style of the "real" Jesus in order to present Jesus' words in such a different language? When merely imagining these consequences, it seems much easier to reckon with a process of transformation from the synoptic tradition to the Johannine presentation.

Especially with regard to language and style, the argument is, in my view, quite clear:[158] apart from few "synoptic-like" sayings in John and the single "Johannine" saying in the synoptic sayings tradition (Matt 11:25-28 // Luke 10:21-22), the character of Jesus' language in John is overwhelmingly different from his language and style in the Synoptics. The genres of the teaching of the synoptic Jesus—prophetic and sapiential sayings, brief apophthegms and especially parables—are absent in John and seem to be replaced by longer, repetitive, spiraling discourses or lengthy dialogues that create larger webs of metaphors throughout the whole Gospel.[159] From those discourses and dialogues, some sayings can be isolated and considered to be traditional,[160] but even the style of these "kernel" sayings (e.g., the "I am" sayings) usually differs from that of the synoptic sayings of Jesus. Linguistic observations widen the gap even further: while some of Jesus' words from the synoptic tradition suggest the possibility of retroversion into his original Aramaic idiom,[161] this is almost impossible for the speech of the Johannine Jesus, even though there are some Aramaic terms and names presented in the Fourth Gospel.[162]

Thus, the decision is clear: Jesus spoke either in the style and the forms of the synoptic tradition, in brief sayings or parables, or in the style of the Fourth Gospel, in lengthy discourses and extensive exemplary

[158] The following paragraph is largely adopted from Frey, "From the 'Kingdom of God' to 'Eternal Life'," 441.

[159] On those "metaphorical networks" in John, see Jan G. van der Watt, *Family of the King: Dynamics of Metaphor in the Gospel of John*, BIS 44 (Leiden: Brill, 2000).

[160] See, comprehensively, Theobald, *Herrenworte im Johannesevangelium*.

[161] Cf. the important work by Joachim Jeremias, *Neutestamentliche Theologie: Erster Teil: Die Verkündigung Jesu*, 3rd ed. (Gütersloh: Gerd Mohn, 1973). See also Matthew Black, *An Aramaic Approach to the Gospels and Acts*, 3rd ed. (Cambridge: Clarendon, 1967); more recently, Maurice Casey, "The Role of Aramaic in Reconstructing the Teaching of Jesus," in Holmén and Porter, *Handbook for the Study of the Historical Jesus*, 2:1343–75.

[162] There were attempts to suggest an Aramaic original of the Fourth Gospel, but they did not find wider acceptance in scholarship. See, for example, Charles Fox Burney, *The Aramaic Origin of the Fourth Gospel* (Oxford: Clarendon, 1922).

dialogues. All the attempts of distinguishing, for example, between a style of public preaching (as in the Synoptics) and an esoteric style of internal teaching (as in John, especially in the farewell discourses) are unsupported by the texts, since the Johannine style of discourses and dialogues is coherent and since Jesus' public teaching in John 2–12 differs from the synoptic style in the aspects mentioned above. If we observe, then, that in the Fourth Gospel Jesus speaks to individuals as well as to groups in the same style as the Baptizer (cf. John 1:30-34; 3:31-36), the Johannine narrator, or the author of the Johannine Epistles, the conclusion is unavoidable that this is the language of the Johannine community, and that the traditional words of Jesus have been transformed into the diction and style of the Johannine community or author(s).

The direction of the transformation is suggested by linguistic and theological considerations: The synoptic tradition in its earliest strata is closer to the teaching of the Jesus of history.[163] Compared with the Synoptics, the Johannine words and speeches of Jesus have undergone a more thorough transformation with regard to their language and quite likely also with regard to content and theology. This is the literary explanation for the observation that John's high Christology is so strongly expressed in the Johannine discourses and that the christological self-presentation of the Johannine Jesus stands in such a marked contrast with the more veiled and mostly implicit messianic or christological claims of Jesus according to the Synoptics.

This is also valid for the declarative statements of the Johannine Jesus, including such well-known and highly regarded sayings like the "I am" sayings or the "It is completed" (John 19:30) utterance from the cross, which are all expressed in the style and terminology of the Fourth Gospel. All these sayings cannot be proven to be "authentic" sayings of the earthly Jesus in the strictest sense of the word,[164] but

[163] See Jeremias, *Neutestamentliche Theologie*, 123–46; and also Maurice Casey, *Jesus of Nazareth: An Independent Historian's Account of His Life and Teaching* (London: T&T Clark, 2010), 108–20.

[164] Peter W. Ensor, "The Johannine Sayings of Jesus and the Question of Authenticity," in *Challenging Perspectives on the Gospel of John*, ed. John Lierman, WUNT 2/219 (Tübingen: Mohr Siebeck, 2006), 14–33, tries to introduce various categories of "authenticity," from *ipsissima verba* through *ipsissima dicta* to *ipsissimae sententiae* (25–33), but this is more an attempt to "save" the category of "authenticity" or "save"

have undergone a thorough process of not only translation but also transformation before they were shaped and integrated into the web of the Fourth Gospel.

One last aspect deserves consideration. If the evangelist did not just unconsciously adopt a tradition that had gone wild but actively interpreted his traditions and shaped his gospel in awareness of the differences from the Synoptics or even composed his work for an audience familiar with those different traditions and views, we must theologically consider the fact that the evangelist deliberately did not harmonize nor conceal the differences[165] but preserved or even created them afresh. Of course, the transformation of traditions had already begun in the earlier periods of the Jesus movement and also in the earlier Johannine community tradition, regardless of how intensely the evangelist himself was part of the process of shaping the Johannine proclamation. But in the composition of the Gospel, the transformation was deliberately accepted and continued, and the new Johannine shape of Jesus' teaching was given a literary form. If this is true, we can only ask how the evangelist could justify such a procedure, or with what legitimacy he could even feel free to change historical and chronological data and modify the plot of the Jesus story that had been transmitted from earlier tradition.[166] At stake here are our views and prejudices about what an evangelist or even "historian" of the Jesus story might be "allowed" to do.

4.2 Methodological Considerations

But how is it possible to identify historical traditions in the Johannine work in spite of its rather coherent language and style and the fact that

John from the accusation of forgery and does not bring any more substantial clarity. The process of translation and transformation is, in any case, presupposed in John's sayings of Jesus. See also the apologetic attempt to prove some similarities between the synoptic and the Johannine discourses by Philipp Bartholomä, *The Johannine Discourses and the Teaching of Jesus in the Synoptics* (Tübingen: Francke, 2012).

[165] In John 3:24, where he mentions a simultaneous activity of Jesus and the Baptizer, John inserts an explanation that seems to be directed to readers who know a different sequence of events from the synoptic tradition.

[166] On these issues, see below in chapter 3.

the evangelist has woven "his sources together so thoroughly that they usually remain shrouded behind his complete document"?[167] How can we identify, isolate, and evaluate historically valid traditions and information in John?

If we want to remain intellectually honest, it is clear that simple harmonization or arbitrary eclecticism are excluded. It is also clear that mere possibilities or narrative plausibility cannot be a valid argument for historical accuracy since a plausible narration is by no means necessarily a historically accurate narration. Even though John's narration is crafted as a factual story, this does not mean that it actually represents the history of the ministry of Jesus "as it was."

Reconstructing historical traditions and evaluating the historical source value of the Johannine narrative shares the difficulties of historical research in general, and in particular the well-known aporias of the quest(s) for the "Historical Jesus."[168] A verdict is only possible since we have other sources about the Jesus story apart from John. However, things are more difficult in John than in the Synoptics because John's use of sources is obviously much more selective and free than Luke's or Matthew's use of their sources Mark and Q.

a) In any case, the precondition for historical evaluation is to get clarity about the *sources* underlying the narrative. But clarity is limited here due to John's obvious liberty in his usage of sources. Although John knows Mark (as I have argued for above), he departs from that source at numerous points. It is our task to decide whether these deviations are best explained from his theological interests, his narrative or dramaturgical strategy, or whether there is enough reason to assume additional written or oral sources. If Mark is presupposed as the

[167] Thus Keener, *Gospel of John*, 1:xxvii; also adopted by Painter, "Memory Holds the Key," 231–32.

[168] On the history of Jesus research and the periods of the early quest, the period of "no quest" (under the influence of Bultmann), the "new quest," the "third quest," and beyond, see Casey, *Jesus of Nazareth*, 1–61; see also Jörg Frey, "Der historische Jesus und der Christus der Evangelien," in *Von Jesus zur neutestamentlichen Theologie: Kleine Schriften II*, ed. Benjamin Schliesser, WUNT 368 (Tübingen: Mohr Siebeck, 2016), 29–84 (31–51); David S. du Toit, "Redefining Jesus: Current Trends in Jesus Research," in *Jesus, Mark, and Q: The Teaching of Jesus and Its Earliest Records*, ed. Michael Labahn and Andreas Schmidt, JSNTS 214 (Sheffield: Sheffield Academic, 2001), 82–124.

continuous narrative source underlying the Johannine narration, other continuous sources such as a signs source or a distinct pre-Johannine passion account can no longer be demonstrated. While some of the narratives can be explained as transformations and expansions of synoptic texts or traditions,[169] others might have been taken from distinct oral or written narratives that the evangelist could have received from his community tradition.[170]

b) The usage of additional sources can be taken into consideration when there are textual elements that do not fully fit into the Johannine narrative or are not "used" in the further context, such as the mention of Jesus' brothers next to his disciples at the wedding of Cana (2:1–2, 12).[171] Additional sources may also be present where material exists in some tension with John's overall theological interests. Without entering the debate about the criteria used in the quest for the historical Jesus (which are primarily criteria for historically evaluating the words of Jesus),[172] we can generally say that traditions can be considered old if they basically fit into a Palestinian Jewish context and, secondly and

[169] Thus, for example, the healing of the royal servant in John 4:46–54, or the Sabbath healing at Bethesda in John 5:1–16, or possibly even the healing of the man born blind in John 9:7.

[170] On the source-critical issues of John's miracle stories, see the thorough discussion in Labahn, *Jesus als Lebensspender.*

[171] On the source criticism behind that story, see Frey, "Das prototypische Zeichen," 172–78.

[172] On the activities of Jesus, see Craig A. Evans, "Authenticating the Activities of Jesus," in *Authenticating the Activities of Jesus*, ed. Bruce Chilton and Craig A. Evans (Leiden: Brill, 1999), 3–29. On the criteria of Jesus research, see further Martin Hengel and Maria Schwemer, *Jesus und das Judentum*, vol. 1 of *Geschichte des frühen Christentums* (Tübingen: Mohr Siebeck, 2007), 262–70; Casey, *Jesus of Nazareth*, 101–42; see also Gerd Theissen and Dagmar Winter, *Die Kriterienfrage in der Jesusforschung: Vom Differenzkriterium zum Plausibilitätskriterium*, NTOA 34 (Freiburg Schweiz: Universitätsverlag; Göttingen: Vandenhoeck & Ruprecht, 1997); Stanley E. Porter, *The Criteria for Authenticity in Historical-Jesus Research: Previous Discussion and New Proposals*, JNTS 191 (Sheffield: Sheffield Academic, 2000); Dale C. Allison, "How to Marginalize the Traditional Criteria of Authenticity?" in Holmén and Porter, *Handbook of the Historical Study of Jesus*, 1:3–30; Stanley E. Porter, "How Do We Know What We Think We Know? Methodological Reflections on Jesus Research," in *Jesus Research: New Methodologies and Perceptions*, ed. James H. Charlesworth (Grand Rapids: Eerdmans, 2014), 82–99.

more importantly, stay in contrast with the general development of the gospel tradition or Johannine theology. One example to be discussed later is the account of Jesus' baptizing activity in John 3:22, 26 (and 4:2). Such activity neither corresponds to the Johannine image of John the Baptist, who is primarily depicted as a witness to Jesus, nor to the general development of the gospel tradition in which the traces of an original closeness between Jesus and the Baptizer have been gradually removed. This may point to an old tradition and probably to the historical validity of the tradition recorded in John 3:22 and 3:26. But in most cases of narrative traditions, the degree of certainty is limited, and it seems almost impossible to precisely reconstruct such traditions.

c) Even more difficult is the attempt to isolate traditional sayings behind the Johannine dialogues and discourses. Here, we may draw on particular features of a shaped language, elements such as the double "Amen" introduction, the existence of variations in the Gospel (e.g., John 3:3 and 3:5), or parallel phrases in the Johannine Epistles (cf. John 3:16 with 1 John 4:9, 10). Criteria for identifying traditional sayings have been cautiously expressed by Michael Theobald,[173] who mentions the aspect of multiple attestation within the New Testament and beyond, including intratextual resumptions or citations, stylistic or formal independence of a unit within its literary context, or tensions in a given context. In most cases, however, we can only get back to traditions that are more or less shaped by the language of the Johannine community, without any direct connection between those sayings traditions and the linguistic forms of the earliest available Jesus tradition, let alone with his *ipsissima vox*. Therefore, the verdict cannot be avoided that all the words of Jesus in John have undergone a thorough theological transformation, and the claim that they represent the words of the Jesus of history cannot, in most cases, be substantiated. It is mandatory, not least with regard to intellectual honesty, to maintain this critical differentiation as clearly as possible.

[173] Theobald, *Herrenworte im Johannesevangelium*, 56–58.

5. Historically Valid Information in John

Scholars in the past century or so have claimed historical validity for a number of traditions in John. These claims are made on various levels, with reference to various kinds of sources, and with various degrees of certainty.

5.1 Indirect Hints at the Author

First, there is the attempt to collect some evidence about the evangelist, his knowledge, and, more tentatively, his background and origin. Of course, caution is needed here, as it is always possible that such knowledge in the text draws on traditions the author adopted and not merely on the author's proper knowledge. But from some of the details in language, topography, and cultural knowledge, we may conclude the author had some familiarity with the Hebrew and Aramaic languages, with Palestinian Judaism, and with the topographical setting of the narrative.

Thus, Martin Hengel has suggested that the evangelist was a Palestinian Jew who had come to the diaspora in Asia Minor, possibly in the period around the Jewish Revolt.[174] As evidence, he points to the fact that the Gospel presents a number of Aramaic names in transliteration, such as Thomas-Didymus (John 11:16; 20:24; 21:2), Cephas (1:42), Mariam (20:16), Siloam (9:7), Gabbatha (19:13), and Golgotha (19:17), and Aramaic terms such as Messias, which is given in its transliterated form only in John (1:41; 4:25), Rabbi, and the intensified form Rabbuni (20:16; cf. Mark 10:51). Some of these names and terms are translated into Greek,[175] some are precisely decoded,[176] and some are explained with a symbolic meaning (Siloam, 9:7).

With regard to Jerusalem and its environs (but not to Galilee), the knowledge about localities is particularly dense.[177] There are references to other places hard to locate but probably also situated in

[174] Hengel, *Johannine Question*, 109–10; see idem, *Die johanneische Frage*, 278–81.

[175] Messias (1:41; 4:25), Cephas (1:42), Thomas (11:16; 20:24), Gabbatha (19:13), and Golgotha (19:17).

[176] Thus Simon, son of John (1:42; 21:15, but cf. Barjona, Matt 16:17) and Judas, son of Simon Iskariot (John 6:1; 13:2, 26).

[177] The treasury in the temple (8:20), the portico of Solomon (10:23), the houses of Hannas and Caiaphas (18:13, 24), and Golgotha close to the city (wall) (19:17, 20).

the south rather than in Galilee such as "Bethany beyond the Jordan" (1:28; cf. 10:40) and "Aenon near Salim" with much water or many springs (3:23). Together, these details make up a remarkable concentration of topographical information from Judea and Jerusalem. Furthermore, the author displays an impressive amount of knowledge about Jewish feasts,[178] customs, and laws. He is aware of the relevance of stone vessels for Jewish (more precisely Pharisaic[179]) purity practice (2:6), knows that the law of circumcision breaks the Sabbath law (7:37), and hints at the prohibition against breaking the bones of a Passover lamb (19:36-37). He also knows about the schism between Jews and Samaritans (4:9), the importance of the last day of Sukkot and the water poured out in front of the altar (7:37), the celebration of Hanukkah in winter (10:22), the "day of preparation for the feast of Passover"[180] (18:28; 19:31), and the "special significance of the Sabbath following Jesus' death, which coincided with the first day of the feast of the Passover."[181] In the Johannine narrative, these details all contribute to the local Palestinian color and also to the author's credibility.

With regard to the historical argument, we must concede that some of these details could simply be taken from various sources or the community tradition, but other references, in particular those within expository narrative asides (such as the translation and explanation of names or the explanations of customs in 4:9 and 10:22) or the scriptural reference that contributes to the chronology of the passion (19:36-37), can be attributed instead to the knowledge and intentions

[178] Cf. Gale A. Yee, *Jewish Feasts and the Gospel of John* (Wilmington, Del.: Michael Glazier, 1989); Luc Devilliers, *La Fête de l'Envoyé* (Paris: Gabalda, 2002); Maarten J. J. Menken, "Die jüdischen Feste im Johannesevangelium," in *Israel und seine Heilstraditionen im Johannesevangelium*, Festschrift Johannes Beutler, ed. Michael Labahn, Klaus Scholtissek, and Angelika Strothmann (Paderborn: Schöningh, 2004), 269–86; Dorit Felsch, *Die Feste im Johannesevangelium. Jüdische Tradition und Christologische Deutung*, WUNT 2/308 (Tübingen: Mohr Siebeck, 2011); and Gerry Wheaton, *The Role of Jewish Feasts in John's Gospel*, SNTSMS 162 (Cambridge: University Press, 2015).

[179] See in particular Roland Deines, *Jüdische Steingefäße und pharisäische Frömmigkeit: Ein archäologisch-historischer Beitrag zum Verständnis von Johannes 2,6 und der jüdischen Reinheitshalacha zur Zeit Jesu*, WUNT 2/52 (Tübingen: Mohr Siebeck, 1993).

[180] Hengel, *Johannine Question*, 111.

[181] Hengel, *Johannine Question*, 111.

of the Johannine author so that they might be counted as evidence for the cultural, legal, and scriptural knowledge of the evangelist. We should note, however, that the evidence about the author's local or cultural knowledge cannot serve as an argument for further substantiating the historical accuracy of his narration. It is possible for even an eyewitness familiar with places, laws, and customs to narrate things quite differently on the basis of a later perspective. Thus, the historical source value of the Fourth Gospel is not confirmed by the affirmation of the evangelist's Palestinian Jewish background.

5.2 John as a Historical Source for Details about Jewish History

As Martin Hengel has demonstrated in an important article,[182] the Fourth Gospel is a historically valid source for some aspects of the history of ancient Judaism.

For example, John 4:5 provides the first attestation of Sychar as the principal village of the Samaritans, before it is mentioned again in the Mishnah (m. Menaḥ. 10:2).[183] More generally, the whole episode in 4:4-42 displays a considerable knowledge about the disputes between Jews and Samaritans with reference to some local traditions about Jacob's well and field (but interestingly not the tomb of Joseph).[184] Likewise, 10:22 provides the first mention of the celebration

[182] Martin Hengel, "Das Johannesevangelium als Quelle für die Geschichte des antiken Judentums," in *Judaica, Hellenistica et Christiana. Kleine Schriften II*, WUNT 109 (Tübingen: Mohr Siebeck, 1999), 293–334.

[183] Hengel, "Das Johannesevangelium als Quelle," 300–302, assumes that Sychar (= Askar) became the principal village of the Samaritans after their liberation from Jewish dominance by Pompeius (63 BCE) and until it was surpassed by the originally pagan town Neapolis (= Nablus).

[184] See Hengel, "Das Johannesevangelium als Quelle," 301. The explanation of the local traditions is not totally clear; we can only speculate whether John 4 draws on early traditions about a mission among Samaritans (cf. Acts 8) or from a Christian community in Sychar, as is argued by Jürgen Zangenberg, *Frühes Christentum in Samarien: Topographische und traditionsgeschichtliche Studien zu den Samarientexten im Johannesevangelium*, TANZ 27 (Tübingen: Francke, 1998), 105 (cf., earlier, Kundsin, *Topologische Überlieferungsstoffe*, 29–30), or whether it is merely the cultural knowledge of the evangelist, who shapes the text from a decidedly Judean perspective.

of Hanukkah with its Greek name τὰ ἐγκαίνια in ancient sources. John is also the only New Testament author who mentions the town Tiberias (6:1, 23f.; 21:1), which had been founded in 17 CE by Herod Antipas to become the new capital of his tetrarchy in 19 CE. Furthermore, John's description of the pool of Bethesda with five porticoes, which had long caused questions among scholars, "fits well with the archaeological remains of the pool as they exist today."[185] Finally, the Johannine passion account draws a realistic image of the situation in Jerusalem and the arrangement between the Roman authority under Pilate and the high priestly aristocracy, with Hannas as the "grey eminence" of his clan even during the tenure of his son-in-law Caiaphas.[186]

This does not mean, however, that John's account is historically closer to the events than Mark's. To take just the example from the passion narrative, John's insertion of Hannas' interrogation of Jesus (18:12-27) does not necessarily draw on a more accurate tradition. It can be explained instead as an addition to the earlier tradition which only included a meeting of the Sanhedrin (Mark 14:53-65), in which Jesus is interrogated by the unnamed high priest about his messiahship until he is finally sentenced to death due to the charge of blasphemy. In John, the meeting of the Sanhedrin under the actual officeholder Caiaphas is already narrated in 11:47-53, for quite conceivable narrative and theological reasons: the Jewish authorities decide on his death immediately after his plain demonstration of his divine authority to raise the dead. But since the evangelist had used up this material about the meeting of the Sanhedrin in chapter 11, he needed to fill the lacuna in the passion narrative in a different way. Interestingly, he still presents a very brief note in 18:24, 28 that Jesus is sent to Caiaphas before being forwarded to Pontius Pilate, but in this scene nothing happens, probably because there was no further tradition available that could be presented. Therefore, he had to create a new scene in the place of Mark's Sanhedrin scene, now with another high priest, Hannas, the grey eminence of the

[185] Shimon Gibson, "The Excavations at the Bethesda Pool in Jerusalem," in *Sainte-Anne de Jérusalem: La Piscine Probatique de Jésus à Saladin: Le Projet Béthesda (1994–2010)*, Proche-Orient Chrétien, Numéro Spécial (Beirut: Faculté des sciences religieuses, 2011), 17–44 (23).

[186] Hengel, "Das Johannesevangelium als Quelle," 322–34.

ruling clan and father-in-law of Caiaphas. The encounter with Hannas is intertwined with Peter's denial, as is the Sanhedrin scene in Mark (cf. Mark 14:54, 66-72). But since the death sentence of the high priest and the Sanhedrin has already been narrated, it cannot include a real trial or decision but only an interrogation, which then provides a retrospective confirmation of Jesus' public teaching. This is, of course, not implausible, and the evangelist demonstrates a good knowledge of the actual situation of the priestly families and the Romans in good business agreement as well as the importance of Hannas and his family, but the literary observations lead to the conclusion that the scene is probably a fictional addition to the earlier tradition.

We can see here that the evangelist's cultural and historical knowledge does not prevent him from crafting fictional scenes but rather enables him to produce a plausible and credible narrative. The same is true for the subsequent scene of Jesus' encounter with Pilate (John 18:28–19:16a), which is carefully structured in seven scenes but has to be considered a largely fictional, theological expansion of the brief scene from Mark.[187] We should notice that at least the private dialogues between Pilate and Jesus (18:33-38a; 19:9b-12a) about Jesus' kingdom and his real origin cannot draw on any witnesses as authentication of the Gospel, not even the beloved disciple, with the result that they are most probably crafted to provide aspects of the evangelist's theological interpretation of the story. In this case, the creative stance of the author becomes undeniable. But although the scenic composition and especially the private dialogue between Pilate and Jesus must be considered a narrative fiction of the evangelist, his depiction of the Jewish leaders pressing Pilate with the threat to denounce him to Caesar draws on a firm knowledge of the political tensions in Judea. It is likely that the evangelist was aware of the fact that Pontius Pilate was actually removed from his office only a few years later due to a complaint by the Jewish authorities. As Hengel has rightly argued, one of the most striking riddles of John is the unique combination of precise historical details and

[187] Cf. my interpretation of the pericope in Jörg Frey, "Jesus und Pilatus: Der wahre König und der Repräsentant des Kaisers im Johannesevangelium," in *Christ and the Emperor*, ed. Gilbert van Belle and Joseph Verheyden, BTS 20 (Leuven: Peeters, 2014), 337–93.

creative theological elaboration of the material,[188] so that, in a thorough historical evaluation of the Gospel, both sides have to be considered.

5.3 Historical Traditions about Jesus and His Mission

Apart from the information regarding the background of the Johannine author and some aspects of the history of ancient Judaism where John displays some often-neglected historical source value, we must now discuss at least a selection of elements in John's story of Jesus where there is some good reason to believe that the Fourth Gospel contains historically valid information. The most compelling collection of such elements is still C. H. Dodd's monograph on *Historical Traditions in the Fourth Gospel*.[189] Despite the fact that Dodd ultimately supports the view of John's independence from the Synoptics,[190] his argument for the historical validity of certain elements of the Johannine narrative is not merely based on that presupposition. A good number of traditions identified by Dodd can also be understood within the framework of John's dependence on Mark. Others, especially in the context of the passion narrative, can be better explained as a theologically motivated renarration of the synoptic account.[191] In the following, I can only mention some aspects where I consider the Johannine data historically valid.[192]

[188] Hengel, "Das Johannesevangelium als Quelle," 334: "die in der urchristlichen Erzählliteratur wohl einzigartige Kombination von präzisem historischem Detail und schöpferischer theologischer Gestaltung des Stoffes." Hengel even uses the term "Jesus-Midrash" to characterize the work.

[189] It is "a work not likely soon to be superseded" (thus Smith, "Jesus Tradition," 2000).

[190] Dodd, *Historical Tradition*, 8–9 and 423. On Dodd's support for the views of his Cambridge colleague Gardner-Smith, see above, p. 68.

[191] In my view, the episode of the arrest of Jesus in 18:1-11 in its differences from Mark is better explained as a theologically motivated variation. See Sabbe, "Arrest of Jesus in Jn 18,1–11"; and Lang, *Johannes und die Synoptiker*, 61–86; against Dodd, *Historical Tradition*, 80–81. It also seems doubtful to postulate a different tradition for the footwashing (as does Dodd, *Historical Tradition*, 64). On the interrogation by Hannas and the trial before Pilate see above, pp. 53–54.

[192] See also my article on the source value of John in Jesus research: Frey, "Johannesevangelium," esp. 144.

a) A very promising field for historical consideration is the data on Jesus' and his disciples' relation to John the Baptizer.[193] Unlike the Synoptics, John provides evidence for the view that the background of some of Jesus' disciples (including Andrew, and thus possibly also Peter) was originally within the prophetic movement of John the Baptizer (cf. John 1:35).[194] This implies a certain closeness of Jesus himself to the Baptizer and his movement,[195] which is also suggested by further Johannine passages (cf. 3:22-30). If this is true, Jesus' baptism by John was not just a one-off encounter but was possibly preceded and certainly followed by a longer relationship or even fellowship, which seems to be suppressed by the synoptic accounts due to their tendency to strengthen Jesus' uniqueness by distancing him from his temporary "mentor." Whereas the synoptic narrative insists on the idea that Jesus began to preach only after the Baptizer had been imprisoned (Mark 1:14; but cf. John 3:24), the close analogies between some sayings and (especially apocalyptic) elements of the teachings[196] of John and Jesus, on the contrary, suggest a certain closeness between both figures. The synoptic chronology is, in this aspect, too schematic and led by the interest of securing Jesus' unique salvation-historical position by suppressing the influence of the Baptizer, whom Jesus himself had spoken about quite highly using the title "Elijah" (Matt 11:14). Therefore, the information presented in John about the personal links between

[193] See the comprehensive discussion in Dodd, *Historical Tradition*, 248–312; cf. also Smith, "Jesus Tradition," 2003–5.

[194] Cf. also John P. Meier, *Companions and Competitors*, vol. 3 of *A Marginal Jew: Rethinking the Historical Jesus* (New York: Doubleday, 2001), 222: "The Fourth Gospel's indication that Peter and other disciples first met Jesus in the circle of the Baptist's disciples may well be true. . . ."

[195] On this, cf. the thorough discussion in John P. Meier, *Mentor, Message, and Miracles*, vol. 2 of *A Marginal Jew*, ABRL (New York: Doubleday, 1994), 100–30; Hengel and Schwemer, *Jesus und das Judentum*, 320–39; somewhat differently, Casey, *Jesus of Nazareth*, 178–85.

[196] Cf. Hengel and Schwemer, *Jesus und das Judentum*, 326–29. The common elements include in particular apocalyptic views about the coming judgment: Israel and its leaders are subject to the judgment that will suddenly happen (Luke 12:16-20; 13:1-5; cf. 10:13-15; 11:31), bring about a division in the midst of Israel (17:34-35), and change the situation in favor of the poor, weeping, and hungry (14:11; 17:33; cf. 6:20-22), and only immediate conversion can save from that judgment (13:5).

the Baptizer's movement and the Jesus movement seems to be a relic of an early awareness of Jesus' connection with the Baptizer, which is already minimized and suppressed in Mark and the other Synoptics.[197] It is the "criterion of embarrassment" which forces us to consider these splinters of information more trustworthy than the narrative and chronological design of the Synoptics.

b) Closely related is the tradition about a chronologically simultaneous ministry of the Baptizer and Jesus (John 3:22-23), which openly contradicts Mark's presentation of Jesus starting his ministry only after the imprisonment of the Baptizer. Drawing on the criterion of embarrassment, we have to consider this a reliable piece of information about the Jesus of history.

This is confirmed by the fact that Mark's separation of the periods of the Baptizer and Jesus raises considerable doubts. The question is how we should plausibly imagine that, after Jesus' baptism by John and the time of forty days in the wilderness (Mark 1:12-13), Jesus only began preaching after the Baptizer was imprisoned. Does Mark want his readers to imagine that Jesus waited somewhere until he could start his own ministry? Obviously, the narrative technique bridges or veils an uncertain span of time where Mark links the traditions about Jesus' baptism (vv. 9-11), the subsequent temptation in the wilderness (vv. 12-13), the beginning of the narrative of his public ministry with a kerygmatic summary (vv. 14-15), and the calling of the first disciples (vv. 16-20). But in spite of the narrative connection, the note in verse 14a inserts a clear temporal separation between the ministry of Jesus and the ministry of John.

The other Gospels widen the gap between John and Jesus by use of various techniques. Luke does not adopt the remark from Mark 1:14 but separates the ministries of John and Jesus by inserting the genealogy in Luke 3:23-38. Furthermore, he introduces a salvation-historical divide between the period of the law and the prophets, including John as the last prophet, and the period of the kingdom emerging in the ministry of Jesus (16:16). Matthew, while simply adopting Mark's chronological schema, arrives at a categorical distance between Jesus and the Baptizer when he creates a problem concerning Jesus' baptism (Matt 3:14-15),

[197] On the tradition of Jesus baptizing (3:22, 26), see below, pp. 121–24.

suggesting that John should rather be baptized by Jesus. The Fourth Gospel goes even beyond this, suppressing the narration of Jesus' baptism and changing the image of the Baptizer into a mere witness (John 1:19–34). Thus, the overall tendency of all four canonical Gospels is to present Jesus in a category of his own, to distance him from his precursor, and to avoid any direct comparison between the two whereby the Baptizer could possibly appear superior to Jesus. In view of this overall tendency, the splinter of information in John 3:22–23, 25–26 is even more remarkable: according to these verses, Jesus and John acted simultaneously, at least for a certain time, and even more that Jesus himself practiced an immersion rite (i.e., "baptized") at least for a certain time (3:22, 26). This is also unknown to the Synoptics and, thus, a possible redactional narrative aside problematizes this notion in 4:2.

The passage in John 3:22–24, however, is quite significant with regard to the manner the evangelist utilizes the historical traditions available to him. John 3:24 explicitly explains the difference between his account and another version of the beginnings of Jesus that the evangelist expects to be known among his readers, and in this case he seems to defend his tradition against the synoptic view. We will have to come back to this point in the next paragraph.[198]

c) Given Mark's chronological schema, we can also try to find a clue to evaluate the chronological differences between John and the Synoptics, first on the issue of the timespan of Jesus' ministry: only less than one year, according to the Synoptics, or two to three years, according to John. We do not have any external clues to decide between the two versions or to determine the duration of Jesus' ministry. In John, the extended chronology is most probably the result of literary or redactional operations. The first Passover is "created" by the transposition of the temple incident from its original context immediately before Jesus' passion to the beginning of his ministry, so that an "additional" Passover is now mentioned in John 2:13. The second Passover in 6:4, making up the "milestone"[199] for the chronology of two to three years, is mentioned plainly, without initiating a festival journey of Jesus. Nevertheless, there is good reason to assume that the narrative aside

[198] See below, pp. 122–23.
[199] Thus Wellhausen, *Das Evangelium Johannis*, 28: "Meilenzeiger."

in which the Passover is mentioned is inspired by the narrative of the feeding of the multitude and its continuation of the bread discourse; that is to say, it is intended to connect that material with the Passover or even Jesus' Last Supper. Thus, the constitution of the extended chronology is due to literary, rather than "historical," reasons.[200]

But if, on the other hand, Mark's short chronology is also a schematic one, the Synoptics cannot claim greater historical source value at this point. In spite of the christological function of the festival journeys in John, there is some probability that Jesus, as a pious Galilean Jew, made the festival pilgrimage more frequently,[201] before and also during his public ministry, so he might have been already known to the Jerusalem authorities at the time of his last Passover.[202] John's account, therefore, is generally more plausible than the Synoptics, at least in the sense that Jesus' ministry lasted longer than only one year. However, a lack of information does not allow us to be any more precise at this point.[203]

d) The most difficult chronological issue, however, is the date of Jesus' death. While all Gospels agree that Jesus died in the context of Passover on a Friday, the day before the Sabbath, the precise relation between the day of his death and the Passover holidays differs. According to the Synoptics, Jesus celebrates the Passover meal before

[200] On this, see below, p. 125–27.

[201] Cf. also Luke 2:41. Another hint at a better acquaintance of Jesus with Judea and Jerusalem is the fact that, even according to Mark, Jesus seems to have a special relation to people in Bethany (Mark 14:3-9). See Hengel and Schwemer, *Jesus und das Judentum*, 556.

[202] Thus the argument by Paula Fredriksen, *Jesus of Nazareth, King of the Jews: A Jewish Life and the Emergence of Christianity* (New York: Knopf, 2000), 238–41; cf. also Smith, "Jesus Tradition," 2002–3.

[203] A possible further argument is the mention of the forty-six years in John 2:20, which could point—if the beginning of the building activities was in the eighteenth year of Herod's reign (Josephus, *Ant.* 15.380), that is, 20/19 BCE—to the year 27/28 CE, thus roughly matching Luke's dating of the appearance of the Baptizer in the fifteenth year of Tiberius in Luke 3:1. If this is connected with the oft-suggested year of Jesus' crucifixion in 30 CE (cf. Hengel and Schwemer, *Jesus und das Judentum*, 556), we would also arrive at a period of roughly three years. It is unclear, however, how the relatively exact number in John 2:20 can be explained. Cf. Frey, *Die johanneische Eschatologie*, 2:154, n. 3.

he is arrested and sentenced to death during the night and the morning of the first Passover holiday. Thus, he dies on Friday, the 15th of Nisan. In John, however, the trial and death of Jesus is still on the day of preparation (i.e., Friday, the 14th of Nisan), so the last meal cannot be a Passover meal (John 18:28; 19:14, 31).

There have been some attempts to harmonize these two versions. For example, some interpreters reference the calendric differences between the official temple calendar and the solar calendar, which was probably followed by the Qumran community and the related movement (not only at Qumran but also elsewhere in Judea and Jerusalem).[204] Such suggestions, however, did not find wider approval, neither from Qumran scholars[205] nor from exegetes. Accordingly, the chronological contradiction cannot be easily eradicated.

Historically, it is possible to argue in favor of Mark *or* John. Joachim Jeremias, in his seminal study of the Last Supper, has strongly argued for the view that Jesus' last meal was indeed a Passover meal, so that the synoptic chronology is historically correct;[206] Martin Hengel follows the related chronology, although he admits that there are some inconsistencies in Mark's schematic account.[207] John P. Meier has made a case instead for the Johannine chronology.[208] His main point is that "it is inconceivable that the events of Jesus' arrest, trial, and death should have occurred on the evening when the Passover meal was eaten."[209] According to Meier, it is improbable that "at the time of Jesus, the supreme Jewish authorities in Jerusalem would arrest a person suspected of a capital crime, immediately convene a

204 Cf. Annie Jaubert, *La Date de la Cène* (Paris: Gabalda, 1957); idem, "Jésus et le calendrier de Qumrân," *NTS* 7 (1960/1961): 1–30; Josef Blinzler, "Qumran-Kalender und Passionschronologie," *ZNW* 39 (1958): 223–51; Eugen Ruckstuhl, "Zur Chronologie der Leidensgeschichte Jesu," SNTU 10 (1985): 27–61; 11 (1986): 97–129.

205 Cf. James C. VanderKam, "The Origin, Character, and Early History of the Qumran Calendar: A Reassessment of Jaubert's Hypthesis," *CBQ* 41 (1979): 390–411.

206 Joachim Jeremias, *The Eucharistic Words of Jesus*, trans. Norman Perrin (Philadelphia Fortress, 1966), 20–23, 62–84; also Hengel and Schwemer, *Jesus und das Judentum*, 582–586.

207 Hengel and Schwemer, *Jesus und das Judentum*, 556.

208 John P. Meier, *The Roots of the Problem and the Person*, vol. 1 of *A Marginal Jew* (New York: Doubleday, 1991), 390–401.

209 So the summary by Smith, "Jesus Tradition," 2022.

meeting of the Sanhedrin to hear the case (a case involving the death penalty), hold a formal trial with witnesses, reach a verdict that the criminal deserved to die, and hand over the criminal with a request for execution on the same day—all within the night and early hours of Passover day, the fifteenth of Nisan!"[210] Furthermore, the amnesty for the Passover could only make sense before the Passover meal and the holidays. The Johannine date of Jesus' death before Passover is further supported by other early Christian (Gos. Pet. 5) and Jewish (b. Sanh. 43a) sources.

On the other hand, the Johannine chronology, in which the time of Jesus' death or rather his final surrender to crucifixion is mentioned with suspicious accuracy,[211] probably points to the time when the Passover lambs were slaughtered for the Passover meal in the evening. This would fit quite well with the predication of Jesus as "the Lamb of God" (John 1:29, 36) and the application of Passover regulations about not breaking the bones of a Passover lamb (Exod 12:10 LXX, 46; Ps 34:20; Num 9:12) to the crucified Jesus (John 19:36). Thus, in John, a rather coherent web of passages suggests that Jesus actually died at the time when the Passover lambs were slaughtered in the temple, typologically signifying that he was the true eschatological Passover lamb.[212]

So, if we simply had to decide who changed the chronology into his own version, John is more "suspect" of altering the dates to match his christological typology. But, as Moody Smith rightly infers, "it is equally possible that John is assuming such a chronology as factual and interpreting it."[213] The question of alteration should be posed also in the other direction: Can we assume that Mark (followed by the other Synoptics) or his passion source already changed the tradition about a "normal" last meal of Jesus with his disciples into the form of a Passover meal? This would also require changing a number of narrative elements, not only the words interpreting the bread and the cup but also the mention of the *hallel* psalms. Therefore, the evidence for the idea that

[210] Meier, *Marginal Jew*, 1:396.

[211] Cf. Frey, *Die johanneische Eschatologie*, 2:181–86.

[212] On the sources from Philo, Josephus, and the Mishnah, see Frey, *Die johanneische Eschatologie*, 2:184.

[213] Smith, "Jesus Tradition," 2023.

the last meal of the Jesus of history was actually a Passover meal is quite strong, and if Jesus could not simply celebrate a Passover meal one day earlier, the weight of the argument suggests a decision in favor of the synoptic date of Jesus' death against the Johannine "theologized" version. But both reconstructions have their strengths and their problems, and commentators and historians are still divided.[214] It is striking that at this pivotal point of Jesus' ministry a clear historical decision between the two contradictory chronologies is impossible.

e) Most of the other single traditions in the Fourth Gospel are difficult to evaluate historically, but the information that Peter, Andrew, and Philip came from Bethsaida (John 1:44)—which is only included in the Fourth Gospel—appears at least historically plausible. Also, the note in 21:2 that Nathanael was from Cana in Galilee might go back to a Palestinian tradition which was possibly linked with the location of two miracles at Cana (2:1-11; 4:46-54). However, the origin and age of that tradition can no longer be ascertained. As with other place names, the issue is instead a matter of whether these places had some relevance in an early period of the Jesus movement, so that local traditions or early sources could connect certain events with those places.

5.4 Historical Traditions Rooted in the History of the Early Community

We have already seen that some of the historical traditions cannot be traced back to the history of the earthly Jesus but may originate in the period of the early post-Easter community within Jewish Palestine or elsewhere. Thus, for example, the Samaritan episode might point back to an early mission in the Samaritan region (which is

[214] A preference for the Johannine chronology of the passion is expressed, for example, by Rudolf Schnackenburg, *Das Johannesevangelium*, 4 vols., HTK 4/1–4 (Freiburg im Breisgau: Herder, 1965–1984), 3:306–7; Raymond E. Brown, *The Death of the Messiah, from Gethsemane to the Grave: A Commentary on the Passion Narratives in the Four Gospels*, ABRL (New York: Doubleday, 1998), 2:1351–73. A preference for Mark's chronology is maintained by Rudolf Pesch, *Das Markusevangelium*, 3rd ed., 2 vols., HTK 2/1–2 (Freiburg im Breisgau: Herder, 1984), 2:323–28; Donald A. Hagner, *Matthew*, 2 vols., WBC 33 (Dallas: Word, 1993–1995), 772–73; Barrett, *Gospel according to John*, 50–51; Keener, *Gospel of John*, 2:1100–103.

also confirmed by Acts 8:4-25),[215] but it is difficult to imagine such an episode within the historical life of Jesus, and in particular the dialogues with the woman are presented as private dialogues, with no other people around, so that their content is not supported by any of the Gospel's claims about witnesses providing an authentication of the narration.[216]

The same is true for the Johannine image of "the Jews" (Ἰουδαῖοι) and "the Pharisees." Regarding the latter, J. Louis Martyn, followed by numerous other scholars, has rightly stated that their Johannine image as opponents of Jesus, especially in John 5–12, and in particular their "official" function including the power to expel members from the synagogue (9:22), mirrors a later situation.[217] But it would be too one sided to simply attribute the entirety of the material about "the Jews" in the Fourth Gospel to the period of the evangelist or to the challenges the Johannine communities had to face around or shortly before the composition of the Fourth Gospel. Even the mention of the ἀποσυνάγωγος (9:22; 12:42; 16:2) might refer to processes of conflict and separation between Jewish Jesus followers and the authorities of the local synagogue in the diaspora that had already begun earlier, maybe in or shortly after the Pauline period,[218] and that continued to exist for a considerably longer time, far into the second century.[219] Furthermore, the debates about Jesus' messianic claims, adopting a wide range of Jewish ideas on the origin and appearance of the messiah,[220] seems to go back to an earlier period in Jewish Palestine rather than in the

[215] See above, pp. 107–8.

[216] The same is true for the dialogue between Jesus and Nicodemus in 3:1-21 and also for the private dialogues between Jesus and Pilate in 18:28–19:16.

[217] Cf. Martyn, *History and Theology*; cf. Frey, *Glory of the Crucified One*, 13–14 and 52.

[218] Rather than corresponding to the "present" of the evangelist and his addressees, these events had probably already taken place some years (perhaps even one or two decades) before the composition of the Gospel. Especially relevant as support for this view is the fact that there are already gentile "Christians" among the addressees and that the community consists of sheep from "this" sheepcote and others from beyond (10:16; cf. 11:51-52). This suggests that the traumatizing parting of the ways had already happened some time ago.

[219] See Frey, "*Toward Reconfiguring Our Views on the 'Parting of the Ways'.*"

[220] Cf. Bauckham, "Messianism according to the Gospel of John," and above, pp. 29–33.

diaspora, although the debates and dialogues are now shaped according to the Johannine style and embedded into the narrative framework of the Gospel. The same is true for the motif of rivalry between the followers of John the Baptist and the Jesus movement adopted in John 3:25-26, where it is expressed within the context of the simultaneous activity of John and Jesus but seems to fit more appropriately in the early period of the Jesus movement in Jewish Palestine when there was still a group of followers of the Baptizer.

5.5 Not Two but at Least Three Levels

In light of all these considerations, we have to conclude that the Fourth Gospel is a complex web of elements referring to various historical levels:

a) First of all, there is the level of the time and history of the earthly Jesus, which is generally maintained through the markers of space and time, and the figures of the story, Jesus, his disciples, and contemporary Jews who live and act in the narrated world of early first-century Palestine. Like the other Gospels, John also claims to tell the story of the earthly Jesus, and in spite of the well-known difficulties, it is possible, at least at a few points, to trace some historically valuable information back to the time and history of Jesus.

b) Other historical traditions incorporated in the Gospel text cannot be traced back to the level of the time and history of Jesus but represent conflicts, discussions, or experiences of the community of Jesus followers from the early post-Easter period until the formation and development of the Johannine communities. Although it is difficult to precisely locate the origin and context of those traditions, we must consider that the problems, experiences, and insights of a longer history have entered the Johannine text.

c) The third and theologically most influential level, however, is the level of the christological and theological insights of the evangelist, who communicates his views about the true dignity of Christ through the narrative designs of his story, through the discourses of both Jesus and the narrator, and also through the web of statements of the various narrative figures. This is the level on which the christological insight is communicated. This insight has grown through a longer process (and, in Johannine terms, through the teaching of the Spirit) and is narrated not from the world of the author and the addressees but from a remote world: the time and space of the ministry of Jesus of Nazareth.

The interplay between the level of the author and the community of addressees and the level of the historical Jesus and his time has been lucidly described in J. Louis Martyn's term of a "two level drama."[221] However, we should widen the pattern and talk of at least three levels, even if the data in the intermediary layer can only be located quite roughly. The Fourth Gospel is a multilevel narrative that incorporates data from at least three periods: from the time and ministry of the earthly Jesus; from the history of the early communities of his followers in Jewish Palestine and then in the diaspora; and—perhaps most distinctively—from the time and perspective of the evangelist, his communities, and the addressees he has in view. The problem is that in many instances this complicated web can no longer be dissolved, so that it is somewhat possible to read the whole Gospel on the level of the Johannine author, that is, as a theological or symbolic text, or also to read the whole Gospel on the level of the history of the earthly Jesus, in a "historicizing" manner. The methodological challenge, however, is to keep those two levels in view, to attribute the textual references as far as possible, and to reckon with the development of traditions and insights between those two levels, although the allocation of many traditions is no longer feasible.

6. Historical Accuracy Unexploited or Incidentally Achieved

The most important feature to observe, however, is the remarkable freedom with which the author of the Fourth Gospel adopts or drops, uses or leaves aside the historical traditions available to him. These observations demand the conclusion that it is not his first and foremost interest to report most accurately what "really" happened during the time of Jesus' ministry or to correct his predecessors with regard to historical accuracy. His interest is not primarily a historiographical one, neither in ancient terms nor even in modern terms, but is principally determined

[221] Martyn, *History and Theology*, 46.

by his narrative-dramaturgical and theological interests. We can see this when taking a closer look at two phenomena already mentioned.

6.1 Jesus' Baptizing Activity: A Splinter of Historical Information Left Unexploited

First, there is a historically valid tradition that the evangelist adopts and even "defends" against the differing data from the Synoptics, but, strikingly, he does not make much of that tradition nor does he utilize it for his theological purposes. The tradition in view concerns the "baptizing" activity of Jesus, which is mentioned three times, in John 3:22, 26, and 4:1 (where it is immediately "corrected" by the aside in 4:2).[222]

According to the transitional remark in John 3:22, after Jesus' dialogue with Nicodemus, Jesus and his disciples go to the Judean countryside.[223] The author uses two verbs in the imperfect tense to inform us that "[Jesus] spent some time there with them and baptized" (καὶ ἐκεῖ διέτριβεν μετ᾽ αὐτῶν καὶ ἐβάπτιζεν). Apparently, Jesus does not head back immediately to Galilee after the Passover but sojourns a certain time with his disciples in Judea.[224] Even more striking is that he (habitually or repeatedly) "practiced an immersion rite" in that region. This is unique information. None of the Synoptics mention a baptizing activity performed by Jesus himself or by his disciples during his

[222] For further discussion, cf. my article: Jörg Frey, "Baptism in the Fourth Gospel, Jesus and John as Baptizers: Historical and Theological Reflections on John 3:22–30 and 4:1–3," in *Expressions of the Johannine Kerygma in John 2:23–5:18: Historical, Literary, and Theological Readings from the Colloquium Ioanneum 2017 in Jerusalem*, ed. R. Alan Culpepper and Jörg Frey, WUNT (Tübingen: Mohr Siebeck, 2019 [in preparation]).

[223] There is a debate as to whether the itinerary note in 3:22 comes from a source, thus creating a connection with 2:12 (with the implication that according to the source Jesus did not go to Jerusalem but more generally to the Judean territory), but in any case, the present text imagines that Jesus went from Jerusalem (which is, of course, also part of Judea) to the Judean countryside. See, however, Jerome Murphy O'Connor, "John the Baptist and Jesus: History and Hypotheses," *NTS* 36 (1990): 359–74 (363).

[224] Cf. Walter Bauer, *Das Johannesevangelium*, 3rd ed., HNT 6 (Tübingen: Mohr, 1933), 63. A similar stay is presupposed in John 7–10, but this may just be a consequence of the addition of several traditions linked with different Jewish festivals (Sukkot in John 7–8 and Hanukkah in John 10).

earthly ministry. Instead, they all try to distance Jesus from the Baptizer and his ministry,[225] and it is almost impossible to imagine that such a tradition was "invented" later, when the uniqueness of Jesus was beyond question. As a "Christian" Baptism (in the name of Jesus) could not be practiced before Jesus' death and resurrection (cf. Matt 28:18-20), it is difficult to assume that the evangelist simply depicted Jesus baptizing in order to root Christian baptism in the ministry of the earthly Jesus.[226] If the verses convey an early tradition, referring even to the period and ministry of the earthly Jesus, we can only think of a variation of John's baptism with a similar meaning of repentance or forgiveness in face of a coming judgment. So, did Jesus actually "copy" and practice John's baptism for a while?

The subsequent verses present the simultaneous ministry of John (who is not called "Baptizer" in the Fourth Gospel) at a place called Aenon near Salem.[227] Jesus is recorded baptizing in a different, though unspecified, place. This results in a complaint from John's disciples about the unwarranted rivalry of Jesus and his ministry. The notice about the simultaneous and rivaling ministry is certainly a piece of tradition, and it is absolutely unlikely that the evangelist invented such information. This is confirmed by the aside in John 3:24. Obviously, the evangelist feels it is necessary to explain his version of the chronology for readers who know the sequence of Mark 1:14, which claims that Jesus only started his ministry after John's imprisonment. For such readers, the aside explains why John and Jesus could act simultaneously: "because John had not yet been imprisoned."

Interestingly, the evangelist negotiates the chronological pattern of Mark and his own community tradition, and in this case he seems

[225] See above, p. 112–13.

[226] The thought that the evangelist invented the idea of Jesus baptizing in order to highlight the importance of baptism is not plausible. Actually, baptism is not a predominant topic in John but at best hinted at by indirect references and metaphors. Furthermore, the idea of Jesus baptizing is again identified as a problematic point in 4:2. This confirms that the notion of Jesus baptizing is adopted by the evangelist, probably from a community tradition (3:26).

[227] The location is probably somewhat further in the north, east of Mt. Gerizim (see Craig S. Keener, *The Gospel of John: A Commentary* [Grand Rapids: Hendrickson], 1:576).

to prefer and even defend his own (community) tradition. This explanation, however, only addresses the chronological problem. The fact that the other Gospels are completely unaware of any baptizing activity of Jesus is reflected only later (though insufficiently) when a second aside in 4:2 infers that not Jesus did not baptize but only his disciples performed baptisms.[228]

The idea of a simultaneous and analogous activity of John and Jesus was quite embarrassing for later Christian thought. As C. H. Dodd rightly says, "To the mind of the early Church, . . . the suggestion that Jesus at any time put himself on the same level with John . . . would be unwelcome."[229] Given the common tendency of all four Gospels to mark the chronological or salvation-historical difference between John and Jesus, the information about the baptizing Jesus deserves more historical credit than Mark's chronology.[230] It supplements the idea that Jesus was first and for a certain time a follower of John the Baptist and, as such, he not only accepted John's immersion rite of "repentance and forgiveness of sins" (Mark 1:4; Luke 3:3) and adopted elements of his apocalyptic message, but also practiced an immersion rite for a certain length of time that was most likely analogous to John's baptism.

If this is historically valid information, the synoptic tradition has wiped it out. All the canonical Gospels are busy inserting a chronological and theological distance between John and Jesus in order to secure Jesus' singularity, his sinlessness, and the beginning of a new age with his appearance. The Fourth Gospel shares that interest when

[228] Ultimately, the aside in 4:2 does not offer a real solution, as the Synoptics do not mention a baptizing activity of Jesus' disciples during his lifetime either. Numerous authors have considered 4:2 a late redactional addition of a glossator; cf. already Wellhausen, *Das Evangelium Johannis*, 20; Rudolf Bultmann, *Das Evangelium des Johannes*, KEK 2 (Göttingen: Vandenhoeck & Ruprecht, 1941), 128, n. 4; Schnackenburg, *Das Johannesevangelium*, 1:458; and Schnelle, *Das Evangelium nach Johannes*, 120. See also Dodd, *Historical Tradition*, 285.

[229] Thus Dodd, *Historical Tradition*, 292.

[230] Cf. John P. Meier, *Mentor, Message and Miracles*, vol. 2 of *A Marginal Jew*, ABRL (New York: Doubleday, 1994), 122: "It is precisely the criterion of embarrassment that . . . comes to play here. If the historical Jesus did baptize, the entire Synoptic tradition was so embarrassed by the fact that it simply suppressed this aspect of Jesus' public life (not unlike the way the Fourth Gospel suppressed the fact that Jesus was baptized!)."

it radically changes the image of John the Baptist by erasing all the elements of the prophet of doom, is silent about Jesus' baptism, and makes John a mere witness to Christ, or even a first believer in him.

But while the evangelist consequently reshapes the image of John the Baptist according to his theological concept, he presents a splinter of historical information about the baptizing activity of Jesus which adds an important aspect to our image of the historical Jesus. This splinter of tradition still keeps the information that the Jesus of history, in his beginnings, was much closer to the Baptizer, his synoptic teaching, and even his immersion rite than any of the Gospels are willing to concede. It is a piece of information that is suppressed by the Synoptics and even difficult to integrate for the evangelist, who uses the aspect of rivalry only as a point of departure for John's final testimony about Jesus' supremacy (John 3:27-30). It is for that reason that he preserves the difficult information about Jesus' baptizing activity. And although the evangelist is well aware of baptism as an inauguration rite in his community context (3:5), he does not use the idea that Jesus already "baptized" as a foundation for establishing the practices of the later community. Most strikingly, he does not make anything of that historically valuable tradition, and an aside (from the evangelist or a later glossator) even dismisses the idea that Jesus himself baptized by the note that only his disciples did so.

The important point for the present argument is this: In the passage discussed, we have splinters of valuable historical information, even though the evangelist cannot use it for his strongly transformed image of John the Baptist, nor for a teaching about Christian baptism. At a point where John has historically valuable and reliable information, he does not focus on that aspect or make anything of that tradition. He defends his tradition against the rival synoptic version, but neither stresses the point that his version is historically more correct nor utilizes the information for one of his theological purposes. These observations decisively question the views of all the scholars so eager to maintain John's historical interest or even historical accuracy!

6.2 John's Chronology: Historically More Plausible but Incidentally Crafted

A second, complementary observation should be added. At a point where John is probably more historically accurate than Mark, his accuracy is achieved somewhat incidentally, that is, through literary operations that are not guided by the interest of achieving greater historical accuracy.

The aspect we are to address now has already been briefly discussed above: the overall chronological framework of John's Gospel, marked by the three Passovers (John 2:13; 6:4; 11:55) in contrast with only one Passover in Mark. There is good reason to assume that Jesus' ministry lasted longer than one year and that he went to Jerusalem more than once for his last Passover. The chronological and topographical framework of Mark, with Jesus acting only after the imprisonment of John the Baptist, and only in Galilee and its environments before moving to Jerusalem for his final Passover, is quite probably schematic. As we have seen, there is a credible tradition about John and Jesus acting simultaneously for a certain period of time, and a more extended chronology of the ministry of Jesus is also plausible, making John closer to the historical truth in this regard.

But when we consider how John arrives at his three-year chronology, we must conclude that this chronology is not created out of an interest in historically correcting Mark or arriving at a more accurate time frame, but arises for very different reasons. The first Passover in 2:13 is linked with the episode of the cleansing of the temple, and when the evangelist transfers this episode from its passion context to the beginning of Jesus' ministry, he has to mention a reason for his appearance in Jerusalem, the Passover festival. Accordingly, a "first" journey of Jesus is created by a literary operation without reference to any tradition of an additional festival journey. This journey also provides the setting of the encounter with Nicodemus (3:1-11) with the concluding discourse and for the traditional information about Jesus' longer stay in the Judean territory (v. 22). The return journey, then, provides the framework for the encounter with the Samaritan woman and her village. John's aims when creating that journey are not focused on a more accurate representation of Jesus' travels or time frame but rather on the programmatically and dramaturgically effective transposition of the conflict in the temple to the beginning of Jesus' ministry.

Things are similar with the mention of the "second" Passover in John 6:4. Here, interpreters have often been tempted to "purge" the chronological problems by assuming a change of the textual sequence between chapters 5 and 6, but there is no reason for such an assumption.[231] It is striking that the mention of the Passover in 6:4 is not linked with a festival journey. Instead, Jesus remains in Galilee during that time. It is even unclear why the Passover is mentioned here in the narrative aside at the beginning of the feeding episode.

If we read the text as it is without assuming a redactional addition, the mention of the Passover provides a semantic signal for readers[232] to interpret the feeding episode and the subsequent bread discourse within the horizon of Passover, that is, against the background of Jesus' death or even against the background of the community meals alluded to in the feeding narrative (6:11) and probably also in the final passage of the bread discourse (vv. 52-58). Either way, the Passover note is not primarily meant as a marker of narrative time (although it functions as such), but rather as a semantic hint that helps readers grasp the meaning of the episodes and dialogues in the following chapter. It is not inserted to provide greater chronological accuracy, but to produce an appropriate understanding of the traditional narrative of the feeding of the multitude.

[231] If we could identify the Passover of 6:4 with that of 2:13, the result would be a chronology of maybe only little more than one year, so that John's framework would be much closer to Mark. This was the motif behind the often-suggested transposition of chapters 5 and 6 or the assumption that an earlier form or source of the Gospel followed that textual sequence. But these suggestions (e.g., in the commentaries by Wellhausen, Bultmann, or Becker) did not find wide acceptance. Moreover, the result is not convincing: Should Jesus have left Jerusalem during Passover to be soon thereafter in Galilee while there was still Passover time? The events narrated after the Passover of 2:13, with Jesus spending some time in the Judean countryside (3:22-24) and traveling through Samaria, probably require more time than only a few days during the closure of Passover. Moreover, 6:4 points to a time shortly before Passover. The transposition of the chapters cannot solve the problem of John's chronology or harmonize John's chronology with that of Mark.

[232] Cf. Frey, *Die johanneische Eschatologie*, 2:179.

Thus, both mentions of Passover (2:13 and 6:4) are apparently not introduced to craft the narrative time frame and chronology or even to present a better and more accurate historical representation of Jesus' ministry. The effect may be a more probable time frame, but this was not the aim of the evangelist. One could even say he incidentally arrives at this "better" chronology by following different dramaturgical and semantic intentions. John may be closer to the historical truth in this point, but his more historically valid framework is not crafted from his interest in an accurate representation of the history of Jesus but rather from his interest in literary and dramaturgically efficient design.

7. Replotting, Renarrating, and Reimagining: The Modification of Historical Traditions in the Fourth Gospel

From here, we can again conclude that John's narrative is not primarily crafted in the interest of a historically accurate representation of the history of Jesus. Instead, theological and narrative dramaturgical intentions have the priority, and the evangelist uses the traditions available to him with an enormous and bewildering selectivity and liberty. Accordingly, we must ask how the evangelist could feel authorized to alter the tradition to such a considerable extent.

John's modification of his traditions can be described in three basic categories, which I would like to characterize as *replotting*, *renarrating*, and *reimagining*. To illustrate this, I will give one or two significant examples for each of these categories.

7.1 Replotting

The first and quite obvious element, especially when knowledge of Mark is presupposed, is what I call replotting: the transposition of narrative elements from their original context in the Jesus story to a different place for reasons of dramaturgical effects or theological connections. These transpositions are definitely not made to present a historically more accurate placement or according to a supposedly better tradition or historical knowledge.

The temple incident is only one example of many elements from the passion narrative that are now relocated and linked with the narrative of Jesus' whole ministry.[233] The question of the legitimization of Jesus' authority (Mark 11:27-33) is already posed in John 2:18-22, where it is linked with the temple logion (John 2:19) from Mark 14:58; the accusation of blasphemy (Mark 14:61-64) is already dealt with in John 10:22-39; the Sanhedrin's decision about his death (Mark 14: 1-2, 53-64) is already made in John 11:46-54; and Jesus' anointment in Bethany (Mark 14:3-9) is transposed to a position before the beginning of his passion (John 12:12-19) and interpreted as prolepsis of the anointment for his burial. All these transpositions are conceivable from the intention of more closely connecting Jesus' public ministry and his death, thus presenting his ministry as already under the shadow of his death,[234] or conversely his death as the completion of his sending and ministry (19:28-30). These transpositions are not made due to the sources the evangelist used, but they are the result of his deliberate decision to make Jesus' death (and its proper understanding) the leading motif of the presentation of his ministry.[235]

This overall technique sheds light on the understanding of the temple incident in John. The narration of the conflict in the temple serves as a programmatic opening of Jesus' encounter with his Jewish contemporaries and their authorities, and from the very beginning his ministry is overshadowed by the end of his earthly path, the "hour" (2:4) of his death and—important for its true understanding—his resurrection (2:20-21).

Whereas in Mark, the temple incident is the external reason for the temple authorities to have Jesus arrested and finally accused, which makes perfect sense in historical terms, the occasion for the Jewish leaders' decision about Jesus' death in John is his greatest sign, the proof of his divine identity and authority in the raising of Lazarus. In

[233] Cf. the list in Jean Zumstein, *Das Johannesevangelium*, trans. K. Vollmer-Mateus, KEK (Göttingen: Vandenhoeck & Ruprecht, 2016), 661.

[234] This is also indicated by the numerous proleptic references to his death and resurrection. Cf. Frey, "Die *theologia crucifixi* im Johannesevangelium," 194–200.

[235] Zumstein, *Johannesevangelium*, 661: "Diese Umstellungen sind nicht den vom Evangelisten verwendeten Quellen zuzuschreiben, sondern sie sind Ausdruck seiner willentlichen Entscheidung: Indem er wesentliche Begebenheiten der Passion im ersten Hauptteil des Evangeliums verstreut erzählt, fordert er den Leser dazu auf, den Tod Jesu zum Leitgedanken seiner Lektüre zu machen."

John's conception, the provocation in the temple area does not have such an immediate effect on the events of Jesus' arrest and indictment. So, the tradition about the temple incident can be transferred to the beginning of Jesus' ministry to function as a programmatic prelude to the conflict between Jesus and the Jewish authorities. It also introduces the significant topographical symbolism that Jesus faces the fiercest opposition in Jerusalem, the Jewish religious center, whereas he finds followers elsewhere, in Galilee, Samaria, and among the Greeks.

This is confirmed by a closer look at some of the differences between the Johannine version and the synoptic accounts (Mark 11:15-17 par.).[236]

a) In John, Jesus' actions in the temple are described in a more violent and intensified manner. Only in John is a whip mentioned, and Jesus expels not only sellers and buyers but even oxen and sheep, so that the scene is described as an aggressively powerful, violent act. Furthermore, he not only overturns the moneychangers' tables (as in Mark and Matthew) but also pours out the vessels with the coins (John 2:15). Of course, this does not point to a different act but rather shows John's way of drastically renarrating the story as the opening of the conflict with the Jews.[237]

b) Apart from the scriptural reference within the narrative (2:16), which differs from the quotation from Isaiah 56:7 adopted in Mark 11:16,[238] the incident is interpreted by an additional scriptural reference presented in a narrative aside in John 2:17: "His disciples remembered that it is written: Zeal for your house will consume me (Ὁ ζῆλος τοῦ οἴκου σου καταφάγεταί με)". The reference to the "remembrance" of the disciples indicates that the interpretation presented here is part of the insights the disciples arrived at in the post-Easter period

[236] In the following, I adopt and slightly modify the observations from Frey, "Temple and Identity," 482–85; cf. also Zumstein, "Johannes 2:13–22," 278–280.

[237] The enhanced violence might be compared with the way John's miracle stories are also intensified, compared with their synoptic parallels, with enhancements from the healing of blind people to the healing of a man born blind (John 9), or from healings performed in the presence of the one healed to a healing performed from the distance (4:46-54).

[238] In my view, such a difference is not a compelling argument for assuming an independent tradition. The switch from the quotation from Isa 56:7 LXX to a mere allusion to Zech 14:21 can be explained from the transformation of the pericope.

(cf. 2:22; 12:16), through the "remembering" activity of the Spirit (14:26; cf. 16:13-15).[239] The quotation from Psalm 69:10 (68:10 LXX), a psalm of lament densely cited within the passion tradition (cf. John 15:25; 19:28), follows the Septuagint, with only one significant alteration: while in the Septuagint the lament is recorded in the aorist, "Zeal for your house has consumed me (κατέφαγέν με)," the quotation is now changed to the future tense and made a prophetic anticipation of a future event.[240] The word from the psalm is obviously read as a word of Jesus: he is the one who is zealous for God's house, the temple, but his zeal *will* consume him in future, that is, in his passion. So, the temple incident is linked with the passion, in which the conflict between Jesus and the Jewish authorities will ultimately lead to his death. Thus, the function the temple incident has in Mark, where it is the occasion for Jesus' arrest and indictment, is presupposed and implicitly adopted here, although the narrative is transposed to an earlier situation within Jesus' ministry. John 2:17 is, therefore, a further argument for the view that John is aware of and freely draws on the Markan tradition, even in this pericope.

c) A third aspect deserves consideration. The temple incident is combined here with another tradition from the context of the passion, namely the temple logion from Mark 14:58.[241] This tradition is adopted in a modified form as a saying of Jesus himself, which now functions as part of the interpretation of his temple action (John 2:19). In contrast with the synoptic tradition, the temple action and the temple logion are combined here into one composition: Jesus' cleansing of the temple is followed by a challenge from the Ἰουδαῖοι, who ask for him a sign of his authority (v. 18). Jesus responds with the temple logion, which is articulated here with the imperative, wherein he calls the Jews to tear

[239] Cf. Frey, "The Gospel of John as a Narrative Memory of Jesus," in *Memory and Memories in Early Christianity*, ed. Simon Butticaz and Enrico Norelli, WUNT 398 (Tübingen: Mohr Siebeck, 2018), 278–83.

[240] Cf. Frey, *Die johanneische Eschatologie*, 2:69–71.

[241] While in Mark the saying is presented by false witnesses, John presents it as an actual word of Jesus, even a request (to the Jews) to tear down the temple, with the annunciation that he (Jesus) will rebuild it. The transformation of the logion is possibly caused by the relation to Jesus' own fate established in the explaining narrative aside (2:21): it is Jesus' body that will be torn down by his enemies but rise from the dead by his own authority.

down the temple and promises to rebuild it in three days. Both the Jews and Jesus' disciples misunderstand the logion, which prompts the important interpretive narrative commentary, "He was speaking of the temple of his body" (v. 21). This narrative commentary is combined with a further hint that the disciples only truly understood the import of Jesus' words in the post-Easter period.

d) With the explanation from 2:21, the temple motif is given a further and deeper significance. Jesus' saying implies the idea of a "new" temple, different from the Herodian temple, which is to be erected by Jesus himself, although the precise referent is left open for the moment and is only explained for the readers in a narrative aside. The readers get the idea that Jesus himself—already in his earthly appearance—is the "place" where God dwells and may be encountered. The body of Jesus is itself called a temple, and later it is said that "from his body rivers of living water shall flow" (7:38)—obviously an allusion to the temple river of Ezekiel 47. The body of the crucified and risen one is the place where humans can find communion with God.

With the temple logion, the whole episode, in its combination of the various traditions, is interpreted in its significance with regard to Jesus' death and resurrection. From the transposition and combination of two traditions that were originally separate, but both from within the passion context, the evangelist creates a dense connection between the beginning of Jesus' ministry and the events of his death and resurrection. The zeal of Jesus for the temple is already linked with his path to death, and this is further confirmed by the conspicuously modified quotation from Psalm 68:10 LXX.

The evangelist is apparently well aware that the episode of the cleansing of the temple is closely connected with Jesus' passion and that, in the tradition, it is actually the reason for Jesus' arrest and death. But since, according to John's insight and viewpoint, the real reason for Jesus' death is not a single action in the temple, but his true identity as God and life giver, he changes the plot of his narrative, presenting the resurrection of Lazarus and thus the divine dignity of Jesus as the real reason for his death. The temple incident is now presented instead as a prelude to the conflict with the Jewish authorities, as a proleptic hint to his impending death and, furthermore, as an important foothold for the christological use of the temple metaphor.

As we can see here, the interpretive gains are numerous, and in view of the Johannine theological conception, these gains far outweigh the loss of historical accuracy or fidelity to the sources. Indeed, the Johannine interpretation of the temple incident shows that this incident is by far more than the mere point of departure for the events of Jesus' passion. In John, it is transformed into a paradigmatic episode with strong symbolic overtones which are closely linked with the whole of the Johannine presentation of Jesus' identity and ministry.

7.2 Renarrating

The second category of changes is that of deliberate renarration of traditional stories according to distinct theological insights or interests. Here, we could mention a large number of examples because all the narrative traditions are more or less modified in John.

The category of renarration has already been touched upon in the previous passage of the temple incident, where the transposition of the episode and its connection with other traditions was accompanied by distinctive narrative changes in John 2:14-16: the more violent presentation, the mention of oxen and sheep and the omission of vessels,[242] and the modified scriptural reference with Jesus talking of "my Father's house." All these elements of renarration contribute to the new dramaturgical, christological, and symbolic meaning of the episode.

a) A very clear example is the image of John the Baptist in the Gospel of John.[243] In the synoptic tradition, in Mark and the sayings source, the Baptizer is presented as a prophet of doom who points to the imminent day of judgment and calls for immediate repentance. And although there is good reason to assume that the Johannine author was aware of the synoptic depiction of "the Baptizer," his image in John is completely different. There is no description of John's outward appearance, his clothing and diet, no reference to his preaching

[242] The phrase "and he was not permitting anyone to carry a vessel through the temple" (Mark 11:16) is omitted. The precise meaning of this narrative element is difficult to determine, and possibly it was already unclear to the readers from the beginning. For Johannine purposes, it was not necessary and could be easily omitted.

[243] On the relationship between the image of the Baptizer in Mark and John, see Frey, "Das vierte Evangelium," 271–77.

of the impending judgment and his call for repentance, and no detailed presentation of his immersion rite and its meaning, nor is there any information given about the Baptizer's origin and birth. In the Fourth Gospel, John the Baptist simply denies all the messianic functions and presents himself as a mere voice in the wilderness and as a witness to the unknown one he is sent to reveal in Israel. While Mark's three sayings of the Baptizer are adopted in the same sequence and slightly modified,[244] John freely adds the distinctive testimony about Jesus as the Lamb of God (John 1:29). And while the occasion of the Spirit's descent on Jesus like a dove, his baptism, is certainly known and presupposed, it is not explicitly narrated, probably in order to avoid any kind of "comparison" between John the Baptist and Jesus in which the Baptizer could appear as the "greater" one. In a clear departure from the historical tradition available to him, the evangelist has reshaped the image of the Baptizer with the theological aim of introducing him as a witness to the soteriological function of Jesus, or even to his divine dignity as the giver of the Spirit (3:34). The image is changed from the historically plausible depiction of a Jewish eschatological prophet of repentance and a forerunner in the role of Elijah to that of an initial witness to Christ, or even a first "Christian."

Whereas there are historically valid elements in John's depiction of the Baptizer, especially with regard to an initial closeness between him and Jesus and the background of some of Jesus' disciples in the circle of the Baptizer, the overall shape of the depiction of the Baptizer is certainly less valid in terms of historical accuracy. It is creatively renarrated from a deliberate selection from the earlier tradition. A number of substantial traditions are omitted and others are supplemented, and in the end, the language of the witness is even fused with that of Jesus (3:31-36). The whole renarration is crafted in order to shape John's role as a witness testifying to Jesus' soteriological function (cf. also 10:40) and his truly divine dignity. In the renarration of the Baptizer story,

[244] Cf. Dietrich-Alex Koch, "Der Täufer als Zeuge des Offenbarers: Das Täuferbild von Joh 1,19–34 auf dem Hintergrund von Mk 1,2–11," in *The Four Gospels*, Festschrift Frans Neirynck, ed. F. van Segbroeck et al., 3 vols., BETL 100 (Leuven: University Press, 1992), 3:1963–84. See also Frey, "Das vierte Evangelium," 274.

the conceptual and christological aspects overshadow the historical outlines as transmitted in the earlier Baptizer traditions.

b) A more complicated example of a theologically motivated renarration is the wine miracle episode in John 2:1-11, and we cannot enter the discussion on the numerous problems of that narrative here.[245] Since there are no parallels in the Synoptics, scholars have intensely asked for possible sources of the episode, reconstructing a simpler version of the narrative which was then considered part of either the signs source or, if such a source has become questionable, a separate community tradition which was possibly linked with the tradition of the second miracle at Cana in 4:46-54.[246] Although it is in my view impossible to isolate and precisely determine the text of such a source behind the Gospel text, there is still good reason to assume that the evangelist did not merely "invent" the story as a completely fictional allegory related to synoptic texts (e.g., Mark 2:18-22),[247] but could draw on a narrative tradition available to him in written or oral form. The tradition probably included the setting of a wedding in rural Galilee, the presence of Jesus' family (i.e., his mother and his brothers), and the act of Jesus (possibly at the request of his mother) transforming water from the stone vessels into wine.[248] A particular theological depth cannot be ascertained in the tradition, and it remains unclear and speculative how such a "popular" narrative could come up in Jewish Palestine. Most likely, the tradition was linked with an itinerary note (2:12) mentioning the move of Jesus' family to Capernaum.[249]

[245] Cf. extensively Frey, "Das prototypische Zeichen"; see also Frey, "From the *Sēmeia* Narratives to the Gospel as a Significant Narrative: On Genre-Bending in the Johannine Miracle Stories," in *The Fourth Gospel as Genre Mosaic*, ed. Kasper Bro Larsen, Studia Aarhusia Neotestamentica 3 (Göttingen: Vandenhoeck & Ruprecht, 2015), 209–32.

[246] See the argument in Labahn, *Jesus als Lebensspender*, in particular 469–470.

[247] Thus the assumption by Zbyněk Garský, *Das Wirken Jesu in Galiläa bei Johannes: Eine strukturale Analyse der Intertextualität des vierten Evangeliums mit den Synoptikern*, WUNT 2/325 (Tübingen: Mohr Siebeck, 2012), 134–48; cf. also Hartwig Thyen, *Das Johannesevangelium*, HNT 6 (Tübingen: Mohr Siebeck, 2005), 152, according to whom the episode provides a lively illustration of the saying that the wedding guests cannot keep fasting as long as the bridegroom is with them.

[248] Cf. the considerations in Frey, "Das prototypische Zeichen," 177.

[249] The mention of Capernaum (which is the place of Jesus' first activities in Mark) is somewhat odd in John 2, and the itinerary note in 2:12 does not fit quite well

For the present considerations it is important to see that, regardless of how brief or detailed that tradition was, it is the evangelist who must be credited for the narrative and symbolic elaboration of the tradition as a significant and exemplary "semeion narrative."[250] In this process, the story was designed with numerous textual elements that direct readers to other parts of the Gospel or convey particular aspects of the meaning of the episode. The Johannine narrator is responsible for locating the episode on "the third day," thus linking it to the chronology of days in John 1:29, 35, 43. This is possibly a typological reference to the week of creation, while at the same time hinting at the day of Jesus' resurrection, or even the day of the revelation of the divine glory on Mt. Sinai (Exod 19:10–11, 16).[251] He is responsible for inserting the strange reference to Jesus' "hour," which forces readers to consider which hour might be meant, in order to ultimately connect the Cana episode with the horizon of Jesus' passion and resurrection.[252] The evangelist has probably inserted the reference to "the purification practice of the Jews" in 2:6 and shaped the remark that the bridegroom actually behaved "not as any other human," thus initiating the question of whether the reference to the bridegroom might actually be related to Jesus (who is later in 3:27-30 openly called the bridegroom).

It is the evangelist's skillful literary activity that has elaborated the traditional miracle story into a semeion narrative, a narrative that cannot be read merely as a report about a certain miraculous event in the past but demands a deeper reading with reference to the events of Jesus' death and resurrection, that is, a reading from the general perspective taken in the Fourth Gospel. The narrative shaping of the Cana episode is a significant example of renarrating and reshaping

---

into the context. This is a strong argument that the note belongs to the tradition and that the story in which Jesus' mother and brothers occur must also be traditional.

[250] On the characteristic of the semeion narratives and their difference from the genre of synoptic miracle narratives, see Frey, "From the *Sēmeia* Narratives to the Gospel."

[251] In the Targums, the third day is explicitly interpreted as the day of the revelation of the glory of the Lord. See Birger Olsson, *Structure and Meaning in the Fourth Gospel*, ConBNT 6 (Uppsala: Almquist & Wiksell, 1974), 103–4; and Frey, "Das prototypische Zeichen," 182–83.

[252] On the motif of Jesus' hour in John, see Frey, *Die johanneische Eschatologie*, 2:215–21.

traditions in the service of theological meaning. Thus, the evangelist creates a dense web of references by which the episode is linked with the whole of the Johannine narrative, and various levels of metaphorical or symbolic meaning are opened in order to lead the readers to a deeper understanding of the entirety of Jesus' ministry.

c) The most significant example of Johannine renarrating is, however, the passion account. As indicated above, the particularities of John's passion narrative do not require the assumption of a special Johannine passion tradition or source, but can be generally explained against the background of the synoptic account (in particular Mark), taking into consideration the aims and theological tendencies of the Johannine conception.[253] Numerous elements of the Johannine narrative show that a truthful understanding of Jesus' death (in light of the christological insights gained in the Johannine community tradition) is one of the foremost purposes of the Gospel. The mention of "Jesus' hour," the two Passovers, the betrayer, the opponents' intention to seize or kill Jesus, the mention of "the Lamb of God" (John 1:29), the explanation about tearing down and rebuilding "the temple of his body" (2:21), the announcement of the exaltation of the Son of Man (3:14-15), or the teaching that the Good Shepherd will "lay down his life for the sheep" (10:11, 15, 17) all prepare the readers with the categories necessary for the understanding of Jesus' death. With the extended farewell discourses, John includes a unique portion completely devoted to dealing with the problems of Jesus' "departure" and later "absence," and the beginning of the section in John 13 provides a lengthy and complicated discourse containing the christological "default setting" for comprehending Jesus' passion: Jesus knew what would happen to him (13:1), he knew that he would return to the Father (v. 3), and yet he loved his own unto completion (v. 2).

Consequently, John's passion narrative presents Jesus as an active figure, even in his suffering. He goes deliberately into his death, and at any given moment he is sovereign over the events: he commissions Judas to do his sinister work (13:27), he delivers himself to the cohort arresting him (18:4-8), he answers the high priest in sovereignty (vv. 20-21), and he even speaks as if he were able to judge about his and others'

[253] Cf. above, pp. 72–75.

sin in his trial before Pilate (19:11). Finally, he bears his cross himself (v. 17), without the help of others; fulfills the Scriptures (v. 28); proclaims the fulfilment of everything (v. 30); actively nods when dropping his head;[254] and also actively surrenders his spirit (παρέδωκεν τὸ πνεῦμα) when dying.

All these elements can be understood as a deliberate reshaping of the earlier tradition under the presupposition of Johannine Christology. The critical rejection of Mark is, thereby, most obvious when the Gethsemane story is deliberately excluded from John's narrative but instead is alluded to in three different passages.[255] Jesus' prayer in Gethsemane is openly rejected and replaced with a prayer wherein he asks for the glorification of the divine name (12:27–28). In the later scene of his arrest, he explicitly accepts the cup of death from the hand of the Father (18:10). Consequently, there is no cry of godforsakenness but, instead, the triumph of the fulfillment of not only his own task and mission, but also of the Scriptures and the divine salvific will (19:30).[256] Yet, the τετέλεσται also echoes the fulfillment of God's work of creation on the seventh day, so that the salvation established in Jesus' death (and resurrection) is presented as the divine work of a new creation.[257]

At some points, the departure from the historical tradition is particularly impressive; for example, in the account of Jesus' arrest or, rather, his self-deliverance: First, there is no need for Judas to identify Jesus with a kiss since Jesus delivers himself. Even more striking is the fact that after Jesus' self-presentation with the absolute Ἐγώ εἰμι, the whole troop of armed guards and soldiers shrinks back and falls on the ground. Their involuntary *proskynesis* demonstrates the

[254] See the interesting observations by Bastian Lemitz, "Der Tod Jesu und das Nicken des Zeus: Zur Wendung κλίνας τὴν κεφαλὴν (Joh 19,30)," in *Erzählung und Briefe im johanneischen Kreis*, ed. Uta Poplutz and Jörg Frey, WUNT 2/420 (Tübingen: Mohr Siebeck, 2016), 241–56.

[255] See above, pp. 73–74.

[256] Cf. Frey, *Glory of the Crucified One*, 172–73.

[257] Cf. John 20:22. Cf. also Martin Hengel, "Die Schriftauslegung des 4. Evangeliums auf dem Hintergrund der urchristlichen Exegese," in *Jesus und die Evangelien: Kleine Schriften V*, ed. Claus-Jürgen Thornton, WUNT 211 (Tübingen: Mohr Siebeck, 2007), 601–43 (639–41).

divine authority of Jesus' words and thus his divine identity. This is even more remarkable since the band arresting Jesus in John is substantially larger than the group of servants of the Jewish leaders, the temple guard, as in Mark. In John, the whole world[258] is after Jesus, Jews and gentiles, the servants of the Jewish leaders *and* a Roman cohort (σπεῖρα), which usually consisted of several hundred armed soldiers.[259] The imagined scenario that all those soldiers fall on the ground implicitly venerating Jesus seems rather grotesque, but this is exactly what John wants to communicate in order to present Jesus in his divine dignity, even in his arrest, passion, and death. But this means that John accepts that historically plausible and probable scenarios (and the data from the sources available to the evangelist) are abandoned in order to create an impressive scene that is able to communicate the theological truth.

7.3 Reimagining

The process of renarration includes various fictional additions. For example, there are some passages, such as the private talks between Jesus and Pilate about kingdom and truth (John 18:35-38; 19:8-11), that we must consider clearly fictional. The same is true for the private dialogues between Jesus and Nicodemus or the Samaritan woman, for which the evangelist cannot claim to draw on any eyewitness testimony. Here, we encounter the phenomenon that even in ancient historiography dialogues and discourses are the means by which an author inserts his own interpretation of the events narrated.

But should we even reckon with the possibility of completely fictional episodes, theological fictions, in John? Such an idea is hard to accept for numerous interpreters and readers of the Bible. In my view, however, we cannot escape that consequence in some instances, especially when special sources cannot be assumed. In the present context, I can only mention one important example: the footwashing episode in the context of Jesus' last meal with his disciples (13:4-15). Of

258 Cf. John 12:19.

259 In Mark, the σπεῖρα is only called together to the mock Jesus (Mark 15:16), immediately before his crucifixion. It is not, however, involved in his arrest.

course, the last meal is firmly rooted in the earlier tradition; there, it provides the framework not only for the identification of the traitor but also for the institution of the Eucharist.

In John, there is also a meal shared between Jesus and his disciples, albeit not a Passover meal.[260] In this context, Judas is revealed as the one who is about to betray Jesus, and he is even commissioned to go do his work (13:27). But strikingly, the institution of the Eucharist, or more precisely, the interpretation of bread and wine,[261] is omitted and replaced by a different action, Jesus washing the feet of his disciples.[262] Scholars have intensely speculated about the presence of such a rite within the Johannine community[263] or even in the history of Jesus, but there is no plausible reconstruction of an earlier tradition of Jesus' footwashing during his last meal with his disciples.[264]

The possibility arises, therefore, that the narration of the footwashing, together with its two interpretations, is crafted as a fictional and symbolic narrative that replaces the institution of the Eucharist as narrated in the Synoptics. Thus, Hartwig Thyen in his commentary suggests that the whole episode is developed from the saying in

260 On the chronological problems, see above, p. 114–17.

261 Strictly speaking, there is no "institution" in Mark. The command to repeat the meal in remembrance of Jesus is only contained in the Pauline-Lukan branch of the tradition (Luke 22:19; 1 Cor 11:24-25).

262 On the footwashing pericope, cf. Jörg Frey, "'Ethical' Traditions, Family Ethos, and Love in the Johannine Literature," in *Die Herrlichkeit des Gekreuzigten*, 767–802 (793–96); Anni Hentschel, "Die Fusswaschung—ein verhindertes Ritual," *Zeitschrift für Neues Testament* 35 (2015): 66–74; and idem, "Grössere Liebe und grössere Werke—die Fusswaschung als Sinnbild der Liebe im Johannesevangelium," in *Liebe*, ed. Martin Ebner et al., JBTh 29 (Neukirchen-Vluyn: Neukirchener, 2015), 99–117.

263 This was suggested, for example, by Jerome H. Neyrey, "The Foot Washing in John 13:6–11: Transformation Ritual or Ceremony," in *The Social World of the First Christians*, Essays in Honor of W. A. Meeks, ed. L. M. White (Minneapolis: Fortress, 1995), 198–213; and H. Weiss, "Foot Washing in the Johannine Community," *NovT* 21 (1979): 298–325. See also Hentschel, "Die Fusswaschung."

264 Cf. the thorough discussion in Christoph Niemand, "Die Fusswaschungserzählung des Johannesevangeliums: Untersuchungen zu ihrer Entstehung und Überlieferung im Urchristentum," SA 114 (Rome: Pontificio Ateneo S. Anselmo, 1994), 236-56, who assumes a very brief original tradition (without any of the interpretations) in 13:9-10abc.

Luke 22:27, "I am among you as the one who serves."[265] Already in Luke, the paraenetic aspect is present in the context of the dispute among the disciples (22:24-26; cf. Mark 10:41-45). Other aspects may also draw on synoptic passages: the notion of washing the feet as an act of love, for instance, could be inspired by the narrative of the woman anointing Jesus' feet in Luke 7:36-50 (cf. John 12:3-8).

In view of these synoptic parallels, the search for an original non-synoptic footwashing tradition and the question of the "historicity" of the narrated scene appear problematic.[266] While John omits the act of interpreting the bread and the cup during Jesus' last meal, the footwashing appears as a replacement of those acts which were most likely known to John's readers. As in some of the eucharistic traditions, there is also a call for repetition or, rather, imitation (13:14-17), but against the background of the ethical practice of mimesis in antiquity,[267] such a call does not necessarily imply that the addressees should literally practice such a rite but rather imitate the attitude expressed by the example described.

In any case we should assume that the first readers of the Gospel could grasp the "deeper" meaning of the narrated act as suggested in the "christological" interpretation of 13:4-11. Thus, the episode is related to the death of Jesus as a proleptic symbolic interpretation. Jesus' death is interpreted by a narrated act that could be conceived as an act of unexpected love toward the members of the family or toward guests and friends. In this, the act is an example for the disciples who should do as Jesus did (v. 15). That is, they should not simply wash someone's or one another's feet, but love each other as Jesus loved them. And perhaps it is no coincidence that the "new" commandment of love (vv. 34-35) appears in a context in which the hint of a "new" covenant (as it appears in the Pauline and Lukan tradition of the institution of the Eucharist) has been omitted.

[265] Thyen, *Johannesevangelium*, 592.

[266] The question of historicity is abandoned in most of the critical commentaries. The brief remarks in Keener, *Gospel of John*, 2:901, remain unclear.

[267] See Jan G. van der Watt, "Reciprocity, Mimesis and Ethics in 1 John," in *Erzählung und Briefe im johanneischen Kreis*, ed. Uta Poplutz and Jörg Frey, WUNT 2/420 (Tübingen: Mohr Siebeck, 2016), 257–76 (261–66).

Thus, the footwashing episode within the context of Jesus' last meal could have originated in the fictional creation of a symbolic narrative, lacking any "historical" tradition in the background. And yet, even such a narrative invention serves the overall intention of the evangelist to interpret Jesus' death as an unprecedented example of love.

8. "Let John Be John!" The Uniqueness of the Fourth Gospel

It was James D. G. Dunn who, in a remarkable plea for the uniqueness of the Fourth Gospel, coined the slogan, "Let John be John!"[268] In that article, Dunn cautions exegetes against reading the Fourth Gospel either in terms of the other three (i.e., the earlier gospel tradition) or in terms of later church doctrine. Compared with the Synoptics, John marks "a major shift in perspective."[269] Its author apparently felt quite free toward the earlier tradition, even though he was still eager to keep the story of the incarnate Jesus. In Dunn's words, there is a remarkable "interplay of freedom and constraint" in John, "greater freedom than we find in the Synoptics,"[270] but also a greater constraint than we find in some later gnostic gospels and texts. It is the interplay between both that requires detailed study and considerations.

Phrased somewhat differently, John continues to tell the founding story of Christianity, the story of Jesus, which took place in a clearly defined context of space and time. However, he tells that story from a theological conviction about who Jesus really is. This theological view and the evangelist's intention to lead readers to an appropriate understanding of who Jesus is reshapes the memory of Jesus to a remarkable degree. This appears hard to accept for those who stick to a (very modern and "historicist") concept of biblical "truth" being based on historical accuracy. Yet, John obviously neither follows nor advocates for such a concept. His notion of truth is relationally and christologically founded. Therefore, John replots, renarrates, or even fictionally invents

[268] James D. G. Dunn, "Let John be John! A Gospel for Its Time," in *Das Evangelium und die Evangelien*, ed. Peter Stuhlmacher, WUNT 28 (Tübingen: Mohr, 1983), 309–39.

[269] Dunn, "Let John be John," 334.

[270] Dunn, "Let John be John," 339.

narrative images according to his interest in depicting Jesus Christ in his true divine dignity. He does this while remaining consistent with the foundational story of the earthly Jesus, whereas later authors loosened those ties and more freely expressed revelatory discourses of a heavenly savior. These unique features of the Fourth Gospel place it "on the border" between the earthly history of Jesus and post-Easter christological insight, and this unique placement may in fact be the reason for its distinctive narrative design and its sometimes bewildering freedom with regard to historical traditions.

3

THE SPIRITUAL GOSPEL

Reworking the Jesus Story for Deeper Theological Understanding

As has been demonstrated in the previous two chapters, the Fourth Gospel is deeply shaped by its remarkably high Christology, depicting the earthly Jesus, the incarnate one, not only as a human but already as a divine being. John utilizes the historical tradition available to him, from Mark and from his community traditions, in a remarkably free manner, taking the liberty of *replotting* the Jesus story, *renarrating* traditional episodes, and even fictionally *reimagining* new narrative episodes such as the footwashing or the private dialogues of Jesus with Nicodemus, the Samaritan woman, or Pilate that are uncovered by the claim of authentification by immediate witnesses.

From these observations, the question arises, "How could the author feel so free toward the traditions he had received?" Or, "How could he be so 'careless' in terms of historical accuracy?" Even if some of his techniques may be in accordance with the habit of ancient historiographers,[1] the uniqueness of this gospel provides a challenge for our modern desire to get historical facts instead of fiction, particularly in a book that has become part of the Bible and is, therefore, widely considered to be even more truthful.

The numerous attempts to defend John's value as a historical source aptly illustrate the persistence of this underlying desire in a large number of readers and interpreters, but—as we have also seen—the actual

[1] Cf. the studies by Richard Bauckham and Susanne Luther mentioned above, pp. 93.

procedure of the evangelist does not support such a view: in some places, the evangelist integrates historical traditions that are, even in our critical perspective, valuable, adding important aspects to our knowledge of the historical Jesus. But in the case we discussed, he does not make anything out of that tradition. Furthermore, his textual chronology—which is, according to our historical reasoning, generally more plausible than Mark's—is only crafted by literary concerns and operations that are motivated not by a contention for historical accuracy but rather by dramaturgical or theological considerations.

So, how does the author legitimate his enormous liberty with regard to history or to his traditions? How does he explain the fact that he so strongly departs from Mark's story, changing not only the image of Jesus in general but also his language, core terms, and message? Should he not be accused of illicit alteration, perhaps even forgery, as some modern critics have accused John of forging the image of Jesus by transforming him from a human into a divine being, "from Jewish prophet to Gentile God"?[2]

1. The Spiritual Gospel: The Spirit-Paraclete, Memory, and Understanding

1.1 Critical Questions and the Johannine Claim of Authority

In my view, there is even a trace in the Gospel that such debates actually existed within the Johannine communities. There was an awareness that such a transformation of the narrative and discourse material about Jesus was not without problems and needed authorization. The debates can be reconstructed from the last saying about the Spirit, called "Paraclete" (which means "advocate")[3] in the farewell discourses, in John 16:13-15, where Jesus speaks about the future teaching of the

[2] Thus the title by Maurice Casey, *From Jewish Prophet to Gentile God* (Louisville: Westminster John Knox, 1992).

[3] The term implies a certain forensic function, which is most clearly expressed in the Paraclete sayings in John 15:26 and 16:7-11. On the term and its interpretation, see in particular David Pastorelli, *Le Paraclet dans le corpus johannique*, BZNW 142 (Berlin: de Gruyter, 2006). Interestingly, Jesus himself is called παράκλητος in 1 John 2:1. The exalted Christ, therefore, is the first helper or advocate for the disciples,

Spirit, saying, "He[4] will not speak on his own, but will speak whatever he hears" (16:13), and "he shall glorify me, for he shall take what is mine and disclose it to you" (v. 14, partly repeated in v. 15).[5] The rejection of the idea that the Spirit might "speak on his own" is significant. Even in Jesus' ministry, we find the idea that doing something "on his own" is also rejected; instead, he does only what he sees the Father do (5:19) or what he hears from the Father (5:30). This means that Jesus' acts are not performed independently and thus illegitimately but are authorized by the Father.[6] Likewise, the Spirit does not teach "on his own," but rather his teaching is taken from what belongs to Jesus and is, therefore, authorized by Jesus himself. Thus, just as Jesus

---

albeit he resides in the realm of the Father, while the Spirit acts on his behalf on earth (cf. Rom 8:34).

[4] Just for clarification, I must emphasize that I am well aware of the insufficiencies of gendering the Spirit. But as the personal aspects of the Spirit are most obvious in John, with John at the final stage of a longer development of "personalizing" the Spirit in the Jesus movement (cf. Jörg Frey, "How Did the Spirit Become a Person?" in *The Holy Spirit, Inspiration, and the Cultures of Antiquity: Multidisciplinary Perspectives*, ed. Jörg Frey and John R. Levison, Ekstasis 5 [Berlin: de Gruyter, 2014], 243–371), it is clear that the Spirit cannot be treated as neuter (as τὸ πνεῦμα is in Greek). While in the Hebrew tradition, the Spirit (*ruaḥ*) is grammatically female, and the idea of the Spirit as "mother" is also present in some early Christian texts (cf. the fragment from the Gos. Heb., quoted by Origen and Jerome; see Origen, *Comm. Jo.* 2.12 on John 1:3), the use of the male pronoun is suggested not only by the Johannine use of the term ὁ παράκλητος but also by the fact that the "personalization" of the Spirit—that is, the conceptualization of "him" as a willful, acting, and speaking being—is largely brought about by ascribing activities to the Spirit analogous to those of (the incarnate and exalted) Christ. Nonetheless, the inadequacies of "gendering" the Spirit should always be kept in mind.

[5] On this saying, cf. Jörg Frey, *Die johanneische Eschatologie*, vol. 3: *Die eschatologische Verkündigung in den johanneischen Texten*, WUNT 117 (Tübingen: Mohr Siebeck, 2000), 190–95; and in particular Christina Hoegen-Rohls, *Der nachösterliche Johannes: Die Abschiedsreden als hermeneutischer Schlüssel zum vierten Evangelium*, WUNT 2/84 (Tübingen: Mohr Siebeck, 1996), 188–94; and Christian Dietzfelbinger, *Der Abschied des Kommenden: Eine Auslegung der johanneischen Abschiedsreden*, WUNT 95 (Tübingen: Mohr Siebeck, 1997), 192–95.

[6] In 5:19-30, this is in particular the authorization to raise the dead or give life and to enact judgment, the two acts that were reserved for God alone in the Jewish tradition. Such an authorization is claimed for Jesus in 5:22-23 and 5:26-27; cf. Frey, *Die johanneische Eschatologie*, 3:354–69.

is authorized by the Father, so also the Spirit-Paraclete's proclamation is authorized by Jesus.

Apparently, the idea that the Spirit (or, rather, a teacher in the Johannine community) might teach "on his own," in an unauthorized manner, was nearby and manifest, so that there was a need to explicitly reject it. As the farewell discourses are the part of the Gospel in which we can most strongly see the fears, distresses, and problems of the post-Easter community,[7] we can interpret this saying as evidence for internal discussions about the legacy of the Spirit's teaching or, rather, the teaching of preachers and teachers within the Johannine communities. Therefore, we can get some glimpses into the life of the Johannine school, its christological teaching, and the internal debate about it. Against the accusation that the respective teachers had developed their teaching "on their own," and that it was, therefore, unauthorized and illegitimate, the saying emphasizes that the proclamation not only glorifies Jesus but is also taken from the realm of Jesus—that is, it is an expression of the close connection with Jesus and is thus authorized by him, the incarnate and exalted Lord.

More generally, the saying supports the theological claim of the Johannine proclamation that it is materially and formally authorized by Jesus himself and thus provides a legitimate and truthful interpretation of Jesus and his identity and dignity, as well as his ministry and history. The Johannine image of Jesus and the narrated story of Jesus are, therefore, considered truthful and authorized—despite the fact that the evangelist and his community were well aware of the fact that the Johannine narrative is not an accurate representation of the historical tradition or of the history of the earthly Jesus, as it happened before the eyes of his contemporaries.

1.2 The Spirit as the Author of John's Memory of Jesus

The Paraclete saying is also significant because it claims that the Spirit guides the community in all truth. If the dative ἐν τῇ ἀληθείᾳ πάσῃ is

[7] Cf. Frey, *Die johanneische Eschatologie*, vol. 2: *Das johanneische Zeitverständnis*, WUNT 110 (Tübingen: Mohr Siebeck, 1998), 250–52; and Hoegen-Rohls, *Der nachösterliche Johannes*.

the correct reading here,[8] it implies that truth is considered to be a totality,[9] imagined as a space or realm, within which the community can stay or move under the guidance of the Spirit. Due to the christological meaning of the ἀλήθεια terminology in John, the realm of truth is characterized by the relationship with Christ, not by some kind of accuracy or historical correctness.[10] The activity of the Spirit is characterized as maintaining the close relationship between the community and the incarnate and exalted Christ. Furthermore, the Spirit's teaching—even its remarkable freedom with respect to history and its progressive reshaping of the Jesus tradition—is considered appropriate to preserve the community in the truth and in the communion with the risen and exalted Jesus.

If we combine this with the second Paraclete saying from John 14:26 about the Spirit's activity of teaching and reminding the disciples of the words of Jesus,[11] we can get an even clearer image of what the

[8] The Spirit does not lead *into* all truth, but *within* the realm of truth that is, therefore, given. The notion of "truth" is therefore spatially constructed, and it is most probable that "truth" should be understood from the idea that God and also Jesus himself is presented as "the truth" (John 14:6)—that is, as a personal or relational truth, not from the Aristotelian idea of a correspondence between the matter and its understanding, the *adaequatio rei et intellectus* (as defined by Thomas Aquinas, *Quaestiones disputatae de veritate* 1.1). Thus, the Spirit can also be called "Spirit of Truth" in John (14:26; 16:13).

[9] Cf. Frey, *Die johanneische Eschatologie*, 3:192–93.

[10] On the Johannine notion of "truth," see the important article by Rudolf Bultmann, "ἀλήθεια," *TDNT* 1:239–48; further Ignace de la Potterie, *La vérité dans Saint Jean*, 2 vols., AnBib 73–74 (Rome: Biblical Institute, 1977); Christof Landmesser, *Wahrheit als Grundbegriff neutestamentlicher Wissenschaft*, WUNT 113 (Tübingen: Mohr Siebeck, 1999); and Peter G. Kirchschläger, *Nur ich bin die Wahrheit: Der Absolutheitsanspruch des johanneischen Christus und das Gespräch zwischen den Religionen*, HBS 63 (Freiburg im Breisgau: Herder, 2010).

[11] On that saying, see Christina Hoegen-Rohls, *Der nachösterliche Johannes*, 111–34. On the particular function of the Spirit in the Gospel of John, see Frey, *Glory of the Crucified One: Theology and Christology in the Fourth Gospel*, trans. W. Coppins and C. Heilig, BMSEC 6 (Waco: Baylor University Press, 2018), 368–72; Frey, "How Did the Spirit Become a Person?" 364–71; and Dietzfelbinger, *Der Abschied des Kommenden*, 202–26. In my view, the five Paraclete sayings have to be interpreted coherently, although there are slight differences between those in John 14 (where the Spirit is sent by the Father at Jesus' request) and those in John 15 and 16 (where the Spirit is sent by the risen Jesus). But this does not necessarily call for an attribution to different literary

Spirit—as the authority behind the Johannine proclamation or even its real author—is supposed to do. Most interestingly, and in contrast with Paul and Luke–Acts, the Fourth Gospel characterizes the activity of the Spirit not by reference to visionary or ecstatic phenomena or to speaking in tongues and performing miracles.[12] The mention of the Spirit is entirely focused on his verbal effects, the "logos function." He reminds; he teaches the disciples (14:26); he enables them to be a testimony (15:26) by assisting them, like an advocate, in the universal trial about the truth;[13] and he guides them in all truth (16:13-15). As a teacher, the Spirit reminds the disciples in the post-Easter period of the story and the words of Jesus and thus keeps them in communion with the risen Lord.

But what kind of reminding activity is meant here? This could possibly be conceived of as an accurate memory that takes the form of a verbal reproduction of Jesus' words. Such an understanding could be suggested from the ancient cultural practice of learning a fixed tradition by heart in order to reproduce and keep it accurately and verbally. But it is quite improbable that such a practice, as is well-known from rabbinic Judaism and sometimes also suggested for the early synoptic tradition,[14] is meant in the present context. The observation of the

---

strata, as Jürgen Becker ("Die Abschiedsreden Jesu im Johannesevangelium," *ZNW* 61 [1970]: 215–46) has suggested. Within the whole text of the Gospel, it is also necessary to see the coherence between the passages on the Spirit in John 1–12 and 18–20 and the passages in the farewell discourses with the particular term "Paraclete." This term, however, seems to be particularly linked with the form and themes of the farewell discourses (see Dietzfelbinger, *Der Abschied des Kommenden*, 208–9; Pastorelli, *Le Paraclet dans le corpus johannique*, 159–60) rather than point to a completely different concept or origin or these sayings.

[12] There is no reference to the Spirit in the context of Jesus' miracles, nor is there any idea that the disciples should perform miracles through the Spirit in the post-Easter period. Even the "greater works" mentioned in John 14:12 (cf. 5:20) are most probably not miracles but the continuation of the salvific work of Jesus, according to the commissioning in John 20:23, but in a wider and universal context. Cf. Frey, *Die johanneische Eschatologie*, 3:352–54.

[13] The trial motif is predominant in John 16:7-11, but it is a motif that characterizes the whole gospel, as Andrew Lincoln (*Truth on Trial: The Lawsuit Motif in the Fourth Gospel* [Peabody, Mass.: Hendrickson, 2000]) has convincingly demonstrated.

[14] Cf. Birger Gerhardsson, *Memory and Manuscript: Oral Tradition and Written Transmission in Rabbinic Judaism and Early Christianity*, ASNU 22 (Lund: Gleerup,

transformation in the language and style of Jesus and the traces of communal debates about the legacy of such a "progressive" teaching point in another direction. Remembering the words of Jesus seems to be focused not on an accurate verbal representation but rather on a process that discloses a deeper meaning about what Jesus said and thus leads to a better and truthful understanding of his mission and his person.

This is confirmed by two passages that I consider crucial for understanding the character and perspective of the Fourth Gospel. These are the narrative asides in 2:22 and 12:16,[15] where verb ὑπομιμνήσκειν does not occur (as in 14:26) but instead the related verb μιμνήσκεσθαι is used. After the narration of the cleansing of the temple, the demand for a sign of Jesus' legitimacy by the Jews, and the temple saying that makes the Jews wonder, the evangelist adds a first narrative aside in 2:21. He explains that, in the saying about destroying and rebuilding the temple (v. 20), Jesus actually spoke about "the temple of his body" (v. 21), thereby communicating an insight that could be gained and brought to expression only after Jesus' death and resurrection. In a second narrative aside or explanation, the author adds, "When he was raised from the dead, his disciples remembered (ἐμνήσθησαν) that he said this; and they believed the scripture, and the word which Jesus had spoken" (v. 22). A close parallel to this can be found in 12:16. After the narration of Jesus' entry into Jerusalem on a donkey, the hailing of the crowd with palm branches, and the quotation from Zechariah 9:9, the evangelist again states, "These things his disciples *did not understand at the first*; but when Jesus was glorified, then they remembered (ἐμνήσθησαν) that these things were written about him, and that they had done these things to him."

1964); Gerhardsson, "Der Weg der Evangelientradition," in *Das Evangelium und die Evangelien*, ed. P. Stuhlmacher, WUNT 28 (Tübingen: Mohr Siebeck, 1983), 79–102; cf. also Rainer Riesner, *Jesus als Lehrer: Eine Untersuchung zum Ursprung der Evanglien-Überlieferung*, 3rd ed., WUNT 2/7 (Tübingen: Mohr Siebeck, 1988); and Samuel Byrskog, *Jesus the Only Teacher: Didactic Authority and Transmission in Ancient Israel, Ancient Judaism and the Matthean Community*, ConBNT 24 (Stockholm: Almqvist & Wiksell, 1994).

[15] See Frey, *Die johanneische Eschatologie*, 2:221–23; further Hoegen-Rohls, *Der nachösterliche Johannes*, 33–39.

In these narrative explanations, the Fourth Gospel openly concedes that the disciples of the earthly Jesus, during the time of their discipleship, did not understand his words, his actions, and his fate, but only after his resurrection or glorification did they remember (ἐμνήσθησαν, 2:22; 12:16) these things and understand their true meaning. During the ministry of Jesus, it is said that they could not realize that the Scriptures pointed to Jesus and that particular prophetic passages (such as Zech 9:9) foreshadowed even details of his ministry and, in particular, his passion. It was only afterward, in the post-Easter period, that they remembered, reread the Scriptures, and understood their reference to the details of the Jesus story.

More generally, the christological interpretation of the Scriptures, as practiced throughout the Fourth Gospel,[16] and the insights into the true identity and dignity of Christ provided through the sacred writings are quite generally ascribed to the teaching of the Spirit, who, in the process of reading, triggered a new understanding of the Jesus story or, conversely, in the remembrance of Jesus' ministry and death produced a new understanding of the Scriptures as directly testifying about Jesus, his ministry, and his fate.

From the correspondence between these "anamnesis remarks" and the anamnetic and didactic function attributed the Spirit-Paraclete (cf. John 14:26; 16:13-15), it is obvious that the act of remembrance mentioned in 2:22 and 12:16 has to be connected with the post-Easter teaching activity of the Spirit, as is envisaged in the Paraclete sayings of the farewell discourse. Thus, the difference between the Johannine image of Jesus (depicted in the light of the Easter events or of his glorification) and the images of the earlier tradition (which are probably much closer to the historical "facts") is explained and also justified by the reference to the activity of the Spirit. The Gospel's claim is, thus, that the creator of the deeper perception of Jesus, indeed the proper author of the Johannine Christology, is the Holy Spirit, who

[16] Cf. Martin Hengel, "Die Schriftauslegung des 4. Evangeliums auf dem Hintergrund der urchristlichen Exegese," in *Jesus und die Evangelien: Kleine Schriften*, ed. Claus-Jürgen Thornton, WUNT 211 (Tübingen: Mohr Siebeck, 2007), 5:601–43; and Andreas Obermann, *Die christologische Erfüllung der Schrift im Johannesevangelium*, WUNT 2/88 (Tübingen: Mohr Siebeck, 1996).

"reminded" and "taught" the disciples in the post-Easter period and thus opened up their eyes to the true understanding of Jesus' words, history, and person. In other words, the Johannine Christology with its "high" and divine traits is not an arbitrary and unauthorized interpretation but shaped under the guidance of the Spirit and in relation with the earthly Jesus (16:14-15).[17]

1.3 Understanding in Retrospective

Further narrative asides in John, apart from John 2:22 (with 2:17) and 12:16, point to the disciples' lack of understanding during the time of Jesus' ministry. The saying about the streams of living water coming out of his (i.e., Jesus') body (7:37-38) is explained as a reference to the Spirit, which had not yet been given at that time but was only bestowed upon the disciples at the same time as or after his glorification.[18] In the footwashing scene, Peter in particular is caught in misunderstandings, but his misunderstandings point to a future understanding of Jesus' symbolic act "thereafter" (13:7). Finally, in the scene of the two disciples discovering the empty tomb (20:2-10), where Peter is still remarkably slow to understand what happened, the narrator comments that "they did not yet understand the scriptures" that Jesus should rise from

[17] On this, cf. the important article by Christian Dietzfelbinger, "Paraklet und theologischer Anspruch im Johannesevangelium," *ZTK* 82 (1985): 389–408.

[18] The discussion about when and how those living waters came from Jesus' body is complicated. The most obvious scene is the scene where blood and water come out of Jesus' body, after his death, and after his side was pierced. Regardless of how the meaning or symbolism of blood and water is interpreted, the scene is also an allusion to the stream coming out from the temple in Ezek 47, as had been observed very early on by the church fathers since Jerome (*Comm. Ezech.* 14 on Ezek 47:1-5). A second interesting option is when Jesus breathes out at the time of his death (John 19:30), which is referred to by the remarkable phrase παρέδωκεν τὸ πνεῦμα (= surrendered the spirit), which might also imply the notion that the Spirit came out of Jesus' mouth in the hour of his death. The final transfer of the "Holy Spirit" to his disciples is narrated in the context of the Easter Day and the commission of the disciples to forgive or retain sins (20:22-23). This passage is also a relatively bodily one, wherein Jesus blows at or rather into (ἐνεφύσησεν) the disciples; cf. Annette Weissenrieder, "The Infusion of the Spirit: The Meaning of ἐμφυσάω in John 20:22–23," in *The Holy Spirit, Inspiration, and the Cultures of Antiquity: Multidisciplinary Perspectives*, ed. Jörg Frey and John R. Levison, Ekstasis 5 (Berlin: de Gruyter, 2014), 119–51.

the dead (20:9). The problem is that the beloved disciple actually does understand and believe, so a lack of understanding cannot be stated equally for both disciples. But as the beloved disciple understands immediately from seeing the "signs" of the linen and the napkin in the tomb, not because of some scriptural knowledge, the hint to the understanding of the Scriptures, which was "not yet" possible on the Easter day, also points forward to the possibility of understanding thereafter, in the post-Easter period, through the teaching of the Spirit. These small temporal remarks in the Gospel could be easily overlooked, but they are significant because they point to a fundamental change that is linked with the events of Jesus' hour, his death or glorification,[19] in which the lack of understanding in the time of Jesus' ministry is transformed into a new understanding "thereafter," in the time after his departure and in the presence of the Spirit. They also point us to the fact that in John, the true understanding of Jesus' history is presented from a retrospective point of view or, more precisely, from a perspective that incorporates knowledge about his death, his resurrection, and the teaching of the Spirit.

Therefore, the narrative asides focusing on a "not yet" or "now" do not only indicate the temporal perspective or location of the Johannine narrator but also support the view that a truthful understanding of Jesus' words, ministry, and death became possible only in the light of the insights that the community had been granted through the Spirit in the post-Easter period. The Gospel emphasizes, therefore, that the post-Easter community is in an extremely privileged position compared with the disciples of the earthly Jesus, because only through Jesus' "departure" could the Spirit be sent (16:7) and only through the Spirit could the christological understanding of the Scriptures and the post-Easter insights of the community be developed.

In the time before, during the time of Jesus' ministry, such knowledge is limited to Jesus himself and, to some extent, the prophetic

[19] In Jesus' "hour," the events of his passion, death, and resurrection and the gift of the Spirit are taken together, although they are considered different acts in the narrative. But for the effect on the post-Easter community, the whole sequence of eschatological acts is important. Cf. Frey, *Glory of the Crucified One*, 87–88; Frey, *Die Johanneische Eschatologie*, 2:216–21.

figure of John the Baptist (cf. 10:40-42) and the ideal figure of the beloved disciple. In fact, the beloved disciple is the only narrative figure in John (apart from Jesus and the Baptizer) who is never subject to misunderstanding, and, therefore, this disciple appears so strongly, though not completely, as an ideal figure, different from all the other disciples. All the other figures, Peter, Philip, Thomas, as well as the Samaritan women and the Bethany sisters, and also Nicodemus and most of the Jewish contemporaries, often misunderstand his words, and the text presents those misunderstandings quite openly, so that the reader is forced to notice them and arrive at a better understanding than even Peter and his companions could gain.[20] Even on the Easter day, in view of the empty tomb, Peter still lacks understanding (20:7-8), while only his ideal companion gains the true understanding of the risen one, when perceiving the linen and the napkin in Jesus' tomb.[21]

The textual elements that mark a difference between a "now" and a "thereafter" (13:7) or maintain the "not yet" and the lack of a full understanding among Jesus' disciples point to the fundamental difference between the time before and after Jesus' hour (or the Easter events), and thus to the possibility of the "revelation" of Jesus' true identity and the meaning of his ministry only in the time "thereafter," through the Spirit, or through the proclamation of the Johannine community, or—most clearly—through the narrative design of the present gospel

[20] The misunderstandings are not a device of polemics against certain "Petrine," "Thomasine," etc. groups, nor are they thought to discredit the disciples or Nicodemus and the Samaritan woman in general. They simply demonstrate that at their point of time, before the glorification of Jesus and without the teaching of the Spirit, the true understanding of Jesus' identity and ministry was not yet possible, and that the readers in post-Easter times are in a much better situation than the disciples of the earthly Jesus. On the didactic function of the Johanannine misunderstandings, see also Walter Rebell, *Gemeinde als Gegenwelt: Zur soziologischen und didaktischen Funktion des Johannesevangelium*, BET 20 (Frankfurt: Peter Lang, 1987).

[21] Johannine Easter faith, therefore, is not only that Jesus came back to life again but, even more, that in his own authority, he is risen, and therefore he is the one who has divine life in himself—that is, he is God; cf. Jörg Frey, "'Ich habe den Herrn gesehen' (John 20,18): Entstehung, Inhalt und Vermittlung des Osterglaubens nach Johannes 20," in *Studien zu Matthäus und Johannes / Études sur Matthieu et Jean*, Festschrift Jean Zumstein, ed. Andreas Dettwiler and Uta Poplutz, AthANT 97 (Zürich: TVZ, 2009), 267–84.

writing. It is, ultimately, the narrator's voice that points readers to the true understanding of Jesus' acts and words, and it is the narrative design of the Gospel that guides them to the truth that is hidden to physical eyes but now revealed through the Spirit.

These asides, together with the Paraclete sayings in 14:26 and 16:13-15, present a concept of "remembering" or "commemoration" with regard to the disciples and the Jesus story: Jesus' disciples did not understand the true meaning of his acts and sayings during the time of his earthly ministry, nor could they understand the Scriptures with regard to Jesus. Such an insight was possible only when Jesus was "glorified" or "raised from the dead"—that is, in the post-Easter period. The true understanding granted by the Spirit includes an understanding of the Scriptures and their christological meaning and a truthful understanding of Jesus' fate, in particular his death, his acts (the miracles and other episodes narrated), and also his words. The evangelist is, therefore, well aware that access to such an understanding was possible only through a process of remembering (μιμνήσκεσθαι) in the post-Easter period.

1.4 The Core Challenge: Understanding the Death of Jesus

The need for such a new and true understanding is particularly obvious with regard to Jesus' death and resurrection, which could not be grasped by the disciples in the time of Jesus. Thus, the internal references from the various episodes of the Jesus story, his miracles understood as "signs" for the whole of his ministry,[22] or the saying about tearing down and rebuilding the "temple of his body" (John 2:21), could be inserted into the Jesus story only due to the knowledge about the events of his death and resurrection.

Furthermore, Jesus' departure and alleged absence obviously continued to provide a source of trouble and distress for his disciples even in the post-Easter period. Thus, the farewell discourses[23] present the

[22] Thus, for example, the reference to Jesus' hour in the Cana episode (2:1-11).

[23] On the farewell discourses and their point of departure, see Frey, *Die johanneische Eschatologie*, 3:130–31; see also Andreas Dettwiler, *Die Gegenwart des Erhöhten:*

lament of Jesus' disciples about his imminent departure (13:33, 36; 14:5) as an image of the tribulations and distress of the post-Easter community in view of his apparent absence. While the community of disciples is troubled by Jesus' invisibility (16:10), feels left behind as "orphans" (14:18), and feels alone amid an unbelieving and sometimes hostile world (15:18), its most prominent aim is in providing readers with a truthful understanding about Jesus' departure, the coming of the Spirit-Paraclete, and the hope for a reunion with Jesus. Such an understanding is meant to provide a novel foundation for the faith community in the post-Easter period and to enable disciples not to stumble but to continue their mission (and the mission of Jesus) in the world.[24]

This understanding of the real meaning and salvific implications of Jesus' life, death, and resurrection is expressed with reference to the events in Jesus' "hour" and to the "glory" bestowed on him in his "glorification."[25] Therefore, it is stressed that, in Jesus' death and resurrection, he is not just detached but indeed glorified (13:31-32; 17:1) and thus confirmed in his eschatological function and dignity. Only on this basis can the last words of Jesus on the cross be so thoroughly rephrased in order to express the completion accomplished in these events. But also when the Gospel states that in his "signs" Jesus "revealed his glory" (2:11), it actually refers not only to some miraculous deeds but ultimately to the glory Jesus obtained in his "hour" (v. 4).[26] More generally speaking,

---

Eine exegetische Studie zu den johanneischen Abschiedsreden (Joh 13,31–16,33) unter Berücksichtigung ihres Relecture-Charakters, FRLANT 169 (Göttingen: Vandenhoeck & Ruprecht, 1995). The first discourse in John 13:31–14:31 is framed in its main part by the mention of the troubledness of the disciples (14:1, 27), and the discourse passage in 16:4b-33 is framed by the mention of the grief (*lupe*) and distress (*thlipsis*) of the disciples (16:6, 33), which are both linked in the central image in 16:20-22.

[24] This is particularly obvious in the final passages of the farewell prayer (17:20-26), where there is even a hope for the world to come to understanding and belief, in spite of the hostility experienced by the community at present. Concerning these perspectives on Johannine mission, see Enno Edzard Popkes, *Die Theologie der Liebe Gottes in den johanneischen Schriften*, WUNT 2/197 (Tübingen: Mohr Siebeck, 2005), 346–49.

[25] Cf. Frey, *Glory of the Crucified One*, 237–58.

[26] On the interpretation of the semeia stories (and 2:1-11 in particular), see Jörg Frey, "From the *Sēmeia* Narratives to the Gospel as a Significant Narrative: On

the narrative design of all the Johannine miracle or signs stories links them with the whole of Jesus' ministry, his death, and his resurrection, so that they all now not only express information about an event that happened once during the ministry of Jesus but also—and perhaps even predominantly—provide an exemplary clue for understanding the whole of Jesus' ministry, including his death and resurrection.

From here, it is clear that the Johannine narrative is not a representation of the history of Jesus' ministry as it could be observed by his contemporaries. It is hermeneutically important that the evangelist is quite aware of the fact that he does not simply tell the story of Jesus as transmitted by the tradition or traditions, or even naively "as it was."[27] Though crafting a factual narration, he deliberately produces a text thoroughly shaped from the christological and theological insights gained in the post-Easter period. The whole Gospel is a retrospective memory of Jesus, an anamnesis of the Jesus story that is authorized by the Spirit, who is considered the real "author" of the gospel proclamation and who can claim to be in a close relationship with Jesus himself. It is this revelation by the Spirit that enables and justifies the author of the Fourth Gospel to narrate Jesus' ministry so differently with regard to its content, plot, language, and interpretation.

1.5 A Complex Process of Reinterpretation

In the Johannine tradition, that process of "remembering" was not just an anxious or dutiful attempt to preserve the original wording of the tradition, let alone the possible historical "facts" behind it. It was, rather, a creative and dynamic process that led to new insights and also led to a reshaping of the Jesus story that raised questions among the community (as John 16:13-15 suggests). In the Johannine view, however, the process is attributed to and legitimized by the activity of the

Genre-Bending in the Johannine Miracle Stories," in *The Fourth Gospel as Genre Mosaic*, ed. Kasper Bro Larsen, Studia Aarhusia Neotestamentica 3 (Göttingen: Vandenhoeck & Ruprecht, 2015), 209–32.

[27] The remark that his disciples "did not understand" points to the difference between the "historical" events and the post-Easter viewpoint and understanding.

Spirit given to the community (cf. 20:22)[28] but ultimately authorized through the exalted Jesus, who is the divine giver of the post-Easter Spirit-Paraclete.

The process includes several dimensions: There is, first and foremost, a new and creative reading of the Scriptures (cf. 2:17; 12:16) that could bring about a new and deeper understanding of the deeds and fate of Jesus in the horizon of various biblical passages. It also includes the continued reflection of the Jesus story in the process of the ongoing proclamation and in view of the experiences and challenges of the community experience. As a result of both, it also implies a thorough transformation of the tradition that goes beyond the process of a mere translation into new linguistic and cultural contexts, including also the creative renarration and reimagining of several episodes of Jesus' ministry. The last and—for the present Gospel—decisive part of this process is, then, the deliberate creative activity of the Johannine author who is responsible for the narrative design of the Gospel, including the replottings mentioned above, the creation of metaphorical links supporting the deeper understanding of the whole Jesus story, and inserting the large number of explanatory asides or narrative commentaries that lead the readers toward the understanding of the story.

Therefore, the "memory" or teaching of the Spirit is not meant to present an accurate representation of some "historical facts" of the past. There is no textual indication that the (quite modern) question of "how things actually happened" is given any relevance here, nor is "truth" basically linked with historical accuracy or an accurate representation

[28] The openness of the Johannine image of the disciples implies that the gift of the Spirit is not confined to a defined circle of disciples of the earthly Jesus supposed to be present in the Easter scene in John 20:19–23. Since the disciples, not only in the farewell discourses but also in the Easter narrative, represent the entirety of the later community (cf. Takashi Onuki, *Gemeinde und Welt im Johannesevangelium: Ein Beitrag zur Frage nach der theologischen und pragmatischen Funktion des johanneischen 'Dualismus,'* WMANT 56 [Neukirchen-Vluyn: Neukirchener Verlag, 1984], 163–66), the gift of the Spirit and the commissioning to continue the mission of Jesus is addressed to the entire community (i.e., the disciples as well as later generations). In particular, the commissioning to forgive and retain sins in John (20:23) is in marked contrast with the parallel saying in Matt 18:18, which is only addressed to Simon Peter as the key figure of the disciples.

of historical data. What is at stake for the Fourth Gospel is rather the real (christologically correct) understanding of Jesus' words, deeds, and fate (i.e., his death and resurrection or "exaltation").

The insights disclosed by the Spirit imply a dimension of meaning inaccessible to Jesus' disciples during his earthly ministry but only disclosed in the post-Easter context. The images and narratives created in this process, thus, differ from the mere "history" that happened before the eyes of Jesus' contemporaries. The Johannine concept of "memory" encompasses the whole process of theological development from the Easter events through the history of the early communities until the composition of the Gospel. It is not bound to a certain event of disclosure or to a particular group of disciples (e.g., the twelve or other "eyewitnesses"), but, in view of the open concept of "disciples" in the Fourth Gospel, it can encompass a larger number of believers (not only "Johannine") until the present time of the Johannine author.

2. How Does the Spirit Teach?

But how can we imagine the teaching of the Spirit? How did the process of commemoration and interpretation happen? Can we simply imagine teachers and preachers in the Johannine community assemblies, can we think of communal study of the Scriptures or prophetic inspiration, or is the reference to the Spirit simply a means of legitimizing the actual process of writing the Gospel in its present literary design? We do not have much data to answer these questions with regard to the life of the Johannine communities, and it is easier to describe the literary and didactic techniques of the Gospel itself. But we should assume that the mention of the Spirit in the Gospel—notwithstanding its remarkable concentration on verbal, logos-oriented functions—is based on a wider range of experiences of the Spirit in the Johannine communities and its predecessors in the early Jesus movement.

2.1 Spirit Experience in the Johannine Communities

First of all, we should take into consideration that the Johannine communities were aware of the Spirit as a gift to the community and to the individual disciples. Of course, we cannot simply presuppose all the phenomena linked with the Spirit in other New Testament texts, in particular Paul and Luke-Acts, within the Johannine communities, but the awareness of certain "signs and wonders" (John 4:48) as powerful works of God in the ministry of Jesus and perhaps also later in the life of the community should be assumed. Similarly, the awareness of "prophetic" phenomena, in particular in the assemblies of the community, in preaching and in the interpretation of the Scriptures should also be assumed. Such an awareness and—at least partly—experience of the Spirit is the precondition for the Johannine concentration on verbal, logos-oriented activities of the Spirit, giving testimony, proclaiming Jesus' glory, remembering and reinterpreting the Jesus story, interpreting the Scriptures, and confirming the truth of faith. When "the Paraclete" is explained with the well-known term "the Holy Spirit" in 14:26, it is almost inconceivable that the author connecting these two terms was not aware of the differences between his particular concept of the ministry of the Spirit and the experiences and phenomena linked with the Holy Spirit in a wide range of expressions in the Jesus movement, especially in the diaspora.[29]

Traces of such an awareness are still visible in the Gospel and the First Epistle. There is mention of "receiving" the Spirit (John 7:39), in a terminology widely paralleled in other NT writings.[30] The Spirit is linked with the renewal or rebirth of the human being (3:5), with becoming "children of God," regardless of how directly or not this is considered with the act of baptism.[31] Therefore, if the First Epistle explains that the sign of God abiding with us is the Spirit he has given us (1 John 3:24), then it is presupposed that this sign (i.e., the presence of the Spirit) can be perceived. Accordingly, it is quite clear that the Spirit was considered a reality that could be experienced. Unlike Paul in 1 Corinthians 12–14, John does not mention extraordinary gifts, but it might be too modern to assume that in John nothing more than

[29] See, e.g., Dietzfelbinger, *Der Abschied des Kommenden*, 215–16.

[30] Rudolf Schnackenburg, "Die johanneische Gemeinde und ihre Geisterfahrung," in *Ergänzende Auslegungen*, vol. 4 of *Das Johannesevangelium*, HTK 4/4 (Freiburg: Herder, 1984), 33–57 (39–40).

[31] Cf. the discussion above, pp. 82–84.

an "internal" testimony or experience is envisaged.[32] In John 14:17, the disciples are said to recognize and "know" the Spirit given to them, whereas "the world" remains insensitive in this respect. In 1 John, the knowledge of the addressees is metaphorically explained by the reference to an anointing (2:20, 27) they have received and now have; thus the gift and possession of the Spirit is linked with spiritual and theological knowledge. In 4:1, there is even the idea of "testing" various Spirits, an idea that draws on the presence of a variety of prophetic or spiritual utterances.

These textual hints show that the Johannine view of the Spirit's work of interpreting and teaching is deeply rooted in a wider practice also shared by the Johannine communities. Thus, Johannine pneumatology is not a mere theological theory, void of any practical experience, but is also based on various experiences within the related communities. Only the mutual agreement on this between the author and the addressees can support the claim that the interpretations presented in the community proclamation and incorporated in the Gospel—the presentation of a more developed Christology and even creative replotting and renarration of the traditional Jesus story—is actually the work of the remembering Spirit, the helper and teacher of the community.

The reference to the communal experience of the Spirit, however, cannot yet clarify how the Spirit actually could teach. Apart from the regular preaching and teaching in the communities, we have to reckon with the disclosure of insights in the context of communal assemblies, prayer and praise, and—in particular—in the continued reading and rereading of the Scriptures.

2.2 The Disclosure of the Scriptures

Scripture was one of the most important sources for the development of an elaborated Christology, not only in the Fourth Gospel but already much earlier in the history of the Jesus movement. Of course, the very early emergence of a relatively "high" Christology[33] can be explained only by

[32] Thus the suggestion in Schnackenburg, "Die johanneische Gemeinde," 42.

[33] There is no need to discuss here the very early steps of christological development. Cf. the comprehensive and largely convincing work by Larry W. Hurtado, *Lord*

various factors. Apart from the Easter experiences, we have to consider the awareness of the presence and activity of the eschatological Spirit,[34] the communal singing of psalms, and also the formation of new songs and hymns which "commemorate" Jesus alongside God. There, the praise of the exalted Lord could be more exalted or enthusiastic than in regular speech, so that "bold" christological views and predications could be developed and expressed.[35] Within that process, the Scriptures of Israel, altogether read as prophetic writings in the light of the conviction that the period of fulfillment had begun in Jesus and his resurrection, were the inexhaustible stock from which numerous expectations and predictions, correspondences, and allusions could be discovered, further developed, and assembled. Behind those discoveries and disclosures, early interpreters could see the Spirit that was given to the community and put into the heart of the believers (Rom 5:5),[36] inspiring wisdom and prophetic speech and "opening" the Scriptures with regard to their eschatological and christological reference, as a testimony for Jesus. In that respect, some passages such as Psalm 110, Isaiah 53, or Isaiah 61 came to a most prominent position, but many others could be included and "exploited" for

---

Jesus Christ: Devotion to Jesus in Earliest Christianity (Grand Rapids: Eerdmans, 2003); see also the overview by Andrew Chester, "High Christology—Whence, When and Why?" *Early Christianity* 2 (2011): 22–50. Most important for the development of this relatively new tradition of research, particularly in the Anglo-Saxon world, were the works by Martin Hengel; cf. especially his collections *Studien zur Christologie: Kleine Schriften IV* (ed. Claus-Jürgen Thornton, WUNT 201 [Tübingen: Mohr, 2006]) and (a smaller selection of them) in English: *Studies in Early Christology* (Edinburgh: T&T Clark, 1995).

[34] Cf. Hengel, "Die Schriftauslegung des 4. Evangeliums," 603–11.

[35] In particular, cf. Martin Hengel, "Hymnus und Christologie," in *Studien zur Christologie*, 185–204 (ET: "Hymn and Christology," in *Papers on Paul and Other NT Authors: Sixth International Congress on Biblical Studies Oxford 3–7 April 1978*, vol. 3 of *Studia Biblica*, JSNTSup 3 [Sheffield: Sheffield Academic Press, 1980], 173–97); "Das Christuslied im frühesten Gottesdienst," in *Studien zur Christologie*, 205–58 (English trans.: "The Song about Christ in Earliest Worship," in *Studies in Early Christology*, 227–92); and "Abba, Maranatha, Hosanna un die Anfänge der Christologie," in *Studien zur Christologie*, 496–534.

[36] On the Jewish background of the early ideas of the interiority of the Holy Spirit, see Jörg Frey, "Paul's View of the Spirit in the Light of Qumran," in *The Dead Sea Scrolls and Pauline Literature*, ed. Jean-Sébastian Rey, STDJ 102 (Leiden: Brill, 2013), 239–62.

Christology, regardless of what their "original" meaning had been, so that, in the new reception perspective, "all" the Scriptures could be viewed as referring to Christ.

The Fourth Gospel already draws on an extended history of Christian scriptural interpretation, and its utilization of explicit quotations; references to more or less well-known episodes, to biblical figures, and to scriptural traditions; or mere allusions point to a wide and variegated process of reading and interpreting.[37] The Scriptures or even "Moses"[38] are read as a witness to Jesus (John 5:39, 45), and their christological understanding is connected with the "remembering" activity of the Spirit. Whereas the "memory" notices in 2:22 and 12:16 merely point to the understanding of Jesus' words and deeds, the shorter notice in 2:17 explicitly refers to the Scriptures: the disciples remembered that it is written, "Zeal for your house will consume me." Thus, the interpretation of the Scriptures is part of the "commemorating" activity of the Spirit (14:26), who inspired the "memory" of the disciples in order to lead them to a new and deepened understanding in the post-Easter period. The Scriptures were read in the awareness of their "fulfillment" in Jesus, and Jesus' ministry and fate were reconsidered and renarrated in view of the insights from the Scriptures.

In 2:17, the quotation from Psalm 69:10 (68:10 LXX) is read as an utterance of Jesus who speaks with the words of the psalmist but makes a significant change in tense.[39] Interestingly, the psalm is one of the psalms firmly rooted in the earlier passion narrative: John not only adopts the narrative tradition from Mark but also draws on the same psalms that were so prominently used in Mark's passion account, especially Psalms 22 and 69, which both provide a lament of the righteous sufferer.[40] In his reception of the scriptural references, however,

[37] Cf. the survey in Hengel, "Die Schriftauslegung des 4 Evangeliums."

[38] This is not only a reference to the Pentateuch, or even the person of Moses, but to the totality of the Scriptures. If the figure of Moses is highlighted in John 5 or 9, it is because of the debate with the "Jews," who saw their identity, particularly in the diaspora, as "disciples of Moses" (9:28).

[39] See above, p. 129–30. For further details on the quotation; see also Obermann, *Die christologische Erfüllung*, 114–28.

[40] On the psalms in Mark's passion narrative, see Craig A. Evans, *Mark 8:27–16:20*, WBC 34B (Nashville: Thomas Nelson, 2001), 498; and Bernd Janowski,

John freely omits certain references (e.g., the lament of godforsakenness in Mark 15:34, which is taken from Ps 22:2), while inserting others (e.g., Ps 69:5 [68:5 LXX] in John 15:25[41] or Ps 41:10 [40:10 LXX] in John 13:18,[42] both with an introduction stating the fulfillment). The reference to Psalm 22:19 (21:19 LXX) about the distribution of the clothes, which is already used in an abbreviated version in Mark 15:24, is now presented more fully and interpreted differently.[43] Now, the two lines of the parallelism are linked with two different actions: (1) the distribution of Jesus' clothes in four parts and (2) casting the lot to determine who will receive the seamless and, therefore, inseparable tunic. We can even assume that John actually created or fictionally imagined the scene with the seamless tunic, which is unattested in the earlier tradition and seems rather to be "developed" by the unfolding reading of the parallelism. If this is true, "history" was rewritten to fit the Scriptures, which is, of course, only possible based on the conviction that the Scriptures and the way of Jesus correspond. In the Johannine view, this kind of creativity in historical matters is also part of the activity of the Spirit.[44]

In the present context, I can only illustrate the intensity and variability of the utilization of the Scriptures in John by a small selection of observations.

a) In the beginning (John 1:1), John's prologue opens the Gospel with a clear reference to the beginning of the Greek Pentateuch (Gen 1:1) and thus conspicuously links his book with the Scriptures of Israel. The whole prologue, then, provides a dense web of implicit references and allusions to traditions about the creation and the revelation on Mt. Sinai, and to the biblical and postbiblical Jewish wisdom tradition.[45]

Konfliktgespräche mit Gott: Eine Anthropologie der Psalmen, 3rd ed. (Neukirchen-Vluyn: Neukirchener Verlag, 2009), 355–56.

41 For details, see Obermann, *Die christologische Erfüllung*, 271–82.

42 See also Obermann, *Die christologische Erfüllung*, 255–71.

43 For details, see cf. Obermann, *Die christologische Erfüllung*, 282–97.

44 See the considerations on John 16:13-15 above, pp. 144–46.

45 Cf. Craig A. Evans, *Word and Glory: On the Exegetical and Theological Background of John's Prologue*, JSNTSup 89 (Sheffield: Sheffield Academic, 1993); and, on the creation motif, Masanobu Endo, *Creation and Christology: A Study on the Johannine Prologue in the Light of Early Jewish Creation Accounts*, WUNT 2/149 (Tübingen: Mohr Siebeck, 2002).

While the "story line" of the prologue draws on ideas linked with personified Wisdom (Prov 8; Sir 24; Wis 7–9), an often-neglected remark in 1:14aβ adopts the tradition of the *Shekhina*, God's dwelling in the holy tent or the temple, in order to illustrate the more abstract idea of incarnation in terms of the inhabitation of the divine Logos in Jesus and to explain the presence of the divine glory in the ministry of the earthly Jesus.[46] With this sophisticated concept, based on a subtle reference to biblical traditions, the presentation of the Jesus in the Gospel narrative is prepared.

b) It is striking that John can quite briefly allude also to less well-known episodes. Apparently, his intended readers were expected to have a detailed scriptural knowledge. Thus, John 3:14-15 only briefly mentions Moses' lifting up of the serpent in the wilderness (Num 21:4-9) as an analogy to the idea that "the Son of Man must (δεῖ) be exalted." However, only readers who know the story can perceive the set of typological correspondences between the serpent and the Son of Man: (1) the lifting up of the serpent on a high and visible pole and Jesus' "exaltation" on the cross, and (2) the promise of staying alive by looking at the salvific sign in the desert episode and the promise of eternal life through faith in Jesus.[47] By introducing that brief reference, John creatively links the terminology of "being exalted," related in earlier traditions (Acts 2:33; 5:31; cf. Phil 2:9) to the heavenly exaltation or enthronement of the risen one, with the crucifixion of Jesus, which is anticipated here and even visually presented before the eyes of the reader.[48]

c) In John 10:34-36, the evangelist introduces a bold interpretation of an extraordinary passage from the Psalms (Ps 82:6) in which,

[46] On the reception of the *Shekina* tradition in John's prologue, see Jörg Frey, *Glory of the Crucified One*, 261–84; cf. also Frey, "God's Dwelling on Earth: '*Shekhina*-Theology' in Revelation 21 and in the Gospel of John," in *John's Gospel and Intimations of Apocalyptic*, ed. Christopher Rowland and Catrin Williams (London: Bloomsbury T&T Clark, 2013), 79–103.

[47] On the structure of the typology, see Jörg Frey, "'Wie Mose die Schlange in der Wüste erhöht hat . . .': Zur frühjüdischen Deutung der 'ehernen Schlange' und ihrer christologischen Rezeption in Johannes 3,14f," in *Schriftauslegung im antiken Judentum und im Urchristentum*, WUNT 73 (Tübingen: Mohr Siebeck, 1994), 153–205.

[48] Cf. Frey, *Die johanneische Eschatologie*, 3:277–80.

according to the Johannine reading, God addresses the Israelites as "gods."[49] The quotation is utilized as an argument from the greater to the smaller (*a maiore ad minus*) to prove that it cannot be a blasphemy if Jesus claims to be "God's Son."[50] This is a very special argument that may be said to comport with the image of the Spirit-Paraclete as a sophisticated "advocate" reproving the arguments of unbelief (cf. John 16:8).

d) John even draws on sophisticated exegetical connections, for example, between various passages in the book of Isaiah. Thus, after quoting from Isaiah 53:1 and 6:10 in a remarkable double quote in John 12:38-40, he explains that Isaiah "saw his [that is, Jesus'] glory and spoke of him" (12:41). Thus, John not only combines the two passages, which are already connected by terminological links in the Hebrew and the LXX text,[51] but also claims that the prophet, in his description of the divine glory in the temple (Isa 6) or in the song of the servant (52:13–53:12) actually saw Jesus' glory and spoke about Jesus. Such a claim is more difficult to uphold for the temple vision where God is explicitly viewed (at least with the "seam of his robe," or—in the LXX—his "glory"). A better explanation can be found in the song of the servant, three verses before the verse is actually quoted (Isa 52:13 LXX). There, in the opening of the song, the Greek text says: "Behold . . . , my servant/son . . . will be exalted and glorified" (ἰδοὺ . . . ὁ παῖς μου . . . ὑψωθήσεται καὶ δοξασθήσεται). If Isaiah spoke about Jesus, he thus prophesized the exaltation and glorification of the servant (i.e., of Jesus, the crucified one). Isaiah 52:13 LXX prominently combines the two words ὑψοῦν / δοξάζειν, which the evangelist utilized as his predominant paradigms for interpreting Jesus' death.[52] Thus, the most

[49] The history-of-religions background of the psalm is quite different, with Elohim speaking in the midst of an assembly of divine beings, but of course it can be omitted here. For details, see Obermann, *Die christologische Erfüllung*, 168–85.

[50] Cf. Hengel, "Die Schriftauslegung des 4. Evangeliums," 615–17.

[51] See Jörg Frey, "The Use of δόξα in Paul and John as Shaped by the Septuagint," in *The Reception of Septuagint Words in Jewish-Hellenistic and Christian Literature*, ed. Eberhard Bons and Ralph Brucker, WUNT 2/367 (Tübingen: Mohr Siebeck, 2014), 85–104 (102).

[52] Both words are densely introduced in John 12:20-34: δοξάζειν in 12:23, 28 (cf. 13:31-32; 17:1) and ὑψοῦν in 12:32, 34 (cf. already 3:14; 8:28). The proclamation of the

important pattern of interpreting Jesus' death in John is taken from the book of Isaiah, more precisely from a particular verse in the Greek version of the song of the servant, which is not even quoted directly, although the evangelist hints at its scriptural context. From here, he feels authorized to depict Jesus as the exalted and glorified one.

This confirms that the Spirit-Paraclete, who is said to "glorify" Jesus (John 16:14-15), could actually do so by disclosing the relevance of particular motifs from the Scriptures and thus teaching basic insights about the "glorification" of Jesus in his "hour" and about the everlasting glory of the crucified one.[53] This is of decisive importance for the Johannine design of the passion narrative.[54]

2.3 Making Jesus Present

Another aspect of the teaching of the Spirit can be characterized as "making present" the history of Jesus and, thus, also Jesus himself.[55] Narrating a story is, in fact, a way of making past things present. In John, this is immediately connected with the process of commemoration or remembering: when the Spirit reminds the disciples (John 14:26), or they remember elements of the Jesus story in the light of the Easter events, the insights gained in the post-Easter period, and the challenges of their own present, the past story is made present in order to understand the present in the light of the foundational past of the Jesus story. Furthermore, even the past Jesus is made present, as the narration of his earthly ministry in the light of the Easter events and the salvific earnings of his ministry and death presents him as the glorified one, whose word calls for belief and promises life at present. This is in accord with the conviction that Jesus is not actually dead but alive and actively supporting his community in the realm of the Father

"hour" in 12:23 is explicitly linked with the glorification of Jesus; the meaning of the more enigmatic term "being exalted" is disclosed in the explanatory aside in 12:33 by the clarification that "being exalted" means the manner of Jesus' death (i.e., his crucifixion).

[53] On the motif of glory and Jesus' glorification in John, see also Frey, *Glory of the Crucified One*, 261–84.

[54] See below, pp. 186–96.

[55] On this, see Frey, *Glory of the Crucified One*, 97–98.

(cf. 1 John 2:1; John 1:18) and that the Spirit, who "replaces" Jesus among his disciples on earth (14:16-17), is actually the one who mediates the presence of the exalted one and makes the invisible Jesus visible for the spiritual eyes of the disciples (14:20).

Thus, the intention of emphasizing the presence of Jesus can be discovered in a number of aspects of John's usage of tenses and his narrative design:

a) A first and quite interesting hint can be found in the conclusion of the prologue: among the predications attributed to Jesus, there is, apart from "only-begotten" (μονογενής) and "God" (θεός), the phrase ὁ ὢν εἰς τὸν κόλπον τοῦ πατρὸς ("who is toward[56] the bosom of the Father"). The present participle ὁ ὢν functions as a marker of the temporal viewpoint of the community speaking in 1:14-18, so that the phrase actually expresses where Jesus is now—in the present time of the community, Jesus, who has made known the invisible Father, actually is in intimate closeness with and orientation to the Father. From the outset of the Gospel, the focus is not merely on the past story of the earthly ministry of Jesus but on the present Jesus.

b) In the narrative parts, the author can create a fictional presence of the episodes narrated by switching from the regular narrative tense, the aorist, to the *historical present*.[57] In John, the device is used quite frequently, though not systematically, to create a vivid presence of the dialogues in some episodes—for example, the narration of the calling of the disciples (John 1:35-51), the wine miracle (2:1-11), the dialogue with the Samaritan woman (4:4-26), or the Easter narratives in 20–21.

[56] Most English translations just render "in the bosom of the Father" (or German: "im Schoss des Vaters"), but this is insufficient in view of the direction marked in the Greek preposition εἰς. Cf. Michael Theobald, *Die Fleischwerdung des Logos*, NTA 20 (Münster: Aschendorff, 1988), 260. Things are similar with πρὸς τὸν θεόν in John 1:1. In both cases, the close relationship between Jesus or the Logos and God is expressed not merely in a local aspect but with reference to a direction or orientation.

[57] This stylistic device is frequently used also in Mark for creating vividness or highlighting particular aspects, whereas Luke almost totally effaces it, and Matthew uses the historical present almost only for verbs of saying (in order to present the words as words of the present Jesus). See Frey, *Die johanneische Eschatologie*, 2:81–83.

c) Of greater theological relevance is the manner John modifies, or "bends,"[58] the form of his miracle stories.[59] The narratives presenting Jesus' miraculous deeds are all supplemented with references to the events of his death and resurrection, to the whole of his ministry, or to its salvific effects.[60] These textual elements provide stumbling stones for a smooth reading of the narratives at the surface level, they insert additional contextualizations, and they open up various symbolic dimensions that are more clearly defined only within the context of a complete reading of the Gospel. Furthermore, these elements urge readers not to read the episode simply as an account of an event at a certain point in the past ministry of Jesus but to perceive it in the framework of his whole ministry and its ultimate effects—that is, as a representation of the eschatological salvation ultimately fulfilled in his death and resurrection but only exemplified in the various semeia narratives.

d) Statistically, with regard to the use of Greek tenses, John has a higher percentage of present tense forms than the Synoptics.[61] This is partly explained from the higher proportion of discourses in John, but their mere extension is also significant, as they create a fictional presence of the speaker, who thus directly addresses his readers, almost uninterrupted by the mention of details from the past of the Jesus story.[62] Thus, the proclamation of the Johannine Jesus is presented almost as a contemporary address: his word is made present to the readers of the Gospel.

e) In John 3:11, the dialogue with the Jewish leader Nicodemus switches into a monologue, in which the former interlocutor disappears.

[58] On this term, cf. Harold W. Attridge, "Genre Bending in the Fourth Gospel," *JBL* 121 (2002): 3–21.

[59] In particular, cf. Frey, "From the *Sēmeia* Narratives."

[60] Cf. Christian Welck (*Erzählte Zeichen: Die Wundergeschichten des Johannesevangeliums literarisch untersucht. Mit einem Ausblick auf Joh 21*, WUNT 2/69 [Tübingen: Mohr Siebeck, 1994], passim), who calls this level the "salvation dramatic" one (*heilsdramatisch*).

[61] See Frey, *Die johanneische Eschatologie*, 2:24–27; Frey, *Glory of the Crucified One*, 79.

[62] This is particularly true for the farewell discourses and for monologues with a high degree of generality, as, e.g., the kerygmatic passages in John 3:11-21 (and also 3:31-36); 12:44-50; the metaphorical passage 15:1-17; or the farewell prayer 17:1-26.

Throughout this first discourse in the Gospel, Jesus speaks rather generally, in the third person, about "the Son" or "Son of Man"; in verse 11, he even speaks in the first-person plural, with the "we" addressing another plurality of listeners. The most plausible literary explanation is that phrases of the Johannine kerygma (e.g., the preaching of the Johannine community) are presented in the mouth of Jesus.[63] This is confirmed by the fact that in verse 13 the "ascent" of the Son of Man is mentioned in the perfect tense, and, if the phrase does not refer to an ascent before his incarnation,[64] it is also an example for the phenomenon that Jesus speaks from the post-Easter perspective of the community, retrospectively presupposing his whole ministry, from the incarnation until the ascent or return to the Father.

f) This is confirmed by a number of other passages, particularly in the farewell discourses, where Jesus speaks in the perfect tense about his glorification (John 13:31), the victory over the world (16:33) and its ruler (16:11), and the "completion" of his work (17:4; cf. 19:28, 30).[65] These verb forms not only are a marker of the retrospective viewpoint of the discourses and the Gospel in general but also highlight the lasting effect of Jesus' ministry and the present reality of the salvific gains that are now presented to the readers.

g) The most powerful presentation of the person of Jesus is provided in Jesus' "I am" sayings.[66] Here, the divine dignity and salvific function of Jesus are presented in a form that goes beyond time. The words of Jesus, still embedded in a narrated past, are presented in a form that gives them a powerful presence to address quite directly readers and hearers and to call for a decision. The Jesus who utters his divine "I am" is already the risen and glorified one, who is "the resurrection and the life" (11:25) and the "light of the world" (8:12).

[63] See Frey, *Die johanneische Eschatologie*, 2:252–57.

[64] Thus the suggestion in Jan-Adolf Bühner (*Der Gesandte und sein Weg im 4. Evangelium: Die kultur- und religionsgeschichtlichen Grundlagen der johanneischen Sendungschristologie sowie ihre traditionsgeschichtliche Entwicklung*, WUNT 2/2 [Tübingen: Mohr, 1977], 382), who speculates about an ascent in analogy with the entronization of Enoch (1 En. 71), but this is all too speculative.

[65] On this phenomenon, see Frey, *Die johanneische Eschatologie*, 2:98–115 and 2:247–48.

[66] On these, see above, pp. 49–52.

The metaphorical predications of bread, light, shepherd, or vine, though deeply rooted in the biblical tradition, are widely accessible to anyone who listens to his words, so that the invitation and the promise of eternal life is presented in a form that is independent from place, time, or cultural context. In these sayings, not only the past story of Jesus' ministry but also the eschatological future of the addressees are made present whenever these words are pronounced, proclaimed, or read in the Gospel book.

2.4 Explicit and Implicit Commentary

The clearest evidence for the evangelist's interest in providing a better understanding of the Jesus story can be found in the numerous narrative devices that explicitly or implicitly hint to the readers that an understanding exists beyond the surface level. Here, the more recent trend of narratological interpretation, as inaugurated by R. Alan Culpepper's groundbreaking study *Anatomy of the Fourth Gospel* in 1983, has provided invaluable insights.[67] Again, I can only hint at some aspects and selected examples.

a) One of the most obvious explanative elements is the number of explanatory "footnotes" or asides in the Gospel narrative representing the "whispering wizard" of the narrator's voice.[68] Of course, there is need for a theoretical distinction, but, for practical purposes, we can link that voice with the intention of the implied author and, historically, with the narrative skills of the hand that shaped the Gospel, the evangelist. The phenomena discussed above with regard to the knowledge and cultural background of the Johannine author can now be interpreted with regard to their function or their interaction with the (implied and, probably also, real) readers.

[67] See especially R. Alan Culpepper, *Anatomy of the Fourth Gospel: A Study in Literary Design* (Philadelphia: Fortress, 1983).

[68] Thus Culpepper, *Anatomy of the Fourth Gospel*, 18. For the analysis of the narrator's voice, see idem, 17–49, on the Johannine asides; see also Gilbert van Belle, *Les parenthèses dans l'évangile de Jean*, SNTA 11 (Leuven: Leuven University Press, 1985). See also the earlier studies by Merrill C. Tenney, "The Footnotes in John's Gospel," *Biblia Sacra* 117 (1960): 350–64; and John O'Rourke, "Asides in the Gospel of John," *NovT* 21 (1979): 210–19.

Narrative asides are conspicuously numerous in John,[69] and they are somewhat detached from the narrative by the use of a different tense form (often the imperfect)[70] or other marks. In John, these asides provide translations of names and terms;[71] they add precise information about the place (cf. John 1:28; 6:59) or the time (cf. 1:39; 4:6) of an episode, or some further background information about the figures (cf. 11:2; 11:51) or events of the story (4:9b); and at least some of them give special hints to the meaning of the narrated story that goes beyond the surface level. Among those narrative asides, there are also the important hints at the disciples' lack of understanding in the time of Jesus and their post-Easter remembrance (2:22; 12:16; cf. 2:17).

Some of those explanations (e.g., about Jewish feasts or customs) may indeed help readers unfamiliar with Jewish tradition understand particular elements of the story, although the explanations are never indispensable for understanding the point, and the reason for some asides (such as "the tenth hour" in 1:39) is quite hard to find. Others seem to constitute symbolic references—for example, the "sixth hour" in 4:6 or the translation of *Siloam* by "the one who is sent" in 9:7. Still other asides, in particular those providing insights into the thoughts or intentions of various narrative figures (e.g., 12:6 on Judas; or 4:53 on the royal servant) or even into Jesus' mind (cf. 6:6; 11:5; 13:11; etc.), underline the competence of the narrator, not only with regard to external information but also with regard to the mind and intentions of the narrative figures, including Jesus himself. The most important asides, however, are those that establish further links within the Johannine text or refer to a particular "deeper" meaning of the episode narrated, such as the "memory" notice inserting the scriptural reference in 2:17, the meaning of Jesus' temple saying as a reference to "the temple of his body" (2:21), the reference of Jesus' saying about the "streams of living water" (7:37-38) to the post-Easter Spirit (7:39), or the meaning of Caiaphas' words (11:51-52) with regard to the salvific effects of Jesus' death. All those asides share the narrator's temporal (retrospective)

69 Cf. Culpepper, *Anatomy of the Fourth Gospel*, 17–18.

70 On the use of the imperfect in the parentheses, see Frey, *Die johanneische Eschatologie*, 2:35–36 and 2:91–92.

71 See above, pp. 106–7.

and ideological point of view. But it is important to see that "Jesus and the narrator share the same vocabulary and use terms with the same veiled or double meaning":[72] by such asides, the narrator (or, actually, the evangelist) introduces particular terms, such as δοξάζεσθαι (7:39), or clarifies the meaning of others, such as "Jesus' hour" (7:30; 8:20; 12:23). Ultimately, the voice of the narrator, as audible in the asides, and the voice of Jesus himself are blended in the farewell discourses.[73] It is no coincidence, therefore, that the most important themes of the narrative asides in the Gospel are related to the events in Jesus' hour, his death and "glorification," and to the meaning and effects of the whole of Jesus' work.

In the narrative asides of the Gospel and the explicit commentaries, the interpretive and teaching intention of the Gospel is most obvious. But the same intention can also be discovered in many implicit commentaries, in the characterization of the narrative figures and their mutual interaction[74] or, most efficiently, in the obvious misunderstandings of all the narrative figures (with the only exception of the beloved disciple). Here, the "'silent' communication between the author and reader"[75] comes to its most striking effects.

In the skillful design of John's text, the reader cannot fail to see that Nicodemus, with his question about reentering the mother's womb in John 3:4, crudely misunderstands Jesus' words from 3:3. His misunderstanding is not only that he misses the "double entendre" of ἄνωθεν, interpreting the word wrongly as "anew" instead as "from above." It is not only the meaning of words or a certain in-group-language that is at stake here. Nor does the text intend to polemicize against Nicodemus here. In narrative perspective, the text utilizes the figure of Nicodemus to lead readers to a deeper understanding, a level of meaning

[72] Culpepper, *Anatomy of the Fourth Gospel*, 39.

[73] See Culpepper, *Anatomy of the Fourth Gospel*, 41–42.

[74] On the characterization in John, see the recent works *Characters and Characterization in the Gospel of John*, ed. Christopher W. Skinner, LNTS 461 (London: Bloomsbury, 2012); *Character Studies in the Fourth Gospel: Narrative Approaches to Seventy Figures in John*, ed. Steven A. Hunt, D. Francois Tolmie, and Ruben Zimmermann, WUNT 314 (Tübingen: Mohr Siebeck, 2013); and Cornelis Bennema, *Encountering Jesus: Character Studies in the Gospel of John*, 2nd ed. (Minneapolis: Fortress, 2014).

[75] Thus Culpepper, *Anatomy of the Fourth Gospel*, 151.

that Nicodemus is not able to follow. Thus, the interest is not on the views or the fate of the figure of Nicodemus, let alone the "historical person" Nicodemus. This figure can easily disappear when its function in the present dialogue is fulfilled and Jesus, then, directly speaks to the Gospel audience (3:11-21). The focus is, thus, exclusively on the understanding of the readers, and the whole text is only designed to let the readers understand. The same technique underlies the misunderstandings of all the disciples, Thomas (14:5) or Philip (14:22) or even Peter (13:6, 9, 36), who so crudely misunderstand Jesus' actions and words. Again, the intention is not to disqualify or polemicize those disciples or a particular early Christian group possibly linked with them (the majority church, or a "Thomasine" group). The misunderstandings only demonstrate that all the disciples in the pre-Easter period could not yet understand the real meaning of Jesus' words and deeds and that the post-Easter community is actually in a better situation because there, through the teaching of the Spirit, a deeper understanding of the Jesus story has become accessible. For that reason, the departure of Jesus was necessary (cf. John 16:7) so that the Spirit could come and open up a new understanding of Jesus and his death, and a new following of Jesus in the post-Easter period, believing in God and in him, or rather believing in God through him (John 14:1) could take place.[76]

2.5 The Symbolic Language of Dualism and the Fusion of the Temporal Horizons of Jesus and the Community

The interest in bridging the gap between the past of the earthly Jesus and the present of the readers is also supported by the metaphorical and symbolic language developed in the Johannine community and utilized in the Gospel, in which the various metaphors and terms are woven together into larger metaphorical networks or even into a symbolic space readers can enter and dwell in. This language is unique within the New Testament, and it is able to transcend the historical particularities of the tradition and build up a narrative that includes

[76] On the interpretation of John 13:36-38 and John 14:1 as expressing the aim of the Johannine instruction, see Frey, *Die johanneische Eschatologie*, 3:127–28 and 3:131–34.

readers and their situation, so that not only the Jesus story but also the entirety of the "fruits" of his work and eschatological salvation (and, on the other hand, judgment) are presented to the readers.[77]

The most striking feature of this language is the number of "dualistic" oppositions such as the opposition of light and darkness, life and death, community and world, and so forth. Whereas the attempts to explain that language from a certain history-of-religions background have largely failed,[78] it can be understood with regard to its function or impact on the readers. Some scholars have tried to explain the dualistic language from the intention of creating misunderstandings or limit the understanding to "insiders" only,[79] but if we cannot ascertain that the Johannine community was an encapsulated "sectarian" group, we should rather see the language of the Gospel with regard to its general aims at triggering the better understanding of the readers. Thus, the Johannine language of light and darkness also serves the didactic purpose of the Gospel,[80] and it is used to draw readers from darkness to the light or into a deeper understanding of Jesus and his work.

As the Japanese New Testament scholar Takashi Onuki has demonstrated in his work on the theological and pragmatic function

[77] On these aspects of Johannine eschatology, see above, pp. 38 and 44.

[78] This is true for Rudolf Bultmann's attempt to explain the Johannine language as a whole from a gnostic background (see Bultmann, "Johanneische Schriften und Gnosis," in *Exegetica: Aufsätze zur Erforschung des Neuen Testaments*, ed. Erich Dinkler [Tübingen: J. C. B. Mohr, 1967], 230–54), but also for the various attempts to find a coherent background in the dualism (or rather dualisms) found in the library of Qumran (cf. Jörg Frey, "Licht aus den Höhlen? Der 'johanneische Dualismus' und die Texte von Qumran," in *Die Herrlichkeit des Gekreuzigten. Studien zu den Johanneischen Schriften 1,* ed. J. Schlegel, WUNT 307 [Tübingen: Mohr Siebeck, 2013], 147–238; and idem, "Recent Perspecties on Johannine Dualism," in *Text, Thought, and Practice in Qumran and Early Christianity*, ed. Ruth Clements and Daniel R. Schwartz, STDJ 84 [Leiden: Brill, 2008]). On the problems of Johannine "dualism," see most recently Frey, "Dualism and the World in the Gospel and Letters of John," in *Oxford Handbook of Johannine Studies*, ed. Martinus de Boer and Judith Lieu (Oxford: Oxford University Press, 2018), 274–91.

[79] Thus Herbert Leroy, *Rätsel und Missverständnis: Ein Beitrag zur Formgeschichte des Johannesevangeliums*, BBB 30 (Bonn: Peter Hanstein, 1968).

[80] See Walter Rebell, *Gemeinde als Gegenwelt: Zur soziologischen und didaktischen Funktion des Johannesevangeliums*, BET 20 (Frankfurt: Peter Lang, 1987).

of the Johannine dualism,[81] the dualistic language helps to create a language "on the border,"[82] that is, a level of abstraction at which the experiences of the post-Easter community and the experiences narrated from the mission of Jesus can be merged. Thus, the Gospel transcends the view on particular opponents of Jesus or the community by generally speaking of "the Jews" or even "the world" or of an opposition between "light" and "darkness."[83] John's "dualistic" language helps to distance the addressees from the problems and trials of their own daily experience and to reconsider their own situation in the light of the remembered story of Jesus that can now be read as a pattern for understanding the experiences of his later followers. The community that experiences hatred and distress (15:18) is led to the perception that its own problems are similar to what had also happened to the Word incarnate. Thus, readers of the Gospel can now appropriate the Jesus story as a foundational pattern for their own life and faith and as a help for coping with their own experiences of unbelief and rejection. On the other hand, their own experiences are now explained by the pattern of Jesus' ministry, rejection, passion, death, and resurrection.

The phrase that "the light shines in the darkness, and the darkness has not overcome it" (1:5) is, therefore, a programmatic reference to the post-Easter reality: the evil powers were not successful in their attempt to extinguish the light of the world, but, due to his

[81] Onuki, *Gemeinde und Welt im Johanneseangelium*, 26–28; see also Frey, *Glory of the Crucified One*.

[82] German: *Grenzsprache*. The phrase nicely fits with a central term in the theology of the German American theologian and philosopher Paul Tillich (1886–1965), since the concept of the "borderline" or "*border* situation" runs through all of Tillich's writings, and insight, particularly religious insight, is disclosed in border situations.

[83] Interestingly, this more general language is predominant in the prologue and the farewell discourses, whereas the narrative of Jesus' public ministry is characterized by the opposition of the "Jews," and the passion narrative mentions even more precisely various groups of Jewish opponents. Here, the narrative is more strongly bound to the situation of the earthly Jesus and his contemporaries (who were, of course, altogether "Jews," with the only exception of Pontius Pilate), while the farewell discourses and also the prologue can take a more general viewpoint. On the use of the term "the Jews" and "the world," see the work by Lars Kierspel, *The Jews and the World in the Fourth Gospel: Parallelism, Function, and Context*, WUNT 2/220 (Tübingen: Mohr Siebeck, 2006).

resurrection, the light shines forth and overcomes darkness or even "the world." Accordingly, the disciples are also encouraged not to be troubled by Jesus' "absence" (14:1, 27) or by the hatred of the world but rather to be strong in tribulation (16:33) and to continue their mission and the proclamation of the word. Interestingly, the farewell discourses (in 17:21-23) and the Gospel story as a whole (in 20:19-23) end with a positive confirmation of the mission of the disciples.

Following the ideas of the hermeneutical philosopher Hans-Georg Gadamer, Onuki has labeled the Johannine technique of connecting the Jesus story with the world and experiences of the community of addressees a hermeneutical "fusion of horizons."[84] Thus, he can describe how John manages to bridge the gap between the time and situation of the Jesus story and the time and situation of the Johannine readers. Neither is the horizon of the Jesus story completely swallowed or eliminated by the interests of its application at present, nor is the horizon of the present readers totally abandoned in the reading of the narration of the past; instead, both come together on a new level, in a "border situation," in which understanding the past also helps to understand and reshape the present. Thus, the hermeneutical process practiced in the Fourth Gospel is able to secure the relevance of the past history narrated for understanding the challenges of the present.

3. What Does the Spirit Teach? Renarrating the Tradition for the Eyes of Faith

In the preceding survey, we have briefly looked at aspects of the teaching of the Spirit from the early Jesus movement to the Johannine community and at the devices the Johannine author uses to integrate that teaching and its insights into the Johannine text. In the Gospel text, the Spirit teaches by presenting Jesus in the light of a developed Christology and by leading the readers to particular insights, by opening scriptural perspectives on the way and ministry of Jesus, and by

[84] See Onuki, *Gemeinde und Welt im Johannesevangelium*, 12–14; adopted in Frey, *Die johanneische Eschatologie*, 2:249–52; see also Frey, *Glory of the Crucified One*, 90–92. In Gadamer, the term characterizes a hermeneutical process that is foundational for understanding history.

relating the Jesus story to the present questions and experiences of the readers in order to help them cope with their present situation in the light of the ministry of Jesus. Thus, it helps to make present and to keep alive the story of the past but also to make present the risen and exalted Jesus in the community of his followers.

But what did the Spirit teach? What are the theological interests behind John's replotting, renarrating, and reimagining the Jesus story? In the following section, we can again only point at a number of selected aspects,[85] starting from the explicit information on the work of the Spirit-Paraclete. From there, we can move onto the pivotal aspect in the remembrance of Jesus, his passion, and his death, which the Gospels present as his exaltation and glorification or, rather, as the enthronization of the true king. Finally, we will discuss some passages in which the Gospel aims at correcting the views of its addressees or introducing patterns of belief and community life for the post-Easter period, beginning with the passion context, which is, as we have already seen, a particular focus of the evangelist, and then adding a few aspects from other parts of the Gospel.

3.1 The Teaching of the Spirit and the Teaching of the Gospel

For the present purpose, we can take a point of departure again in the five Paraclete sayings of the farewell discourses that focus on the activity of the Spirit, although not all of the theological interests of the Fourth Gospel are represented here. But since the farewell discourses provide the most thorough glimpses into the problems and challenges of the community of addressees, we can look for hints at the teaching of the Spirit, keeping in mind that the Spirit is not mentioned for the first time in the Gospel here and that the addressees had their own experiences with the Holy Spirit, which may go beyond the aspects described in the Fourth Gospel.[86]

[85] There is no need to repeat the discussion of the christological teaching of the Gospel here; see above, pp. 13–54.

[86] See in particular Rudolf Schnackenburg, "Die johanneische Gemeinde"; and Dietzfelbinger, *Der Abschied des Kommenden*, 210–17.

a) In the first one of the five Paraclete sayings (John 14:16-17), the Spirit is introduced as a post-Easter gift of the Father that will be sent to replace or be a substitute for Jesus, after his departure, in order to be among the disciples and stay with them forever. In the context of the disciples' lament at Jesus' departure (13:33, 36; 14:5; cf. 14:18) and invisibility (14:19), which reflects the situation in the post-Easter period, the promise of "another Paraclete"[87] characterizes the Spirit as the "successor" of the earthly Jesus who puts into effect Jesus' prevailing presence within the community and also (invisibly) in the midst of the world, in spite of his physical absence. The Paraclete will abide with the disciples, unlike Jesus who has to depart, in fulfillment of his mission and for the benefit of his disciples. However, due to the provision of Jesus, the Spirit will be sent to comfort[88] them in their distress and to abide with them forever, unlike the earthly Jesus, who was present for a limited time. It is further stressed that the Spirit, as the invisible presence of the exalted Jesus, cannot be received by the world, so that the gift of the Spirit actually marks the borders between the "anointed" community of disciples[89] and the unbe-

[87] Most likely, the term "another Paraclete" is related to the idea that Jesus is the first Paraclete (advocate) of his disciples. Two versions of this idea can be considered: First, the Spirit-Paraclete is "another" Paraclete since he is asked to be a substitute for the earthly Jesus and to stay with his disciples in the time after his departure. The problem is, however, that Jesus has never been called "Paraclete" before, and in his public ministry he does not act as a defender or advocate of his disciples. Only in his passion is he said to ask for the freedom of his disciples when he is arrested (18:8), and, more generally, he takes the place of the disciples when he dies "for their sake" on the cross. If we also consider the testimony of 1 John, where Jesus is called "Paraclete" in 1 John 2:1, the first Paraclete is, rather, the exalted Christ who acts in support of his disciples in the realm of the Father (cf. 14:2-3), while the Spirit-Paraclete acts on their behalf on earth (cf., similarly Rom 8:34). Both options, however, are not mutually exclusive. The remarkable phrase ἄλλος παράκλητος constitutes a relation of the Spirit to both the earthly and the exalted Christ (cf. Hoegen-Rohls, *Der nachösterliche Johannes*, 156–57).

[88] The (philologically wrong) translation of παράκλητος as "comforter" (German: *Tröster*) in numerous Bibles has a certain ring of truth, insofar as the farewell discourses are designed with elements of consolation (cf. George L. Parsenios, *Departure and Consolation: The Johannine Farewell Discourses in Light of Greco-Roman Literature*, NovTSup 117 [Leiden: Brill, 2005]), and insofar as the Spirit-Paraclete is promised as a main figure within these discourses and is a part of the consolatory process.

[89] Cf. the title by Gary M. Burge, *The Anointed Community: The Holy Spirit in the Johannine Tradition* (Grand Rapids: Eerdmans, 1987).

lieving world. This situation of distance, or even conflict, with the world will be further developed in the third and fourth Paraclete saying. In the initial passage, in which the term παράκλητος is introduced for the first time, together with the additional attribute "the Spirit of Truth," the general function of the Holy Spirit as a substitute for Jesus' presence, a comforter and helper of the disciples, is introduced, while the more elaborate mention of his precise works is saved for the subsequent sayings.

b) The second Paraclete saying (14:26) most clearly pronounces the verbal, Logos-related function of the Spirit—that is, his teaching as a commemoration of Jesus' words (and also his deeds). These two terms encompass the whole process of making (and keeping) the Jesus story alive and present, in such a manner that the salvific effects of his death and resurrection are exposed in their foundational function for post-Easter belief and post-Easter communities. Through the Spirit, the community is made aware of the benefits and fruits of the whole work of Jesus, and through the Spirit the eschatological gifts of peace (14:27; 16:33) and joy (15:11; 16:20-22, 24) are communicated. With the mention of the remembering activity of the Spirit, the hook words from the narrative explanations in 2:17, 22, and 12:16 are resumed, so that the disciples' understanding in the post-Easter period is now linked with the activity of the Spirit. The commemoration of the Jesus story through the Spirit thus encompasses the whole process in which the community of Jesus followers arrived at a better and deeper understanding of the Jesus story and a clearer and truthful view of the christological dignity of Jesus and the salvific meaning of his death. With the mention of the activities of commemorating and teaching, the saying stresses the (merely) verbal function of the Spirit that is so characteristic of the Fourth Gospel, wherein the Spirit is linked never with miracles or ecstatic speech but only with phenomena that could be also characterized as proclamation, meditation, or interpretation of the Scriptures and the Jesus story.

c) The third Paraclete saying (15:26)[90] addresses the forensic aspects linked with the term παράκλητος when it describes the function of the Spirit as a witness for Jesus and thereby inspires the disciples to also be

[90] This is the first saying according to which the Spirit-Paraclete is immediately sent by the exalted Jesus, not (as in 14:16-17 and 14:26) by the Father. However, the difference should not be overemphasized. Already in 3:34, according to the grammatically

witnesses.[91] Just as Jesus himself bore witness to the truth during his ministry (cf. 18:37),[92] so also the Spirit-Paraclete will now bear witness for Jesus in the period after his departure and exaltation. He thus joins and strengthens the testimony of the disciples and, at the same time, enables them to give testimony, inspiring both its content and its form: the testimony of the disciples is, therefore, not only related to what they have seen and heard in their company with Jesus; their memory is also enriched by the new understanding of Jesus they had arrived at through the teaching of the Spirit. So, their testimony, guided by the testimony of the Spirit, proclaims Jesus as the glorified crucified one, with his death and resurrection as the foundation of post-Easter faith.

The link between the Spirit and the testimony further reminds of the earlier tradition in which the Spirit is described as a helper of the disciples in situations of persecution and trial (Mark 13:11). Scholars have assumed that this is the earliest root for the forensic dimension of the ministry of the Spirit, as is implied in the term παράκλητος.[93] However, unlike that tradition, which referred to the experience of inquiries and trials in a situation of persecution, the Fourth Gospel does not explicitly mention worldly or synagogal tribunals. But the placement of the saying within the context of the discussion of the hatred of the world toward the disciples confirms that the evangelist deliberately relates the saying about the testimony to the community's experience of enmity by its unbelieving contemporaries. The more generalizing language of the Gospel, then, widens the view and relates the testimony of the Spirit to the universal trial on truth, in which the

---

correct interpretation of the text, the subject who gives the Spirit is Jesus, and this is in perfect accord with the view of Jesus' divine dignity.

[91] The phrase καὶ ὑμεῖς δὲ μαρτυρεῖτε can be seen as a weak marker of a consecutive connection. As the Spirit gives testimony, so will the disciples also give testimony, inspired and guided by the Spirit.

[92] On the topic of testimony (μαρτυρία) in John, see in particular Johannes Beutler, *Martyria: Traditionsgeschichtliche Untersuchungen zum Zeugnisthema bei Johannes*, FThS 10 (Frankfurt: Knecht, 1972).

[93] See also Matt 10:19–20 // Luke 12:11–12. Cf. Raymond E. Brown, *The Gospel according to John*, AB 29/29A (New York: Doubleday, 1970), 2:694; Burge, *Anointed Community*, 205; and Rudolf Schnackenburg, *Das Johannesevangelium nach Johannes*, HTK 4/3 (Freiburg: Herder, 1975), 3:136.

disciples are troubled by the unbelieving world,[94] but confirmed in the truth by their divine advocate, the Spirit-Paraclete, who enables them to testify to Jesus within a hostile environment.

d) The forensic function of the Spirit-Paraclete is further elaborated in the fourth Paraclete saying in John 16:8-11 when it is again said that the Spirit will "reprove" (ἐλέγξει) the world or even conduct the case against the world or, conversely, in favor of the disciples.[95] Here, the Spirit's role of an "advocate" is most clearly defined, and, in contrast to the preceding Paraclete saying, there is no mention of any direct activity of the disciples. Thus, it is even more unclear where the rebuttal of "the world" is thought to happen. All the suggested possibilities—worldly tribunals, community sermons, public missionary proclamation[96]—cannot be confirmed, and this openness is most likely a deliberate choice. The focus of the saying is merely on the revealing function of the Spirit, while the trial addressed is not specified. It may take place within the community or merely within the conscience of individual believers, but it is nonetheless part of the universal trial on the truth of faith.

The Spirit provides the decisive argument that belief in Jesus is right and that unbelief is wrong; he confirms and stabilizes the unsettled disciples in their faith and thus preserves the community in the truth (cf. 16:13). This is unfolded with regard to three aspects—sin, righteousness, and judgment (16:8)—and the explanations given for the three aspects help to get a clearer view of the issues at stake.

First, sin is explained quite clearly as unbelief in Jesus (16:9),[97] and it is the work of the Spirit-Paraclete to conduct the case that belief

[94] There is no mention of worldly or synagogal tribunals, but this is unnecessary in the generalizing language of John, and the placement of the saying in the context of the discussion on the hatred of the world confirms that the evangelist deliberately relates the saying to the testimony borne in the midst of the community's experience of hatred and persecution by their unbelieving contemporaries; cf. Craig S. Keener, *Gospel of John: A Commentary* (Peabody, Mass.: Hendrickson, 2003), 2:1023.

[95] On this saying, see Frey, *Die johanneische Eschatologie*, 3:183–90; Hoegen-Rohls, *Der nachösterliche Johannes*, 176–88.

[96] See the discussion in Frey, *Die johanneische Eschatologie*, 3:183–84.

[97] John notably differs from a "moral" view of sins (in the plural) as unlawful deeds or transgression of certain rules. While large traditions of Christianity have

in Jesus is true and gives life, whereas unbelief keeps humans in separation from God, under his wrath (3:36), and in the state of eschatological death.

In the second phrase, righteousness is explained as the fact the Jesus goes to the Father and the disciples will not see him any more (16:10). Here, the main issue of the farewell discourses is addressed: with Jesus' departure and death and his later invisibility or "absence," it remains unclear where he has gone. Unbelievers can insist on the fact that he died and his ministry has come to an end and that the truth of the conviction that he has risen, was enthroned, and installed into a cosmic rulership cannot be proved by any kind of worldly evidence. So, the invisibility and alleged "absence" of Jesus also leads to the unsettledness and distress of the disciples and the community, and it is the work of the Spirit-Paraclete to provide the community with confirmation of the truth that Jesus has indeed gone to the Father and that he has been glorified and justified. Accordingly, 16:10 speaks about the "justification" of Jesus[98] or the divine confirmation of his work—contrary to the view of the unbelieving world, he has not been eliminated as a criminal but been enthroned as the true king to reign over the universe. His invisibility does not mean that he has passed away but means, on the contrary, that he has indeed entered the realm of God to reign over the universe. By confirming the truth of Jesus' exaltation, the Spirit-Paraclete advocates the truth of faith against the objections of the unbelieving world.

The third explanation continues the universal dimension addressed in the preceding line: "judgment" is now explained by the phrase that

---

preserved such an understanding, John (as before him also Paul) has developed a much more theological understanding of sin (in the singular), conceptualized precisely as unbelief in Jesus. Cf. also 3:36.

[98] In John, δικαιοσύνη is only used in 16:8, 10; but in 1 John 2:1, Jesus as the "righteous one" (δίκαιος) is the (first) Paraclete, the helper of the disciples in the realm of the Father. Here, Jesus, his "righteousness," and his universal rule are also combined. Thus, δικαιοσύνη in John 16:8, 10 can be understood not from the Pauline usage, but, rather, from the parallel in the christological hymn of 1 Tim 3:16: Jesus is "justified in (the) Spirit"—that is, his righteousness is made manifest in the heavenly world or, more precisely, in his heavenly enthronization that substantiates his claim of universal rule.

"the ruler of the world is already condemned" (16:11). This is, of course, not an all-encompassing "definition" of judgment, not even in the Johannine view, but it emphasizes the consequences of the enthronization of Jesus to his universal rulership, namely the disempowerment (cf. 12:31) and condemnation of the "ruler of the world" (i.e., Satan).[99] In the present context, the focus is on the eschatological condemnation of the opposed powers, which is the logical consequence of the eschatological confirmation of Jesus in his glorification. The notable Greek perfect form κέκριται stresses the present effect of the events linked with Jesus' "hour," heavenly justification, and enthronization—the issue is already decided, the victory over Satan and also over the unbelieving world (cf. 16:33) is already won, and there is no uncertainty left for a future decision, an eschatological war (as, e.g., in Revelation) or even a last judgment.[100] If the decisive eschatological event already

[99] This very brief statement, together with the passage on the "excommunication" of the ruler of the world in John 12:31 (ἐκβληθήσεται ἔξω), is strongly debated. The question is, from which realm Satan is thrown out in the "hour" of Christ's exaltation (John 12:23, 32, 34) (the "now" [νῦν] in 12:31), and whether the Gospel really dares to say that he is completely disempowered in the earthly realm, in spite of the fact that the community is still contested or even persecuted at present. The most illuminating parallel is, therefore, in Rev 12:10–12 where a hymnic composition links the enthronization of Christ with the "excommunication" of the "accuser" (i.e., Satan). The term κατήγωρ used in 12:10 is the precise opposite of παράκλητος—if Rev 12:10 and 1 John 2:1 can be used to clarify the view in John 12:31 and 16:11, then the idea is that with the enthronization of the heavenly helper, the παράκλητος Jesus Christ, the "just" one (1 John 2:1), the accuser (i.e., Satan; cf. Job 1–2) has lost his heavenly position and is condemned and excluded from the realm of God. Cf. Jörg Frey, "Erwägungen zum Verhältnis der Johannesapokalypse zu den übrigen Schriften im Corpus Johanneum," in Martin Hengel, *Die johanneische Frage: Eine Lösungsversuch, mit einem Anhang der Apokalypse von Jörg Frey*, WUNT 67 (Tübingen: Mohr Siebeck, 1993), 386–87.

[100] Johannine eschatology is predominantly shaped by its orientation toward the present (although a future dimension, particularly with regard to the resurrection of the dead, is not totally excluded): believers have transferred from death to life (John 5:24) or have eternal life (John 3:18, 36), while those who do not believe have already been judged (John 3:18, 36). This means that any kind of future event can only reveal the decision already made in the encounter of humans with Jesus or his word. Therefore, eternal life is considered a present gift that believers have already obtained rather than a gift only awarded in future, depending on a still imminent final judgment decision. Cf. Jörg Frey, *Die johanneische Eschatolgie*, 3:464–81; Frey, "Eschatology in the Johannine Circle," in *Die Herrlichkeit des Gekreuzigten*, 1:664–98;

happened in the "hour" of Jesus, in his death and resurrection (understood as glorification and enthronization), the revelation of the Spirit can only expose the consequences of those events. That is, it can only expose the fact that the believers (already) have eternal life and that the judgment has also already been decided in Jesus or, with regard to the individuals, in their encounter with Jesus and his word (3:18).

Therefore, 16:8-11 provides a precise summary of the revelatory function of the Holy Spirit in the post-Easter period in which the Spirit is presented as the decisive figure in the trial on the truth, confirming the community (i) of the truth of faith and the falseness and sinfulness of unbelief, (ii) of the exaltation and enthronization of Jesus in the realm of God (i.e., a truth that is hidden from the bodily eyes or even contradicts the views and thoughts of the world), and (iii) of the validity and definitive character of the eschatological decision, the "victory" obtained in the exaltation of Jesus.

e) The last Paraclete saying in John 16:13-15 has already been discussed above with respect to its value as a hint to community discussions about the authorization and legitimacy of the Johannine proclamation and its developed image of Jesus. But there are some more aspects to add here. The Spirit is now presented as one who provides supplementary revelation that could not be expressed in the hour of Jesus' departure, since the disciples were still unable to grasp the meaning or to cope with the difficulties (16:12). But the "many things" that were to be revealed in the subsequent period, and are now revealed by the Spirit, are actually authorized by Jesus himself and keep the community of disciples within the realm of "the whole truth" (16:13)—that is, communion with Jesus.

In the somewhat repetitive structure of the saying, two further aspects should be noticed. First, it is said that the Spirit will glorify Jesus. This adds an important aspect to the idea of Jesus' glorification in the Gospel—while some passages state that the earthly Jesus was already bestowed with and so revealed his glory (2:11), the majority of passages link Jesus' glory with his glorification (i.e., with Jesus'

Frey, "*Johannine Christology and Eschatology*," in *Beyond Bultmann: Reckoning a New Testament Theology*, ed. Bruce W. Longeneker and Mikeal C. Parsons (Waco: Baylor University Press, 2014), 101–32.

"hour" / the events of his cross and resurrection). John 16:14, however, adds the decisive aspect that the glory of the crucified one could be perceived only in the time after his resurrection and was actually disclosed and proclaimed in the post-Easter period. It is, therefore, the work of the Spirit and his revealing activity that Jesus is now presented in his glory, a glory basically rooted in his glorification or exaltation[101] but proclaimed only after his resurrection by the remembering and revealing Spirit. The brief reference to the glorifying work of the Spirit actually encompasses the whole development of the high Christology as presented in the Fourth Gospel, the reinterpretation of Jesus' ministry, words, deeds, and faith, in the post-Easter perspective and in the horizon of the later community.

The second aspect to be considered in this saying is the idea that the Spirit will proclaim the "coming things" (τὰ ἐρχόμενα). Notwithstanding the fact that in other passages, the term τὰ ἐρχόμενα can refer to eschatological events, or generally to "the future,"[102] it is doubtful whether the saying actually wants to attribute prophecy or eschatological expectations to the Spirit-Paraclete. If the "coming things" are mentioned from the perspective of Jesus before his departure, the phrase might also refer to events and challenges in the present of the addressees and their communities that are not altogether forecasted by the Spirit in prophetic utterances[103] but rather explained and interpreted in view of the memory of the Jesus story and the truth of the glorified Jesus.

In conclusion, we can see that the five Paraclete sayings characterize the work of the Spirit in a multifaceted manner: as "replacing" the present Jesus, teaching and commemorating Jesus, bearing witness

[101] See p. 165 above on the reception of Isa 52:13 LXX.

[102] See the discussion in Frey, *Die johanneische Eschatologie*, 3:199–204, where I have argued, perhaps too strongly, for the idea that John 16:14 is part of dimension of future-oriented eschatology, referring to, for example, Jesus' parousia or related events (cf. 16:16-19).

[103] The references to future challenges and events in the farewell discourses, such as the hatred of the world (15:18) or the hostility of the synagogue (16:2-3), are presented as Jesus' words, and as words of Jesus they can be read as prophecy. However, they are in fact explanations from the post-Easter perspective of the Gospel that were put into the mouth of Jesus. In any case, they are not prophesies of the Spirit.

about him and thus glorifying him from the post-Easter perspective, confirming the community in the truth of Christology and in the truthful understanding of his departure and death, helping them to cope with the challenges in the times to come, and enabling them to bear witness or to proclaim Jesus and thus to continue his own work.

Thus, the Holy Spirit is not only the figure authorizing the Johannine preaching and the narrative and didactic techniques of the presentation of Jesus in the Fourth Gospel; it is also linked with the predominant theological aims of the Fourth Gospel, the content that is presented in this work as the teaching of the Spirit. In the subsequent passages, we can only expose a selection of those intentions by reference to a number of selected passages.

3.2 The Understanding of the Death of Jesus: The Crucifixion as the Enthronement of the King of Truth

The first and foremost theological theme of the Fourth Gospel is Christology: the Spirit will "glorify" Jesus by exposing his true divine identity and dignity. The glory that already breaks through in the way of the earthly, incarnate one is revealed in the (thoroughly designed) narratives about his deeds (John 2:11) and throughout the narrative of Jesus' ministry. For this purpose, the evangelist adopts a wide range of christological titles and proclaims Jesus as Messiah, king of Israel, Son of God, or Son of Man from the very beginning of the Gospel narrative but frames all those predications by the use of the θεός category.[104] He presents Jesus as the one who speaks the words of God (e.g., in his "I am" sayings) and does the works of God, when enacting the judgment and raising the dead (ch. 11). In his whole earthly ministry, Jesus is presented in unity with the Father (10:30) and in his divine authority, which was only revealed to the disciples through the Spirit, in the post-Easter memory. Presenting Jesus in his divine dignity is the most prominent aim of the Fourth Gospel.

The most challenging problem, however, which could also be considered a most obvious contradiction to the claim of Jesus' divine dignity, is his death on the cross. In view of Jesus' death, which was

[104] See above, pp. 27–38.

the shameful death of a convicted and abused criminal, any claim of divine dignity could be easily dismissed. Furthermore, the experience of Jesus' "absence" in the post-Easter period (14:18) and his invisibility (16:10) could endanger the faith of the community, and the farewell discourses give evidence of those questions. Therefore, John makes such a strong effort to lead his readers to an appropriate understanding of Jesus' death, which is, structurally and theologically, the "climax" of his whole story.[105]

For that purpose, John allots a larger amount of space within his narrative to the themes related to the death of Jesus than the Synoptics, and the farewell discourses provide a unique form in which the departure of Jesus or, more precisely, the challenges posed by his alleged absence from the post-Easter community can be discussed.[106] This confirms that the evangelist's primary interpretive aim in his gospel is a truthful understanding of the fact of Jesus' death on the cross and its consequences, an understanding in accord with the insights of Johannine Christology but without any "docetic" reduction of the bodily reality of his human life and cruel reality of his death on the cross.[107] The question is, instead, whether Jesus has merely died and his "departure" put an end to his ministry, or whether he was actually glorified, has returned to the Father, and, therefore, started his reign as the true king over those who listen to his voice (18:37). This is the main issue in the trial on the truth of faith that is being conducted, far beyond the earthly trial of Jesus, universally between the Spirit-Paraclete and "the world" and in which the Paraclete refutes the arguments of unbelief and strengthens the disciples in their faith (16:8-11). Thus, in John's passion narrative, we can observe the conflict of two perspectives—the perspective of the cruel liquidation that happened

[105] See Frey, *Glory of the Crucified One*, 172–74.

[106] In Mark 14:43, there is only the brief note that Jesus spoke something before his arrest. Luke 22:24-38 inserts a short series of sayings and exhortations. But compared with these synoptic passages, the Johannine farewell discourses are a remarkable innovation that shows the weight of the themes discussed here. See Jörg Frey, "Die *theologia crucifixi* des Johannesevangeliums," in *Die Herrlichkeit des Gekreuzigten*, 485–554 (508–10).

[107] On the true and unquestioned humanity of Jesus and the confirmation of his bodiliness in John, see Frey, *Glory of the Crucified One*, 224–34.

before the eyes of Jesus' contemporaries and the perspective of faith that perceives in the death of Jesus the event of eschatological salvation and in his "lifting up" on the cross the enthronization of the true king and the inauguration of his kingship. The whole Gospel can thus be characterized as an introduction into that perspective of faith, a "school of perception" in faith.[108]

Much more than Mark, John can be labeled a passion story with extended introduction.[109] The final events of Jesus' death and resurrection are referred to from the very beginning of the Gospel. Thus, unlike Mark, John inserts numerous proleptic hints to the events of Jesus' passion (including his resurrection) and inserts interpretive aspects[110]—for example, his reference to the "lamb of God" (1:29, 36), the "hour of Jesus" (2:4; 7:30; 8:20; 12:24), the "temple of his body" (2:21), the "uplifting of the son of man" (3:14; 8:28, 12:32-34), and his "glorification" (7:39; 11:4; 12:16, 23, 28). Frequently, there is mention of the intention of Jesus' opponents to bring about his death (5:18; 7:1, 19-20, 25; 8:37, 40; 11:53; 12:10), to lay hands on him (7:30, 32, 44; 8:2; 10:39; 11:57), or to stone him (10:31-33; 11:8), and there is also mention of Judas as the one who was to betray or deliver him (6:64, 70f.; 12:4; 13:2). The formulaic ὑπέρ-sayings about Jesus laying down his life "for the sheep" (10:11, 15, 17), "for his friends" (15:13), or even "for the people" (11:51f.) and "for the life of the world" (6:51) provide further anticipatory clues that aid in understanding his passion as a positive, salvific, and vicarious act.[111]

The second part of the Gospel begins with the statement that Jesus "loved his own unto the end" (εἰς τέλος, 13:1)—and the mention of the end (τέλος) already provides a link to the moment of Jesus' death

[108] See Jörg Frey, "Die johanneische Passionsgeschichte als Sehschule des Glaubens," in *Theologische Beiträge* 50 (forthcoming 2019). The main ideas in the present subchapter are taken from that article.

[109] Cf. the dictum by Martin Kähler, who characterized Mark as a "Passionsgeschichte mit ausführicher Einleitung." Kähler, *Der sogenannte historische Jesus und der geschichtliche, biblische Christus*, ed. E. Wolf (Munich: Kaiser, 1953), 59–60, n. 1.

[110] See Frey, "Die *theologia crucifixi* des Johannesevangelium," 510–16. cf. Thomas Knöppler, *Die theologia crucis des Johannesevangeliums: Das Verständnis des Todes Jesu im Rahmen der johanneischen Inkarnations- und Erhöhungschristologie*, WMANT 69 (Neukirchen-Vluyn: Neukirchener Verlag, 1994).

[111] See Frey, *Glory of the Crucified One*, 186–93.

(John 19:30). Thus introduced, in a lengthy and long-winded phrase the act of the footwashing is narrated, which is to be interpreted as a symbolic anticipation of his passion.[112] Then, the farewell discourses provide an extensive discussion of the questions about Jesus' departure (13:33, 36; 14:5), invisibility, or detachedness in the post-Easter period (14:19; 16:10; 16:16-19). His departure is proleptically interpreted as a return to the Father (13:3; 14:2f.; 14:28), and his death is victory over the world (16:33), judgment on its "ruler" (16:11), completion of his mission (17:4), and the precondition of the sending of the Spirit (16:7).

All these interpretive clues are introduced before the passion story begins. So, the passion or rather the death of Jesus is in view from the very beginning of the Gospel (1:29 or even 1:14). Further clues for its proper understanding are given through John's Christology: as the eternal Logos (1:1-2), Jesus is sent into the world because of God's love (3:16); he is not a mere human but one with the Father (10:30) and has the authority to lay down his life and to take it back up again (10:17-18). Consequently, Jesus' passion is not a result of human intrigues—Jesus is not the victim of evil people, neither Judas, nor the Jewish authorities, nor the Roman imperial power. His death is not the result of a scandal of justice but ultimately rooted in the loving will of God who gives his only begotten Son and thus ultimately himself over to death for the sake and salvation of humans. Therefore, Jesus enters his passion voluntarily, in full awareness and even royal sovereignty.[113]

From here, it can be explained that John focuses less on Jesus' suffering and more on the fruits of the events, or even his triumph in the passion. Accordingly, Jesus' last word is not a cry of godforsakenness as in Mark 15:34 but the declaration of triumph: "It is fulfilled" (19:30). In this vein, John openly rejects the idea that Jesus could have tried to escape death (18:11).

John, therefore, renarrates the traditional passion story, inserting numerous elements to open the eyes of his readers for the true meaning

[112] On this episode, see above, pp. 138–41.

[113] On these categories of John's interpretation of the passion, see also Manfred Lang, *Johannes und die Synoptiker. Eine redaktionsgeschichtliche Analyse von Joh 18–20 vor dem markinischen und lukanischen Hintergrund*, FRLANT 182 (Göttingen: Vandenhoeck & Ruprecht, 1999).

of the events, supported by the categories and explanations already communicated in the earlier parts of the Gospel. I can only point to a small selection of the narrative devices and changes in comparison to Mark. John's narrative depicts Jesus as actively entering his passion, in full awareness of what is about to happen (cf. 13:1, 3). Jesus is presented and crucified as the true king, and behind the act of crucifixion readers may recognize a veiled ceremony of enthronization. In all the episodes of the passion, John's focus is on the meaning and the soteriological outcome of the events for Jesus' disciples.

As early as the opening of the passion in chapter 18, we find that the narrative is programmatically designed to show Jesus' sovereignty: he actively crosses the Kedron Valley and enters the garden (18:1) to deliver himself to the opponents (18:6-8). He asks whom they are seeking, he identifies himself with his characteristic "I am," and his only request is for the freedom of his disciples.[114] The famous kiss of Judas is omitted, and Judas virtually loses his traditional function as the betrayer[115] because Jesus is the absolute master of the procedure. As already mentioned,[116] John expands the troops who come to arrest Jesus: whereas in Mark, servants of the high priests and scribes—probably the temple guards—arrest Jesus, he adds the cohort, which in Mark is only mentioned in the mocking scene (Mark 15:16). Since a cohort usually consisted of six hundred to a thousand soldiers, we have to imagine a band of hundreds of armed men, from Jews and gentiles, arriving "with torches and lanterns and weapons" (John 18:3) to arrest Jesus. The grotesque contrast of this scene is unmistakable—the huge mass of armed soldiers from Jews and gentiles stands against one unarmed man and his few friends, but when he utters the mere word "I am," they shrink back and fall to the ground. Thus, the scene of his arrest is changed into a demonstration of his royal honor and of the divine authority of his word: when Jesus articulates his divine identity, his enemies have to fall

114 The scene implies an interesting narratival change of places: Jesus is arrested, whereas his disciples are given freedom. On a deeper theological level, this is just what happens in Jesus' passion and death.

115 Interestingly, he is mentioned as the one who was to deliver Jesus (6:64, 70f.; 12:4; 13:2). And yet, in John, this function is quite limited: Judas is "sent" to do his work (13:27) by Jesus, who is depicted as fully being in control of his passion.

116 See above, pp. 137–38.

to the ground or rather prostrate themselves before him. Finally, the disciple with the sword, who is not identified with Peter, is rebuked, and Jesus confirms—in stark contrast with Mark's Gethsemane story —that he voluntarily takes the cup the Father has given him (18:11). Any sidestepping or even a defense by his adherents is plainly rejected. Jesus gives himself over to death.

This is confirmed by the second scene, the interrogation before Hannas. Since John has already used the scene of the trial before the Sanhedrin and Caiaphas, he inserts another interrogation here. And since there is no evidence about a special tradition, this might be a fictional expansion by the evangelist,[117] who also consciously interlocks Jesus' confession with Peter's denial. While Peter denies, Jesus confirms his message and mission. When asked about his teaching, Jesus does not say anything new but simply refers to his previous public teaching. He does not speak as a culprit but answers in a self-confident and sovereign manner, and, when being slapped for this, he defends himself as if he were not a convict but a free man, even a king.

The most significant passage, however, is the extended trial before Pilate.[118] While Mark narrates only a brief encounter in which Jesus answers the question of whether he is "the king of the Jews" with an opaque σὺ λέγεις (Mark 15:2), which could mean "yes" but also "you say this (but things are different)" or even "are *you* saying this (or someone else)?" John expands the episode into a well-structured composition of seven scenes with the accusers outside the building and Jesus inside, while Pilate is oscillating between both parties, thus appearing throughout as an unstable figure, manipulated by the Jews. Whereas the accusers outside try to enforce the death sentence they have requested, the interrogation of Jesus inside the building is designed as a dense theological dialogue on kingship, truth, and Jesus' real origin. In the very center of the episode is the fourth scene (John 19:1–5), inside the building. But instead of a dialogue, there is only a silent scenic play in which the

[117] See above, pp. 44 and 108.

[118] On this, see the thorough interpretation in Jörg Frey, "Jesus und Pilatus: Der wahre König und der Repräsentant des Kaisers im Johannesevangelium," in *Christ and the Emperor*, ed. Gilbert van Belle and Joseph Verheyden, BTS 20 (Leuven: Peeters, 2014), 355–91.

soldiers first scourge Jesus and then ironically dress him with royal garments, crown him with a crown of thorns, and greet him as king of the Jews all the while they slap him in his face. John relocates the episode from its original place after the trial, before the crucifixion,[119] and makes it the pivotal expression of Jesus' real identity, which is veiled behind the soldiers' cruel and humiliating acts. Within the ironic investiture, crowning, and veneration, his true royal dignity shines through. At the point of his utmost humiliation, Jesus is presented as a king—though not of this world (cf. 18:36-37)—and the reader is supposed to perceive Jesus' real glory in the image of the beaten and abused one in mean and improvised royal insignia, and afterward in the sign of his cross.

The dramatic encounter between Jesus and Pilate is thoroughly ambiguous and causes readers to interact with it on two levels simultaneously: on the surface level, there is the question of whether Jesus is guilty in terms of the accusation that he is a politically dangerous royal pretender, but, behind this surface level, deeper theological questions are at stake. So Jesus explicitly confirms the charge about being a king, saying, "I am a king," but with the important qualification, "My kingdom is not of this world" (18:36-37). Although such a kingdom is not a real, harmful, or dangerous entity to Pilate, readers will grasp that Jesus is the one in whom the "kingdom of God" is erected. Pilate, instead, confirms three times that Jesus is innocent, and the readers will also get the point that he is not only politically harmless but also sinless on a theological level, making it possible for him to carry the sin of the world. Jesus claims that those who are of the truth will hear his voice, but Pilate skeptically rejects such a truth unsupported by mundane power (18:38).[120]

[119] In Mark, the scene is located after the death sentence, immediately before the crucifixion (Mark 15:17-20). Here, the abusing of the convict could have its place, when the delinquent was already sentenced to death, and the soldiers were allowed to do so with the person to be crucified. During the course of the trial, the scene is useless. Exegetes have suggested various interpretations of the act, related with the phrase of presenting Jesus as "human" (*ecce homo*) in John 19:5 (cf. Lang, *Johannes und die Synoptiker*, 192–95). The view that the image of the abused Jesus should evoke the compassion of the accusers is unconvincing. Rather, the phrase shows, on the level of the judicial trial, that Jesus is innocent in terms of the accusation. He is a mere human, not a royal pretender, and therefore he is innocent. Of course, the phrase also has a deeper meaning on the theological level.

[120] As a mere *homo politicus*, Pilate has no appreciation for a king without real power.

In the following scenes, however, the roles are reversed: Pilate learns that this convict might be a son of a god, a numinous figure, and when fearfully asking about his true identity and origin, he receives no answer. And despite Pilate insisting on his power to convict or pardon, Jesus tells him that this power is only his because it has been given to him "from above" and that the sin of Jesus' accusers is greater than that of Pilate. The readers will get the point that the defendant, Jesus, is a judge on a deeper level, and the judge in the trial, Pilate, is not free to decide. In the final scene, it is even linguistically ambiguous whether Pilate takes his judgment seat or rather presents Jesus on a podium, seat, or throne, while he is presented to the Jews as their "king."[121]

The focus on Jesus' kingship, densely discussed in the trial scene, is confirmed in the crucifixion. Jesus carries his cross without the help of others, he is "uplifted" on the cross, and the inscription about him being "king of the Jews," which is fiercely rejected by the accusers, is officially confirmed by Pilate (19:21-22). Just as Caiaphas already confirmed the efficiency of Jesus' self-sacrificial offering in the trial scene (11:51-52), in a manner that goes far beyond the horizon of a Jewish high priest, Pilate now confirms a theological truth that goes far beyond the horizon of the historical Roman ruler but is attributed to him by the Gospel narrative to make even him a testimony to Jesus' true kingship.

Up until the point of his death, Jesus remains active in his passion. He cares for his mother (19:25-27), fulfills the Scriptures (19:28-29), and then (19:30) speaks his final word of completion, the τετέλεσται ("It is completed"), bows his head,[122] and actively surrenders the spirit

[121] In the phrase ἐκάθισεν ἐπὶ βήματος, the verb ἐκάθισεν can be interpreted as an intransitive verb with the meaning that Pilate (himself) sits on a (judgment) seat to pronounce the judgment, but it can also be read as a transitive verb, with the meaning that Pilate seats Jesus on an elevated place (ἐπὶ βήματος) to present him. In fact, there is no judgment pronounced by Pilate. Instead, Jesus is presented to the accusers with the words "Behold, (this is) your king!" It is likely that the ambiguity was deliberately created; cf. Jean Zumstein, *Das Johannesevangelium*, trans. K. Vollmer-Mateus, KEK (Göttingen: Vandenhoeck & Ruprecht, 2016), 711. See also Ignace de la Potterie, "Jésus roi et juge d'après Jn 19,13 ἐκάθισεν ἐπὶ βήματος," *Bib* 41 (1960): 217–47.

[122] It is even possible to interpret κλίνας τὴν κεφαλὴν as an affirmative nod, as it is reported about kings or even Zeus; cf. Bastian Lemitz, "Der Tod Jesu und das Nicken des Zeus: Zur Wendung κλίνας τὴν κεφαλὴν (Joh 19,30)," in *Erzählung und Briefe im*

(παρέδωκεν τὸ πνεῦμα).[123] Through that deeply ambiguous wording, readers will certainly grasp the idea that the gift of the Spirit, which is passed on to the disciples on Easter day (20:22), originates in Jesus' death. When the Gospel, then, adduces the testimony under the cross, pointing to the "blood and water" that came out from the wound in Jesus' side, this is meant to confirm the salvific outcome of Jesus' death, depicted and connected with the stream of life that comes out of the temple in Ezekiel 47. This ultimately confirms that the crucified one, or more precisely his body (cf. John 2:21), is ultimately depicted as the *place* of God's salvific presence on earth and as the *origin* of new life.

The whole of John's account of Jesus' passion is shaped by distinct features of the post-Easter spiritual interpretation of the Jesus narrative. The categories communicated earlier in the narrative are resumed here and continued in the redesigned narrative of the passion.

a) Jesus' death happens in the divinely determined "hour" and signals the completion of the divine will or the Scriptures, and yet it is depicted as an act of his loving commitment for his friends and a proof of God's love for the world.
b) Jesus' death is characterized as an exaltation, which is already inherently present in the depiction of him being "lifted up" in the air on the cross. But this physical exaltation also implies his exaltation to the Father.
c) Jesus' death is further presented as "glorification," which itself implies a knowledge of the Easter events and involves a combination of two terms that are taken from the Scriptures (Isa 52:13 LXX) where there is testimony about God's servant: "My servant . . . will be exalted and exceedingly glorified" (ὁ παῖς μου . . . ὑψωθήσεται καὶ δοξασθήσεται σφόδρα).[124]
d) Jesus' death is also characterized as a vicarious death that is done "for the people" (John 11:51) or "for his friends" (15:13) and "for the sheep" (10:11). In the passion narrative, there are several scenes that involve such a substitution: Jesus is arrested, but his disciples are permitted to go free (18:8-9); the innocent is convicted, while the "robber" Barabbas

johanneischen Kreis, ed. Uta Poplutz and Jörg Frey, WUNT 2/420 (Tübingen: Mohr Siebeck, 2016), 241–56.

[123] Most translations do not render the active meaning of the phrase παρέδωκεν τὸ πνεῦμα, but render it insufficiently as a mere paraphrase of dying.

[124] See above, p. 165.

is released (18:38-40); and Jesus dies on the cross, while the one whom he loves now takes his place as the son of the mother (19:25-27).

e) Particularly significant is the aspect that Jesus is depicted not as the suffering one who laments about his godforsakenness (as in Mark 15:34) but instead as a sovereign who knows about his fate and remains active until his last breath. He is in control of what happens when he commissions Judas to act, delivers himself to the soldiers, answers Hannas and Pilate with dignity, carries his own cross, and even when he dies.

f) Most important, however, is the aspect of his kingship that is present in his encounter with Pilate, in his crucifixion, and in the royal burial he receives. Within the trial and the crucifixion narratives, we can even discover a kind of royal ritual, partly presented in terms of an ironic reversal but clear enough for the readers to discover the deep truth of Jesus' kingdom.[125] While the unbelievers accuse him of having made himself a (messianic) king, the evangelist depicts him as the true king who rules—in a totally different manner—from the cross over those who listen to his voice. This is indicated by a number of narrative elements: Jesus himself proclaims, "I am a king" (John 18:36); he is (ironically) crowned; he is clothed with a royal overcoat; he is (ironically) venerated with the phrase, "χαῖρε, king of the Jews" (19:3-4); he is presented to the people by Pilate with the expression, "Behold, your king!" (19:14), to which the people respond with the (negative) acclamation, "Away with him, crucify him!"; and, finally, he is "enthroned" on the cross and universally proclaimed as king in three world languages (19:21-22). This last act functions as an "official" confirmation by Pilate concerning the truth of Jesus's kingdom, which is paradoxically presented and even visually stage-managed in his trial and "exaltation" on the cross.

As already mentioned, this passion narrative is presented with a considerable freedom regarding the historical traditions. The evangelist not only moves certain elements of the traditional passion account to earlier places in his narrative and changes Jesus' last words—he also redesigns the scene of Jesus' arrest; creates a new interrogation scene with Hannas; expands the encounter with Pilate, which is now designed in a scenic structure in which at least the theological dialogues must be considered fictional; inserts the beloved disciple as a witness under the cross; and concludes the scene with a dense double quotation from

[125] Cf. Frey, "Jesus und Pilatus," 386–88; see also Frey, *Die johanneische Eschatologie*, 3:273–76.

the Scriptures. All these creative changes against the earlier tradition are, however, motivated by the intention to provide a truthful interpretation of Jesus' death and its real meaning, as the exaltation and glorification of Jesus and as the act of the eschatological salvation.

3.3 The Post-Easter Way of Following Jesus: Faith in Jesus as God

One further aspect of John's teaching can be added here, and it is linked with the "border situation" of Jesus' hour, with the gap between the time of the earthly ministry of Jesus and the period thereafter, inaugurated by his death and exaltation and characterized by the presence of the Spirit.

The Johannine farewell discourses not only explain Jesus' departure in order to comfort his disciples, but, as discourses actually addressed to their post-Easter readers, they are directed at that audience, helping them cope with their situation of distress. One important part of their strategy is to convince the post-Easter disciples that they are in a better situation than the disciples of the earthly Jesus are: They are not left behind as orphans (John 14:18) but guided and taught by the "other Paraclete," the Spirit (14:16-17, 26). They can "see" Jesus with spiritual eyes (14:19) and are granted the eschatological gifts of peace (14:27), joy (16:24), and plain understanding (16:25-26).[126] Furthermore, 16:7 clearly states that Jesus' departure was necessary, not only due to a divine plan (cf. 3:14) but also in view of the benefits of the community. Even in distress and grief, the post-Easter community should not be tempted to think that keeping faith would have been easier if Jesus had stayed with them. On the contrary, the misunderstandings of the disciples of the earthly Jesus presented in the Gospel inevitably show that Peter and the disciples were unable to grasp the meaning of Jesus' ministry and words. They could not understand what had been revealed and explained to the post-Easter community through the "remembering" Spirit (cf. 2:22; 12:16). Thus, the post-Easter community is actually in a better situation than Peter and the other disciples during their

[126] On the strategy of comforting the community in John 16:23-33, see Frey, *Die johanneische Eschatologie*, 3:218–22.

time with the earthly Jesus. The addressees of the Gospel are therefore urged to accept the change of times, not to shrink back but to appreciate the benefits granted through the work of Jesus and through the Spirit. This is ultimately illustrated in the Easter narratives when Mary is called not to look for the corpse of Jesus (cf. 20:15)[127] or to cling to his physical body (20:17)[128] but to accept the new situation inaugurated by the Easter events.

But there is also a fundamental change regarding the object of the disciples' faith and the nature of their discipleship. This is most clearly demonstrated in the obvious misunderstanding of Peter in the opening section of the farewell discourses (13:36-38). When Jesus had announced his departure and the consequences for his disciples (13:33) and, on special request, also for Peter (13:36), namely that they cannot follow him *now*, Peter reacts quite resolutely, uttering his firm intention to follow Jesus everywhere, even into death. Jesus' reaction, a subtle rebuke, silently points readers to a deeper dimension: Peter not only claims to follow Jesus everywhere but boldly expresses his readiness even to "lay down his life" for Jesus. His words adopt the ὑπέρ-formula, which is already well introduced in the Gospel with regard to Jesus' death "for the sheep" (10:11) or "for the life of the world" (6:51). When Peter says, "I will lay down my life for you" (τὴν ψυχήν μου ὑπὲρ σοῦ θήσω, 13:37), Jesus' answer is conspicuously similar: it is merely a subtle reversal of the phrase, now formed as a question, so that the focus is laid on the changed pronouns, "*You* will lay down *your* life for *me*?" (τὴν ψυχήν σου ὑπὲρ ἐμοῦ θήσεις; 13:38). The question is immediately followed by the announcement of Peter's denial, which makes it clear that Peter's

[127] In John 20:15, Mary is still in grief, looking for the body of Jesus. But when Jesus addresses her by her name, she undergoes a change and is able to perceive the risen Lord and to become a testimony to the other disciples (20:18). On the making and contents of the Easter faith in John 20, see Frey, "Ich habe den Herrn gesehen."

[128] The phrase μή μου ἅπτου in John 20:17 is most likely not a prohibition against touching his body (as the famous Latin rendering *noli me tangere* suggests), nor can the phrase be used for speculations about the physical nature of the risen one. Rather, the phrase is to be understood as an exhortation not to hold Jesus back. A possible parallel is Matt 28:9, where the women hold Jesus' feet.

idea of laying down his life for the sake of Jesus[129] is impossible. Here, the implicit message is that "laying down one's life for" others, in the deeper soteriological meaning of the phrase, is only possible with Jesus as subject and the disciples, friends, sheep, and so forth as object.[130] This construction cannot be reversed.

Apart from the soteriological teaching included in this small dialogue, readers are pointed to the inevitable insight that discipleship, as the disciples of the earthly Jesus came to know, comes to a definitive end in Jesus' death. Following Jesus locally, in his physical presence, is now becoming impossible, and the disciples have to accept this. The evangelist chooses the figure of Peter, the leading figure of the group of the disciples, to demonstrate not only the lack of understanding of the pre-Easter disciples but also the impasse of the form of pre-Easter discipleship. It is no coincidence that the immediate continuation of the discourse in 14:1 is about the new way of discipleship in the post-Easter period: "Let not your heart be troubled: Believe in God and believe in me!" Now, the term "following" (ἀκολουθεῖν) is replaced by "believing" (πιστεύειν), with the implication that the new way of "following" Jesus can only be "believing in him" or, as it is expressed here in a dyadic (or even "binitarian") manner, "in God and in Jesus." John's Gospel not only wants its readers to believe in Jesus as "the Messiah," "the Son of God" (20:31). It introduces a new understanding according to which true faith in God can only be faith in God as Jesus has revealed him (1:18), faith in Jesus as the "image" of the invisible God, and thus faith in God who is in unity with his Son, the exalted and glorified Jesus. John not only teaches Christology but, even more, theology[131] and "pistology," the new way of venerating God "in Spirit and truth" (4:24).

129 Cf. also Peter's action with the sword and Jesus' rebuke in 18:10-11.

130 See Frey, *Die johanneische Eschatologie*, 3:127–28; Frey, *Glory of the Crucified One*, 184–85.

131 On the consequences of Johannine Christology for the understanding of God, see Frey, *Glory of the Crucified One*, 313–44.

3.4 "Come and See!" The Calling of the Disciples as Introduction into Post-Easter Communal Life

But how can humans in the post-Easter period come to belief? In several passages, the Fourth Gospel seems to show a special consideration of the post-Easter situation, as in its notable difference from the situation during the earthly ministry of Jesus. One of those passages is also thoroughly renarrated, or even reimagined, in notable difference from the earlier gospel tradition: the episode of the calling of the first disciples (John 1:35-51).

In Mark, Jesus begins his ministry after the imprisonment of the Baptizer, and, at the very beginning, he is depicted walking by the Sea of Galilee, where he sees two pairs of brothers and charismatically calls them to be his disciples. The pairs of brothers respond to this call by immediately following Jesus (Mark 1:16-20). Somewhat later, Mark also mentions the "creation" of the circle of the Twelve and their names (3:14-19).

In John, the calling of the first disciples is completely different with respect to place, names, and procedure. There is no mention of the Sea of Galilee. Instead, the calling starts from the spot where John has been baptizing: Bethany beyond the Jordan. More important are the differences regarding the names of the disciples—although John knows about the circle of the Twelve, he never gives a list of twelve names.[132] Even though he omits the names of the majority of the Twelve, he adds other named and unnamed disciples,[133] and even changes the most prominent positions: instead of Peter and Andrew, the first two disciples in Mark 1:16, John's first disciples are Andrew and another anonymous disciple (John 1:40). Peter is only "found" by Andrew thereafter, in a second step. This alteration might be interpreted as part of the author's strategy of placing Peter in the shadow of the beloved disciple, and the question naturally arises as to whether this unnamed disciple is to be identified with the beloved disciple first mentioned in chapter 13 and whether it is appropriate for readers to fill this narrative gap accordingly.[134] The fourth disciple now called directly

[132] The most extensive list of disciples in John is given in 21:2, with seven disciples.

[133] Cf. Martin Hengel, *The Johannine Question* (London: SCM Press, 1989), 17–19.

[134] These problems need not be discussed here, as other aspects are more important for our purposes.

by Jesus is Philip, and the central role of Andrew and Philip in the Fourth Gospel is again confirmed in 12:20-22.[135] With the last disciple mentioned in this scene—Nathanael (who is unknown from the Synoptics and painted as a paradigmatic believer from Israel)—John also considers another angle: Jews who follow Jesus. At the opening of John's narrative, Nathanael programmatically shows the way for possible readers and believers from a Jewish background.

Even more obvious than the variation in the names is the change in the calling. With the one exception of Philip, the disciples are not immediately called by Jesus. They are, instead, pointed to Jesus by another witness, and, because of that testimony, they enter into an encounter with Jesus. Only after that experience, or after being addressed by Jesus himself, do they come to faith and discipleship. Thus, the Baptizer points the first two disciples to Jesus (1:36). Then, Peter is found by his brother Andrew, and Nathanael is found by Philip. The first two disciples are addressed by Jesus and then stay with him for a day or night (1:39); Peter and Nathanael are addressed by Jesus with a new name ("Cephas," 1:42) or an attribute ("a true Israelite . . .," 1:47), and so they come to a proper encounter with Jesus himself. Moreover, there is something like a relay from one disciple to the next: each one who is found and comes to an encounter with Jesus gives testimony to others and leads them to Jesus, and thus the pattern repeats itself.[136]

The pattern presented here recurs in John 4 when the Samaritans finally say that they do not merely believe because of the woman's testimony, but because they heard Jesus' word (4:41-42). By hearing Jesus' words, they have a proper encounter with Jesus. Again, in chapter 20, the message about the risen one is proclaimed to the disciples by Mary (20:18), but they believe only when they have their own encounter with Jesus (v. 20). The same is true of Thomas' encounter with Jesus in the final episode (vv. 25-27).

[135] Perhaps it is no coincidence that they are the only two disciples with Greek names, and we can also speculate whether their prominence has to do with their relevance for Greek-speaking or even gentile addressees in Asia Minor where the tradition about Philip (Hierapolis) and Andrew (Pontus) points. Cf. Hengel, *Johannine Question*, 17 with n. 103, and 19 with nn. 114–15.

[136] On this pattern, see Annegret Meyer, *Kommt und seht: Mystagogie im Johannesevangelium ausgehend von Joh 1,35–51*, FB 103 (Würzburg: Echter, 2005).

The pattern is also linked with characteristic terms. In John 1:37, the disciples who are listening to John's testimony and following Jesus are invited with the words "come and (you will) see" (1:39). The same words are repeated by Philip when he invites Nathanael (v. 46). Similarly, the Samaritans "come," "hear," and then "know" (4:41-42), and the Greeks in John 12 "come near" and want to "see" Jesus (12:21). Although it is not narrated that the Greeks could actually encounter Jesus and come to pre-Easter faith, in Jesus' following discourse he announces that he will "draw all humans," possibly also Greeks, unto himself after his exaltation (v. 32), so that they finally also come to see, albeit only with spiritual eyes, in the post-Easter period. The particular concern for those who live in the post-Easter period and do not have the chance to see and meet Jesus physically seems to be also important in the Thomas episode in 20:24-28. Thomas is characterized as a disciple who was not there when Jesus met his disciples; this is not to emphasize that he did not believe but simply to note that he was late. But Jesus honors the late disciple with a special treatment, so that in the end he also can perceive the risen Lord and express his belief in Jesus as "my Lord and my God" (v. 28).[137] The concluding word of Jesus, the benediction of those "who believe although they do not see" (v. 29), is not primarily a rebuke of Thomas because of the doubts he previously uttered but rather conceived more positively as a promise to all those who do not have the chance to encounter Jesus physically but will anyway be brought to belief in the post-Easter time, through the Spirit.

We can see that, in various passages, the Fourth Gospel seems to mirror the manner in which belief in Jesus can be transmitted only in the post-Easter period—through the testimony of other believers or through the written testimony of the book (cf. 20:30). There is only one important difference: the personal encounter with Jesus and his word, which was immediately possible for Jesus' contemporaries (including Thomas as the "last" one), can happen only through the agency of the Spirit. Only with spiritual eyes can he be "seen," and the book that makes Jesus present and depicts him vividly to the imagination of its readers is the medium of the teaching of the Spirit.

[137] On the Thomas episode, see Frey, "Ich habe den Herrn gesehen," 280–81.

John's renarration of the calling story, with the significant changes with regard to not only the names and number of the disciples but also to the process of coming to faith, may be explained from the interest in providing a pattern for the post-Easter community of addressees. John radically changes the synoptic tradition, and there is no evidence that he could draw on a different source for the pattern described, particularly if this pattern is repeated several times in the Gospel. But according to his renarration, coming to belief in the post-Easter community is already foreshadowed and prestructured in the narration of the first disciples. Thus, the Fourth Gospel again provides a paradigmatic story that retells aspects of the ministry of Jesus with the situation of the post-Easter community in view in order to enable its readers to connect their situation with the foundational story of the earthly Jesus.

4. The Spirit's Creative Transformation of the Jesus Story

A number of further examples could be added to illustrate the multifaceted theological aspects of the Fourth Gospel in its design of the Jesus story and its various episodes. From the presentation of the Samaria episode—regardless of what the tradition behind that episode looked like—we could see the Johannine focus on the movement of the gospel message from its Palestinian and Jewish context to its universal acceptance, among gentiles and in "the world" (John 4:42), independent of any sacred region or place. From the Johannine presentation of the temple incident (2:13-22), further symbolic dimensions of the temple theme could be developed, not only with regard to Christology, but also with implications for ecclesiology and eschatology (cf. 14:2-3).[138] But this might lead to a developed presentation of the theology of the Fourth Gospel—a task that would widely exceed the present context.

[138] On these aspects, see Jörg Frey, "Temple and Identity in Early Christianity and in the Johannine Community: Reflections on the 'Parting of the Ways,'" in *Was 70 CE a Watershed in Jewish History? On Jews and Judaism before and after the Destruction of the Second Temple*, ed. Daniel R. Schwartz and Zeev Weiss, AJEC 78 (Leiden: Brill, 2012), 485–88; cf. also G. McCaffrey, *The House with Many Rooms: The Temple Theme of Jn 14:2–3* (Rome: Pontificio Istituto Biblico, 1988).

The preceding examples have shown, however, that John's "spiritual" Gospel is not merely restricted to Christology and closely related teachings, such as the present-oriented form of eschatology, nor are John's didactic interests limited to merely correcting "insufficient" views of Jesus, his miracles, or his dignity. The activity of the "remembering" Spirit—who re-presents Jesus by connecting the present of the community to the past story of the ministry and death of Jesus and by renarrating the Jesus story into the present of the community—includes a wide range of interests focused on, but not limited to, Christology. And these theological interests, aiming at the present of the readers, are the ultimate reason for John's reshaping and creative transformation of the Jesus story into a proclamation of his life-giving presence.

CONCLUSION

In the preceding chapters, based on the series of three Shaffer Lectures delivered at Yale Divinity School in January 2018, I started with a glimpse at the situation of Johannine scholarship fifty years ago, in particular in North America, with J. Louis Martyn and also Raymond E. Brown explaining the Johannine theology from the history of the community. History, therefore, was given priority over theology, and the idea of John as a drama on two levels, the level of the narrated story and the level of the narrator and his recipients, was established as an effective pattern of interpreting the Gospel.

During the following decades, the optimism of reconstructing the history of the Johannine community was increasingly questioned. Furthermore, the inspiring pattern of the drama on two levels called for modification and clarification. Which level is the dominating one, and how are the two levels connected, in John's narrative and also with regard to the historical "truth"? If John really aims at narrating the story of the earthly ministry of Jesus, while actually doing so from a programmatic post-Easter perspective, the question remains open to what extent the Gospel actually narrates history. To what extent is it "fictional," a narrative in which history "as it was" is overshadowed (or "overshone") by the perspective of the post-Easter period, a perspective of faith that notably differs from the earlier tradition and even more from the history of the earthly Jesus as his contemporaries could perceive?

The point of my argument is that in John *not history but theology has the priority*: a distinct and developed theology, based on a high christological view of Jesus as a human and divine being. While adopting a wide range of earlier messianic and christological traditions, all of them are programmatically embedded in a high christological perspective, which causes the author also to renarrate and reshape the traditional Jesus story to a considerable extent. For these insights, the author adopts a longer process of christological development that was not only limited to the Johannine communities but had started much earlier in the post-Easter period. Among his addressees, in the Johannine communities and also beyond, the evangelist presupposes an awareness of the differences between the traditional Jesus story as presented—for example, in Mark—and the perspectives given in his gospel writing. And occasionally, he even provides his readers with hints at those differences. They are not veiled by attempts of harmonization or false claims of complete agreement but left open for the readers to notice and—regardless of the historical accuracy—to follow the insights of the present work.

When asked for the legacy of his own teaching, the author claims that the particular christological insights and the changes against the tradition result from the process of "remembering" the Jesus story in the post-Easter retrospective under the guidance of the Holy Spirit. Thus, he claims that his story, even where it differs from the earlier tradition or contradicts other narratives, is authorized by the Spirit. The Spirit is, therefore, considered the ultimate author of the post-Easter "glorification" of Jesus, of the deeper and truthful understanding of his death, and of the new insights into the Scriptures.

The most obvious theological differences can be discovered in the passion narrative, which is well prepared by numerous anticipatory hints and designed in a deliberate contrast with Mark and the other Synoptics. According to John, Jesus dies not in godforsakenness but triumphantly and in fulfillment of the Scriptures. His death is not a death of mere dishonor but in fact a death of glorification, wherein he is bestowed with divine glory. It is not the epitome of humiliation but truly an exaltation of Jesus, which is visibly illustrated in advance by the image of the "uplifted" serpent (John 3:14).

This is communicated in a particularly skillful manner in the passion narrative. As demonstrated above, the dramatic Johannine presentation of Jesus' trial and passion works on two levels: On the surface, the historical reality of Jesus' humiliating execution and the cruel reality of his death is affirmed and is by no means questioned. But there is a second level operating behind the surface, which points to a reality that can be perceived only by faith in the light of the Easter events. On this level, the narrative communicates the truth of faith that in his "exaltation" on the cross, viewed in the perspective of Easter, Jesus is actually exalted to the Father, bestowed with divine righteousness and glory, and enthroned as the true king who invisibly reigns over those who listen to his word. In this perspective, Jesus' death and departure was not the end of his ministry but a new beginning; it is the foundation of a continued life in faith, and the precondition of the sending of the Spirit, who is at work and can be experienced at present within the community of disciples.

Johannine readers are supposed to perceive that truth of faith in the narration of Jesus' trial and crucifixion, and the interpretive hints given in advance as well as the design of the narrative help grasp the deeper meaning. Thus, the renarration of the Jesus story and, in particular, his passion, death, and resurrection are supposed to strengthen the identity and faith of the post-Easter community, a community unsettled by Jesus' invisibility and alleged absence and suffering from the unbelief in the surrounding world.

But the narrative is not only addressed to a particular situation but generalized as to apply to any community of disciples in the post-Easter period. In their life and distress "in the world," readers are invited to freshly remember and reconsider the fate of the incarnate Word and to apply it to their situation (cf. 15:18). Under the guidance of the Spirit, they can now reconsider the way of the light that came into the world and shines forth, because darkness could not overtake it (1:5). John's story is designed to proclaim the truth of faith to a community in distress, but the image of that community is open, and the metaphorical language of John gives this gospel a wider appeal to the Christian community in the world between Easter and Jesus' "coming."

For those theological reasons, the Jesus story is narrated not as a mere episode in a remote past but in in a manner that bridges the gaps between the past and the present to address the post-Easter situation of its readers. All the episodes, in particular the "signs" stories, are designed as exemplary narratives that convey the whole of Jesus' ministry, especially the "fruit" of his death and resurrection. A mere reading of these events as episodes of the past history of Jesus would, therefore, be completely insufficient.

As I tried to demonstrate in these lectures, the evangelist is well aware of the fact that he does not merely tell things "as they were" or simply stick to the "historical tradition" available to him. He deliberately renarrates, replots, and even in some parts fictionally reimagines the traditional Jesus story, claiming the authority of the Spirit for his version of the memory of Jesus. It is a version designed to help the views of the readers switch, as in a kaleidoscope, from distress to confidence and joy—or, to use another comparison, like an icon in which the image of the person depicted is outshone by rays of glory.

The question remains of whether this is forgery, production of "alternative facts," or betrayal of the "real" history. We could make this claim if it were possible to get back to a historical "truth" that is void of any interpretation. But such a "truth" would also be completely meaningless to the present. Telling history in a meaningful manner necessarily includes levels of selection, arrangement, perspective, and interpretation. It necessarily means the intrusion of the horizon of the present, with its challenges and insights. Telling history in a meaningful manner necessarily means that the tradition is recontextualized and renarrated. This is, of course, true for all the Gospels, but John does it in a hermeneutically conscious manner. He gives testimony about the process of "remembering" and the growth of the new understanding of Jesus in the later community, and this is probably the most decisive difference between John and the other Gospels. Hermeneutically, John can be considered the most "progressive" of our canonical Gospels, and interpreters of the Enlightenment era were not totally wrong when they claimed that this gospel, to a certain extent, transcends space and time to proclaim the universal truth of the gospel.

The quest for historically valid information in John is, of course, by no means illegitimate. But the theological conceptualization of the Gospel and its linguistic unity provide serious and in many instances insurmountable difficulties for any attempt at reconstructing and isolating sources or extracting historically valid information. Furthermore, as I tried to demonstrate in the central second part of these lectures, John's way of dealing with historical tradition does not support the assumption that he is interested in correcting Mark or presenting a historically more valid presentation. At a point where he presents a very valuable piece of tradition—the information that Jesus himself "baptized" as did John the Baptist—he does not make much of it. Furthermore, in an aspect where John is quite probably closer to the historical "truth"—in his more extended chronology—he arrives at that time frame by utilizing literary techniques that are motivated by other intentions than merely improving historical accuracy.

Therefore, Johannine interpretation will miss the intention of the Gospel and the evangelist's level of hermeneutical awareness if it merely asks questions about its historical accuracy or aims at crediting John with as much historical source value as possible. Such interests are rather motivated by modern concerns or rooted in certain tendencies of a conservative apologetics. But the related concerns about the author, his aims, and his techniques fail to meet not only the intention of the Gospel but also the manner in which it actually deals with the historical tradition it is based upon.

If the hermeneutical task is to "let John be John," we are left with the task of accepting and appreciating John's unique design, his claims about the remembering Spirit, and the ultimate priority of theology over history in the Fourth Gospel.

BIBLIOGRAPHY

Albright, William F. "Recent Discoveries in Palestine and the Gospel of St. John." Pages 153–71 in *The Background of the New Testament and Its Eschatology*. Festschrift C. H. Dodd. Edited by W. D. Davies and David Daube. Cambridge: Cambridge University Press, 1956.

Allison, Dale C. "How to Marginalize the Traditional Criteria of Authenticity?" Pages 3–30 in *Handbook of the Historical Study of Jesus*. Edited by Stanley E. Porter and Tom Holmén. 4 vols. Leiden: Brill, 2011.

Anderson, Paul N. "Aspects of Historicity in the Gospel of John: Implications for Investigations of Jesus and Archaeology." Pages 587–618 in *Jesus and Archaeology*. Edited by J. Charlesworth. Grand Rapids: Eerdmans, 2006.

———. *The Christology of the Fourth Gospel: Its Unity and Diversity in the Light of John 6*. WUNT 2/78. Tübingen: Mohr Siebeck, 1996.

———. *The Fourth Gospel and the Quest for Jesus: Modern Foundations Reconsidered*. LNTS 321. New York: T&T Clark, 2006.

———. "Why This Study Is Needed, and Why It Is Needed Now." Pages 13–73 in vol. 1 of Anderson, Just, and Thatcher, eds., *John, Jesus, and History*.

Anderson, Paul N., Felix Just, S.J., and Tom Thatcher, eds. *John, Jesus and History*. Vol. 1: *Critical Appraisals of Critical Views*. SBL Symposium Series 44. Atlanta: SBL, 2007.

———. *John, Jesus and History*. Vol. 2: *Aspects of History in the Fourth Gospel*. SBL Early Christianity and Its Literature 12. Atlanta: SBL, 2009.

———. *John, Jesus and History*. Vol. 3: *Glimpses of Jesus through the Johannine Lens*. SBL Early Christianity and Its Literature 18. Atlanta: SBL, 2016.

Ashton, John. *Understanding the Fourth Gospel*. Oxford: Oxford University Press, 1991.

Attridge, Harold W. "Genre Bending in the Fourth Gospel." *JBL* 121 (2002): 3–21. Reprinted as pages 61–78 in *Essays on John and Hebrews*. WUNT 264. Tübingen: Mohr Siebeck, 2010.

Back, Frances. *Gott als Vater der Jünger im Johannesevangelium*. WUNT 2/336. Tübingen: Mohr Siebeck, 2012.

Backhaus, Knut. "Spielräume der Wahrheit: Zur Konstruktivität in der hellenistisch-römischen Geschichtsschreibung." Pages 1–29 in *Historiographie und fiktionales Erzählen: Zur Konstruktivität in Geschichtstheorie und Exegese*. Edited by Knut Backhaus and Gert Häfner. BThS 86. Neukirchen-Vluyn: Neukirchener, 2007.

Bacon, Benjamin W. *The Fourth Gospel in Research and Debate*. New York: Moffat, Yard, 1910.

Baird, William. *History of New Testament Research*. Vol. 2: *From Jonathan Edwards to Rudolf Bultmann*. Minneapolis: Fortress, 2003.

———. *History of New Testament Research*. Vol. 3: *From C. H. Dodd to Hans Dieter Betz*. Minneapolis: Fortress, 2013.

Ball, David M. *"I Am" in John's Gospel: Literary Function, Background and Theological Implications*. JSSNTS 124. Sheffield: Sheffield Academic, 1996.

Barrett, Charles Kingsley. "'The Father Is Greater than I' (John 14.28): Subordinationist Christology in the New Testament." Pages 19–36 in *Essays on John*. Philadelphia: Westminster, 1982.

———. *The Gospel according to St. John: An Introduction with Commentary and Notes on the Greek Text*. London: SPCK, 1955.

Bartholomä, Philipp. *The Johannine Discourses and the Teaching of Jesus in the Synoptics*. Tübingen: Francke, 2012.

Bauckham, Richard. "The Beloved Disciple as an Ideal Author." *JSNT* 39 (1993): 21–44. Reprinted as pages 73–91 in *The Testimony of the Beloved Disciple: Narrative, History, and Theology in the Gospel of John*. Grand Rapids: Eerdmans, 2007.

———. "Dualism and Soteriology in Johannine Theology." Pages 133–54 in *Beyond Bultmann: Reckoning a New Testament Theology*. Edited by Bruce W. Longenecker and Mikeal C. Parsons. Waco: Baylor University Press, 2014.

———. *God Crucified: Monotheism and Christology in the New Testament*. Carlisle: Paternoster, 1998.

———. "Historiographical Characteristics of the Gospel of John." *NTS* 53 (2007): 17–36. Reprinted in pages 93–112 of *The Testimony of the Beloved Disciple: Narrative, History, and Theology in the Gospel of John*. Grand Rapids: Eerdmans, 2007.

———. "Is There Patristic Counter-evidence? A Response to Margaret Mitchell." Pages 68–110 in *The Audience of the Gospels: The Origins and Function of the Gospels in Early Christianity*. Edited by Edward W. Klink III. Library of New Testament Studies 353. London: T&T Clark, 2010.

———. *Jesus and the Eyewitnesses: The Gospels as Eyewitness Testimony*. Grand Rapids: Eerdmans, 2006.

———. "John for Readers of Mark." Pages 147–71 in *The Gospels for All Christians*. Edited by Richard J. Bauckham. Grand Rapids: Eerdmans, 1998.

———. "Messianism according to the Gospel of John." Pages 34–68 in *Challenging Perspectives on the Gospel of John*. Edited by J. Lierman. WUNT 2/219. Tübingen: Mohr Siebeck, 2006.

———. "Papias and Polykrates on the Origins of the Fourth Gospel." *JTS* 33 (1993): 24–69.

———. "Qumran and the Fourth Gospel: Is There a Connection?" Pages 267–79 in *The Scrolls and the Scriptures: Qumran Fifty Years After*. Edited by Stanley E. Porter and Craig A. Evans. JSPS 26 / RJLP 3. Sheffield: Academic, 1997.

Bauer, Walter. *Das Johannesevangelium*. 3rd ed. HNT 6. Tübingen: Mohr, 1933.

Baur, Ferdinand Christian. *Kritische Untersuchungen über die kanonischen Evangelien.* Tübingen: Fues, 1847.

———. "Über die Composition und den Charakter des Johannesevangeliums." *ThJ* 3 (1844): 1–191, 397–475, 615–700.

Becker, Jürgen. *Das Evangelium nach Johannes.* 2 vols. ÖTBK 4/1–2. Gütersloh: Gütersloher Verlagshaus Mohn, 1978/1980. 3rd ed., 1991.

———. "Die Abschiedsreden Jesu im Johannesevangelium." *ZNW* 61 (1970): 215–46.

Bennema, Cornelis. *Encountering Jesus: Character Studies in the Gospel of John.* 2nd ed. Minneapolis: Fortress, 2014.

Berger, Klaus. *Im Anfang war Johannes. Datierung und Theologie des vierten Evangeliums.* Stuttgart: Quell, 1997.

Bernier, Jonathan. *Ἀποσυνάγωγος and the Historical Jesus in John: Rethinking the Historicity of the Johannine Expulsion Passages.* BibInt 122. Leiden: Brill, 2013.

Betz, Hans-Dieter. "Wellhausen's Dictum 'Jesus Was Not a Christian, but a Jew' in Light of Present Scholarship." *Studia Theologica* 45 (1991): 83–110.

Beutler, Johannes. *Martyria: Traditionsgeschichtliche Untersuchungen zum Zeugnisthema bei Johannes.* FThS 10. Frankfurt: Knecht, 1972.

Blinzler, Josef. "Qumran-Kalender und Passionschronologie." *ZNW* 39 (1958): 223–51.

Blomberg, Craig L. "The Gospels for Specific Communities *and* All Christians." Pages 111–33 in *The Audience of the Gospels: The Origins and Function of the Gospels in Early Christianity.* Edited by Edward W. Klink III. LNTS 353. London: T&T Clark, 2010.

———. "The Historical Reliability of John: Rushing in Where Angels Fear to Tread?" Pages 71–82 in *Jesus in Johannine Tradition.* Edited by Robert T. Fortna and Tom Thatcher. Louisville: Westminster John Knox, 2001.

———. *The Historical Reliability of John's Gospel: Issues and Commentary.* Downers Grove, Ill.: InterVarsity, 2002.

Bock, Darrell L. *Blasphemy and Exaltation in Judaism and the Final Examination of Jesus.* WUNT 2/106. Tübingen: Mohr Siebeck, 1998.

Borgen, Peder. *Bread from Heaven: An Exegetical Study of the Conception of Manna in the Gospel of John and the Writings of Philo.* NovTSup 10. Leiden: Brill, 1965.

Braun, François-Marie. "L'expulsion des vendeurs du temple." *RB* 38 (1929): 178–200.

Bretschneider, Carolus Theophilus. *Probabilia de evangelii et epistolarum Joannis, Apostoli, indole et origine eruditorum iudidiis modeste subiecit.* Leipzig: Stein, 1820.

Brown, Raymond E. *The Community of the Beloved Disciple: The Loves and Hates of an Individual Church in New Testament Times.* New York: Paulist, 1979.

———. *The Epistles of John.* AB 30. New York: Doubleday, 1982.

———. *The Gospel according to John.* 2 vols. AB 29/29A. New York: Doubleday, 1966/1970.

———. "The Qumran Scrolls and the Johannine Gospel and Epistles." *CBQ* 17 (1955): 403–19 and 559–74.

Brown, Raymond E., and Francis J. Moloney. *An Introduction to the Gospel of John.* ABRL. New York: Doubleday, 2003.

Bühner, Jan-Adolf. *Der Gesandte und sein Weg im 4. Evangelium: Die kultur- und religionsgeschichtlichen Grundlagen der johanneischen Sendungschristologie sowie ihre traditionsgeschichtliche Entwicklung*. WUNT 2/2. Tübingen: Mohr, 1977.

Bultmann, Rudolf. "ἀλήθεια." *TDNT* 1:239–48.

———. *Das Evangelium des Johannes*. KEK 2. Göttingen: Vandenhoeck & Ruprecht, 1941. English translation: *The Gospel of John: A Commentary*. Translated by George R. Beasley-Murray. Oxford: Blackwell, 1971.

———. "Johanneische Schriften und Gnosis." Pages 230–54 in *Exegetica. Aufsätze zur Erforschung des Neuen Testaments*. Edited by Erich Dinkler. Tübingen: J. C. B. Mohr, 1967.

Burge, Gary M. *The Anointed Community: The Holy Spirit in the Johannine Tradition*. Grand Rapids: Eerdmans, 1987.

Burkett, Delbert. *The Son of Man in the Gospel of John*. JSNTSup 56. Sheffield: JSOT Press, 1991.

Burney, Charles Fox. *The Aramaic Origin of the Fourth Gospel*. Oxford: Clarendon, 1922.

Byrskog, Samuel. *Jesus the Only Teacher: Didactic Authority and Transmission in Ancient Israel, Ancient Judaism and the Matthean Community*. ConBNT 24. Stockholm: Almqvist & Wiksell, 1994.

Calvin, Johannes. *In Evangelium secundum Johannem Commentarius*. Edited by Helmut Feld. 2 vols. Ioannis Calvini opera omnia denuo recognita, ser. 2, vol. 11/1–2. Geneva, 1997–1998.

Campbell, R. J. "Evidence for the Historicity of the Fourth Gospel in John 2:13–22." Pages 101–20 in vol. 7 of *Studia Evangelica*. Edited by Elizabeth A. Livingstone. Berlin: Academie Verlag, 1982.

Carson, Don A. *The Gospel according to John*. Leicester: InterVarsity; Grand Rapids: Eerdmans, 1991.

———. "Historical Tradition in the Fourth Gospel: After Dodd, What?" Pages 83–145 in *Studies of History and Tradition in the Four Gospels*. Vol. 2 of *Studies of History and Tradition in the Four Gospels*. Edited by R. T. France and David Wenham. Sheffield: JSOT Press, 1981.

Casey, Maurice. *From Jewish Prophet to Gentile God*. Louisville: Westminster John Knox, 1992.

———. *Jesus of Nazareth: An Independent Historian's Account of the Life and Teaching*. New York: T&T Clark, 2010.

———. "The Role of Aramaic in Reconstructing the Teaching of Jesus." Pages 1343–75 in vol. 2 of *Handbook for the Study of the Historical Jesus*. Edited by Stanley E. Porter and Tom Holmén. 4 vols. Leiden: Brill, 2011.

Chapman, David W., and Eckhard J. Schnabel. *The Trial and Crucifixion of Jesus: Texts and Commentary*. WUNT 344. Tübingen: Mohr Siebeck, 2015.

Chapple, Allan. "Jesus' Intervention in the Temple: Once or Twice?" *JETS* 58 (2015): 545–69.

Charlesworth, James H. "The Dead Sea Scrolls and the Gospel according to John." Pages 69–97 in *Exploring the Gospel of John*. Festschrift D. Moody Smith. Louisville: Westminster John Knox, 1996.

———. "The Historical Jesus in the Fourth Gospel: A Paradigm Shift?" *JSHJ* 8 (2010): 3–46.

Chester, Andrew. "High Christology—Whence, When and Why?" *Early Christianity* 2 (2011): 22–50.

———. *Messiah and Exaltation: Jewish Messianic and Visionary Traditions and New Testament Christology*. WUNT 207. Tübingen: Mohr, 2007.

Collins, Adela Yarbro. *Mark: A Commentary*. Hermeneia. Minneapolis: Augsburg Fortress, 2007.

Collins, John J. *The Scepter and the Star: The Messiahs of the Dead Sea Scrolls and Other Ancient Literature*. New York: Doubleday, 1995.

Cook, John Granger. *Crucifixion in the Mediterranean World*. WUNT 327. Tübingen: Mohr Siebeck, 2014.

Cross, Frank Moore. *The Ancient Library of Qumran and Modern Biblical Studies*. London: Duckworth, 1958.

Culpepper, R. Alan. *Anatomy of the Fourth Gospel: A Study in Literary Design*. Philadelphia: Fortress, 1983.

———. *John the Son of Zebedee: The Life of a Legend*. Edinburgh: T&T Clark, 2000.

Dauer, Anton. *Die Passionsgeschichte im Johannesevangelium*. SANT 30. Münich: Kösel, 1972.

de Jonge, Henk J. "The Loss of Faith in the Historicity of the Gospels." Pages 409–21 in *John and the Synoptics*. Edited by Adalbert Denaux. BETL 101. Leuven: Peeters, 1992.

Deines, Roland. *Jüdische Steingefäße und pharisäische Frömmigkeit: Ein archäologisch-historischer Beitrag zum Verständnis von Johannes 2,6 und der jüdischen Reinheitshalacha zur Zeit Jesu*. WUNT 2/52. Tübingen: Mohr Siebeck, 1993.

Dettwiler, Andreas. *Die Gegenwart des Erhöhten: Eine exegetische Studie zu den johanneischen Abschiedsreden (Joh 13,31–16,33) unter Berücksichtigung ihres Relecture-Charakters*. FRLANT 169. Göttingen: Vandenhoeck & Ruprecht, 1995.

Devilliers, Luc. *La Fête de l'Envoyé*. Paris: Gabalda, 2002.

Dewey, A. J. "The Eyewitness of History: Visionary Consciousness in the Fourth Gospel." Pages 59–70 in *Jesus in Johannine Tradition*. Edited by Robert T. Fortna and Tom Thatcher. Louisville: Westminster John Knox, 2001.

Dexinger, Ferdinand. "Samaritan Eschatology." Pages 266–92 in *The Samaritans*. Edited by Alan D. Crown. Tübingen: Mohr Siebeck, 1989.

Dietzfelbinger, Christian. *Der Abschied des Kommenden: Eine Auslegung der johanneischen Abschiedsreden*. WUNT 95. Tübingen: Mohr Siebeck, 1997.

———. "Paraklet und theologischer Anspruch im Johannesevangelium." *ZTK* 82 (1985): 389–408.

Dodd, C. H. *Historical Tradition in the Fourth Gospel*. Cambridge: Cambridge University Press, 1963.

———. *History and the Gospel*. London: Nisbet, 1938.

———. *The Interpretation of the Fourth Gospel*. Cambridge: Cambridge University Press, 1953.

du Toit, David S. "Redefining Jesus: Current Trends in Jesus Research." Pages 82–124 in *Jesus, Mark, and Q: The Teaching of Jesus and Its Earliest Records*. Edited by Michael Labahn and Andreas Schmidt. JSNTS 214. Sheffield: Sheffield Academic, 2001.

Dunderberg, Ismo. *Johannes und die Synaoptiker*. Annales Academiae Scientiarum Fennicae / Dissertationes humanarum litterarum 69. Helsinki: Akateeminen Kirjakauppa, 1994.

Dunn, James D. G. "Let John Be John! A Gospel for Its Time." Pages 309–39 in *Das Evangelium und die Evangelien*. Edited by Peter Stuhlmacher. WUNT 28. Tübingen: Mohr, 1983. Reprinted as "Let John Be John! A Gospel for Its Time." Pages 293–323 in *The Gospel and the Gospels*. Edited by Peter Stuhlmacher. Grand Rapids: Eerdmans, 1991.

———. *The Partings of the Ways: Between Christianity and Judaism and Their Significance for the Character of Christianity*. London: SCM Press, 1991. 2nd rev. ed., 2006.

Endo, Masanobu. *Creation and Christology: A Study on the Johannine Prologue in the Light of Early Jewish Creation Accounts*. WUNT 2/149. Tübingen: Mohr Siebeck, 2002.

Ensor, Peter W. "The Johannine Sayings of Jesus and the Question of Authenticity." Pages 14–33 in *Challenging Perspectives on the Gospel of John*. Edited by John Lierman. WUNT 2/219. Tübingen: Mohr Siebeck, 2006.

Evans, Craig A. "Authenticating the Activities of Jesus." Pages 3–29 in *Authenticating the Activities of Jesus*. Edited by Bruce Chilton and Craig A. Evans. Leiden: Brill, 1999.

———. "The Historical Reliability of John's Gospel: From What Perspective Should It Be Assessed?" Pages 91–119 in *The Gospel of John and Christian Theology*. Edited by Richard J. Bauckham and C. Moser. Grand Rapids: Eerdmans, 2008.

———. *Mark 8:27–16:20*. WBC 34B. Nashville: Thomas Nelson, 2001.

———. *Word and Glory: On the Exegetical and Theological Background of John's Prologue*. JSNTSup 89. Sheffield: Sheffield Academic, 1993.

Evanson, Edward. *The Dissonance of the Four Generally Received Evangelists, and the Evidence of Their Respective Authority Examined*. Ipswich: George Jermyn, 1792.

Felsch, Dorit. *Die Feste im Johannesevangelium: Jüdische Tradition und christologische Deutung*. WUNT 2/308. Tübingen: Mohr Siebeck, 2011.

Fortna, Robert T. *The Gospel of Signs: A Reconstruction of the Narrative Source Underlying the Fourth Gospel*. MSSNTS 11. Cambridge: Cambridge University Press, 1970.

Fredriksen, Paula. *Jesus of Nazareth, King of the Jews: A Jewish Life and the Emergence of Christianity*. New York: Knopf, 2000.

Frey, Jörg. "Auf der Suche nach dem Kontext des vierten Evangeliums." Pages 45–87 in *Die Herrlichkeit des Gekreuzigten*.

———. "Baptism in the Fourth Gospel, Jesus and John as Baptizers: Historical and Theological Reflections on John 3:22–30 and 4:1–3." In *Expressions of the Johannine Kerygma in John 2:23–5:18: Historical, Literary, and Theological Readings from the Colloquium Ioanneum 2017 in Jerusalem*. Edited by R. Alan Culpepper and Jörg Frey. WUNT. Tübingen: Mohr Siebeck, forthcoming.

———. "Continuity and Discontinuity between 'Jesus' and 'Christ': The Possibilities of an Implicit Christology." *RCT* 36, no. 1 (2011): 69–98.

———. "Das Corpus Johanneum und die Apokalypse des Johannes: Die Johanneslegende, die Probleme der johanneischen Verfasserschaft und die Frage der Pseudonymität der Apokalypse." Pages 71–133 in *Poetik und Intertextualität der Apokalypse*. Edited by St. Alkier, T. Hieke, and T. Nicklas. WUNT 346. Tübingen: Mohr Siebeck, 2015.

———. "Der Christus der Evangelien als der 'historische Jesus': Zum Jesus-Buch des Papstes." Pages 111–29 in *Der Papst aus Bayern: Protestantische Wahrnehmungen*. Edited by Werner Thiede. Leipzig: Evangelische Verlagsanstalt, 2010.

———. "Der historische Jesus und der Christus der Evangelien." Pages 29–84 in *Von Jesus zur neutestamentlichen Theologie: Kleine Schriften II*. Edited by Benjamin Schliesser. WUNT 386. Tübingen: Mohr Siebeck, 2016.

———. *Die Herrlichkeit des Gekreuzigten: Studien zu den johanneischen Schriften I*. Edited by Juliane Schlegel. WUNT 307. Tübingen: Mohr Siebeck 2013.

———. "'Docetic-like' Christologies and the Polymorphy of Christ: A Plea for Further Consideration of Diversity in the Discussion of 'Docetism.'" Pages 27–49 in *Docetism in the Early Church: The Quest for an Elusive Phenomenon*. Edited by Joseph Verheyden et al. WUNT 402. Tübingen: Mohr Siebeck, 2018.

———. "Dualism and the World in the Gospel and Letters of John." Pages 274–91 in *Oxford Handbook of Johannine Studies*. Edited by Martinus de Boer and Judith Lieu. Oxford: Oxford University Press, 2018.

———. "Eine neue religionsgeschichtliche Perspektive. Larry W. Hurtados *Lord Jesus Christ* und die Herausbildung der frühen Christologie." Pages 117–68 in *Reflections on Early Christian History and Religion—Erwägungen zur frühchristlichen Religionsgeschichte*. Edited by Cilliers Breytenbach and Jörg Frey. AJEC 81. Leiden: Brill, 2012.

———. "Erwägungen zum Verhältnis der Johannesapokalypse zu den übrigen Schriften im Corpus Johanneum." Pages 326–429 in *Martin Hengel, Die johanneische Frage: Ein Lösungsversuch, mit einem Anhang zur Apokalypse von Jörg Frey. WUNT 67*. Tübingen: Mohr Siebeck, 1993.

———. "Eschatology in the Johannine Circle." Pages 664–98 in *Die Herrlichkeit des Gekreuzigten.*

———. "'Ethical' Traditions, Family Ethos, and Love in the Johannine Literature." Pages 767–802 in *Die Herrlichkeit des Gekreuzigten.*

———. "Ferdinand Christian Baur and the Interpretation of John." Pages 206–35 in *Ferdinand Christian Baur and the History of Early Christianity*. Edited by Martin Bauspiess, Christof Landmesser, and David Lincicium. Translated by R. F. Brown and P. C. Hodgson. Oxford: Oxford University Press, 2017.

———. "From the 'Kingdom of God' to 'Eternal Life': The Transformation of Theological Language in the Fourth Gospel." Pages 439–58 in vol. 1 of Anderson, Just, and Thatcher, *John, Jesus, and History.*

———. "From the *Sēmeia* Narratives to the Gospel as a Significant Narrative: On Genre-Bending in the Johannine Miracle Stories." Pages 209–32 in *The Fourth Gospel as Genre Mosaic*. Edited by Kasper Bro Larsen. Studia Aarhusia Neotestamentica 3. Göttingen: Vandenhoeck & Ruprecht, 2015.

———. *The Glory of the Crucified One: Christology and Theology in the Gospel of John*. Translated by W. Coppins and C. Heilig. BMSEC 6. Waco: Baylor University Press, 2018.

———. "God's Dwelling on Earth: '*Shekhina*-Theology' in Revelation 21 and in the Gospel of John." Pages 79–103 in *John's Gospel and Intimations of Apocalyptic*. Edited by Christopher Rowland and Catrin Williams. London: Bloomsbury T&T Clark, 2013.

———. "The Gospel of John as a Narrative Memory of Jesus." Pages 261–84 in *Memory and Memories in Early Christianity*. Edited by Simon Butticaz and Enrico Norelli. WUNT 398. Tübingen: Mohr Siebeck, 2018.

———. "How Could Mark and John Do without Infancy Stories? Jesus' Humanity and His Divine Origins in Mark and John." Pages 189–215 in *Infancy Gospels: Story and Identity*. Edited by Claire Clivaz et al. WUNT 281. Tübingen: Mohr Siebeck, 2011.

———. "How Did the Spirit Become a Person?" Pages 243–371 in *The Holy Spirit, Inspiration, and the Cultures of Antiquity: Multidisciplinary Perspectives*. Edited by Jörg Frey and John R. Levison. Ekstasis 5. Berlin: de Gruyter, 2014.

———. "'Ich habe den Herrn gesehen' (Joh 20,18): Entstehung, Inhalt und Vermittlung des Osterglaubens nach Johannes 20." Pages 267–84 in *Studien zu Matthäus und Johannes / Études sur Matthieu et Jean*. Festschrift Jean Zumstein. Edited by Andreas Dettwiler and Uta Poplutz. AthANT 97. Zürich: TVZ, 2009.

———. "Jesus und Pilatus: Der wahre König und der Repräsentant des Kaisers im Johannesevangelium." Pages 337–93 in *Christ and the Emperor*. Edited by Gilbert van Belle and Joseph Verheyden. BTS 20. Leuven: Peeters, 2014.

———. *Die johanneische Eschatologie*. Vol. 1: *Ihre Probleme im Spiegel der Forschung seit Reimarus*. WUNT 97. Tübingen: Mohr Siebeck, 1997.

———. *Die johanneische Eschatologie*. Vol. 2: *Das johanneische Zeitverständnis*. WUNT 110. Tübingen: Mohr Siebeck, 1998.

———. *Die johanneische Eschatologie*. Vol. 3: *Die eschatologische Verkündigung in den johanneischen Texten*. WUNT 117. Tübingen: Mohr Siebeck, 2000.

———. "Die johanneische Passionsgeschichte als Sehschule des Glaubens." In *Theologische Beiträge* 50 (forthcoming 2019).

———. "Die johanneische Theologie zwischen 'Doketismus' und 'Antidoketismus': Auseinandersetzungen und Trennungsprozesse im Hintergrund der johanneischen Schriften und ihrer Rezeption." Pages 129–56 in *Erzählung und Briefe im johanneischen Kreis*. Edited by Uta Poplutz and Jörg Frey. WUNT 2/420. Tübingen: Mohr Siebeck, 2016.

———. "Johannesevangelium." Pages 137–45 in *Jesus Handbuch*. Edited by Jens Schröter and Christine Jacobi. Tübingen: Mohr Siebeck, 2017.

———. "Johannine Christology and Eschatology." Pages 101–32 in *Beyond Bultmann: Reckoning a New Testament Theology*. Edited by Bruce W. Longeneker and Mikeal C. Parsons. Waco: Baylor University Press, 2014.

———. "The Johannine Prologue and the References to the Creation of the World in Its Second Century Receptions." Pages 221–44 in *Les judaïsmes dans tous leurs états aux Ier–IIIe siècles (Les Judéeens des synagogues, les chrétiens et les rabbins): Actes du colloque de Lausanne 12–14 décembre 2012*. Edited by C. Clivaz, S. C. Mimouni, and B. Pouderon. Judaïsme ancien et origines du christianisme 5. Turnhout: Brepols, 2015.

———. "Licht aus den Höhlen? Der 'johanneische Dualismus' und die Texte von Qumran." Pages 147–238 in *Die Herrlichkeit des Gekreuzigten*.

———. "Paul's View of the Spirit in the Light of Qumran." Pages 239–62 in *The Dead Sea Scrolls and Pauline Literature*. Edited by Jean-Sébastian Rey. STDJ 102. Leiden: Brill, 2013.

———. "Das prototypische Zeichen (Joh 2,1–11)." Pages 165–216 in *The Opening of John's Narrative (John 1:19–2:22): Historical, Literary, and Theological Readings from the Colloquium Ioanneum in Ephesus*. Edited by R. Alan Culpepper and Jörg Frey. WUNT 385. Tübingen: Mohr Siebeck, 2017.

———. "Recent Perspectives on Johannine Dualism and Its Background." Pages 127–57 in *Text, Thought, and Practice in Qumran and Early Christianity*. Edited by Ruth Clements and Daniel R. Schwartz. STDJ 84. Leiden: Brill, 2008.

———. "Sehen oder Nicht-Sehen? (Die Heilung des blind Geborenen)—Joh 9,1–41." Pages 725–41 in *Kompendium der frühchristlichen Wundererzählungen*. Vol. 1 of *Die Wunder Jesu*. Edited by Ruben Zimmermann. Gütersloh: Gütersloher Verlagshaus, 2013.

———. "Die *theologia crucifixi* des Johannesevangeliums." Pages 169–238 in *Kreuzestheologie im Neuen Testament*. Edited by Andreas Dettwiler and Jean Zumstein. WUNT 151. Tübingen: Mohr Siebeck, 2002. Reprinted as "Die *theologia crucifixi* des Johannesevangeliums." Pages 485–554 in *Die Herrlichkeit des Gekreuzigten*.

———. "Temple and Identity in Early Christianity and in the Johannine Community: Reflections on the 'Parting of the Ways.'" Pages 447–507 in *Was 70 CE a Watershed in Jewish History? On Jews and Judaism before and after the Destruction of the Second Temple*. Edited by Daniel R. Schwartz and Zeev Weiss. AJEC 78. Leiden: Brill, 2012.

———. "Towards Reconfiguring Our Views on the 'Parting of the Ways': Ephesus as a Test Case." Pages 221–41 in *John and Judaism: A Contested Relationship in Context*. Edited by R. Alan Culpepper and Paul N. Anderson. Resources for Biblical Study 87. Atlanta: SBL, 2017.

———. "The Use of δόξα in Paul and John as Shaped by the Septuagint." Pages 85–104 in *The Reception of Septuagint Words in Jewish-Hellenistic and Christian Literature*. Edited by Eberhard Bons and Ralph Brucker. WUNT 2/367. Tübingen: Mohr Siebeck, 2014.

———. "Von Paulus zu Johannes: Die Diversität 'christlicher' Gemeindekreise und die 'Trennngsprozesse' zwischen der Syynagoge und den Gemeinden der Jesusnachfolger in Ephesus im ersten Jahrhundert." Pages 235–78 in *The Rise and Expansion of Christianity in the First Three Centuries of the Common Era*. Edited by Clare K. Rothschild and Jens Schröter. WUNT 301. Tübingen: Mohr Siebeck, 2013.

———. "'Wie Mose die Schlange in der Wüste erhöht hat . . .': Zur frühjüdischen Deutung der 'ehernen Schlange' und ihrer christologischen Rezeption in Johannes 3,14f." Pages 153–205 in *Schriftauslegung im antiken Judentum und im Urchristentum*. WUNT 73. Tübingen: Mohr Siebeck, 1994.

Gadamer, Hans-Georg. *Wahrheit und Methode: Grundzüge einer philosophischen Hermeneutik*. 5th ed. Tübingen: Mohr Siebeck, 1986.

Gardner-Smith, P. *Saint John and the Synoptic Gospels*. Cambridge: Cambridge University Press, 1938.

Garský, Zbyněk. *Das Wirken Jesu in Galiläa bei Johannes: Eine strukturale Analyse der Intertextualität des vierten Evangeliums mit den Synoptikern*. WUNT 2/325. Tübingen: Mohr Siebeck, 2012.

Gathercole, Simon J. *The Pre-existent Son: Recovering the Christologies of Matthew, Mark, and Luke*. Grand Rapids: Eerdmans, 2006.

Gerhardsson, Birger. "Der Weg der Evangelientradition." Pages 79–102 in *Das Evangelium und die Evangelien*. Edited by P. Stuhlmacher. WUNT 28. Tübingen: Mohr Siebeck, 1983.

———. *Memory and Manuscript: Oral Tradition and Written Transmission in Rabbinic Judaism and Early Christianity*. ASNU 22. Lund: Gleerup, 1964.

Giblin, Charles H. "Suggestion, Negative Response, and Positive Action in St. John's Portrayal of Jesus (John 2,1–11; 4,46–54; 7,2–14; 11,1–44)." *NTS* 26 (1979/1980): 197–211.

Gibson, Shimon. "The Excavations at the Bethesda Pool in Jerusalem." Pages 17–44 in *Sainte-Anne de Jérusalem: La Piscine Probatique de Jésus à Saladin: Le Projet Béthesda (1994–2010)*. Proche-Orient Chrétien, Numéro Spécial. Beirut: Faculté des sciences religieuses, 2011.

Godet, Frederic. *Kommentar zu dem Evangelium des Johannes.* 4th ed. 2 vols. Hannover: Meyer, 1903.

Haenchen, Ernst. *A Commentary on the Gospel of John.* Translated by R. W. Funk. Hermeneia. Philadelphia: Fortress, 1984.

———. *Johannesevangelium.* Edited by U. Busse. Tübingen: Mohr, 1980.

Hagner, Donald A. *Matthew.* 2 vols. WBC 33. Dallas: Word, 1993–1995.

Hengel, Martin. "Abba, Maranatha, Hosanna un die Anfänge der Christologie." Pages 496–534 in *Studien zur Christologie.*

———. "Bishop *Lightfoot* and the *Tübingen School* on the Gospel of John and the Second Century." *Durham University Journal: Supplement* (1992): 23–51. Reprinted as pages 329–58 in Lightfoot, *Gospel of St. John.*

———. *Crucifixion: In the Ancient World and the Folly of the Message of the Cross.* Translated by John Bowden. Minneapolis: Fortress, 1977.

———. "Das Christuslied im frühesten Gottesdienst." Pages 205–58 in *Studien zur Christologie.* English translation: "The Song about Christ in Earliest Worship." Pages 227–92 in *Studies in Early Christology.* Edinburgh: T&T Clark, 1995.

———. "Das Johannesevangelium als Quelle für die Geschichte des antiken Judentums." Pages 293–334 in *Judaica, Hellenistica et Christiana: Kleine Schriften II.* WUNT 109. Tübingen: Mohr Siebeck, 1999.

———. *Die johanneische Frage: Ein Lösungsversuch, mit einem Beitrag zur Apokalypse von J. Frey.* WUNT 67. Tübingen: Mohr Siebeck, 1993.

———. "Die Schriftauslegung des 4. Evangeliums auf dem Hintergrund der urchristlichen Exegese." Pages 601–43 in *Jesus und die Evangelien: Kleine Schriften V.* Edited by Claus-Jürgen Thornton. WUNT 211. Tübingen: Mohr Siebeck, 2007.

———. *Die vier Evangelien und das eine Evangelium von Jesus Christus.* WUNT 224. Tübingen: Mohr Siebeck, 2008.

———. "Hymnus und Christologie." Pages 185–204 in *Studien zur Christologie.* English translation: "Hymn and Christology." Pages 173–97 in *Papers on Paul and Other NT Authors: Sixth International Congress on Biblical Studies Oxford 3–7 April 1978.* Vol. 3 of *Studia Biblica.* JSNTSup 3. Sheffield: Sheffield Academic, 1980. Reprinted in Martin Hengel, *Between Jesus and Paul: Studies in the Earliest History of Christianity.* Translation by J. Bowden. London: SCM Press; Philadelphia: Fortress, 1983.

———. "Jesus as Messianic Teacher of Wisdom and the Beginnings of Christology." Pages 73–118 in *Studies in Early Christology.* Edinburgh: T&T Clark, 1995.

———. "Jesus, the Messiah of Israel." Pages 1–72 in *Studies in Early Christology.* Edinburgh: T&T Clark, 1995.

———. *The Johannine Question.* London: SCM Press, 1989.

———. *The Son of God.* Philadelphia: Fortress, 1983.

———. *Studien zur Christologie: Kleine Schriften IV.* Edited by Claus-Jürgen Thornton. WUNT 201. Tübingen: Mohr, 2006.

———. *Studies in Early Christology.* Edinburgh: T&T Clark, 1995.

Hengel, Martin, and Anna Maria Schwemer. *Jesus und das Judentum.* Geschichte des frühen Christentums 1. Tübingen: Mohr Siebeck, 2007.

Hentschel, Anni. "Die Fusswaschung—ein verhindertes Ritual." *Zeitschrift für Neues Testament* 35 (2015): 66–74.

———. "Grössere Liebe und grössere Werke—die Fusswaschung als Sinnbild der Liebe im Johannesevangelium." Pages 99–117 in *Liebe*. Edited by Martin Ebner et al. JBTh 29. Neukirchen-Vluyn: Neukirchener, 2015.

Herder, Johann Gottfried. "Von Gottes Sohn, der Welt Heiland, nach Johannis Evangelium. Nebst einer Regel der Zusammenstimmung unserer Evangelien aus ihrer Entstehung und Ordnung." Pages 253–424 in vol. 19 of *Sämmtliche Werke*. Edited by B. Suphan. Berlin: Weidemann, 1880.

Hoegen-Rohls, Christina. *Der nachösterliche Johannes: Die Abschiedsreden als hermeneutischer Schlüssel zum vierten Evangelium*. WUNT 2/84. Tübingen: Mohr Siebeck, 1996.

Hofius, Otfried. "Die Auferweckung des Lazarus: Joh 11,1–44 als Zeugnis narrative Christologie." Pages 28–45 in *Exegetische Studien*. WUNT 223. Tübingen: Mohr Siebeck, 2008.

———. "'Einer ist Gott—Einer ist Herr': Erwägungen zu Struktur und Aussage des Bekenntnisses 1 Kor 8,6." Pages 167–80 in *Paulusstudien II*. WUNT 143. Tübingen: Mohr Siebeck, 2002.

———. "Jesu Zuspruch der Sündenvergebung: Exegetische Erwagungen zu Mk 2,5b." Pages 38–56 in *Neutestamentliche Studien*. WUNT 132. Tübingen: Mohr Siebeck, 2000.

Holtzmann, Heinrich Julius. "Das schriftstellerische Verhältnis des Johannes zu den Synoptikern." *ZWT* 12 (1869): 62–85, 155–78, 446–56.

———. *Die synoptischen Evangelien, ihr Ursprung und geschichtlicher Charakter*. Leipzig: Engelmann, 1863.

Horbury, William. "The Benediction of the 'Minim' and Early Jewish-Christian Controversy." *JTS* 33 (1982): 19–61.

———. "Jewish Messianism and Early Christology." Pages 3–24 in *Contours of Christology in the New Testament*. Edited by Richard N. Longenecker. Grand Rapids: Eerdmans, 2005.

———. *Jewish Messianism and the Cult of Christ*. London: SCM Press, 1998.

———. "Jüdische Wurzeln der Christologie." *Early Christianity* 2 (2011): 5–21.

Howard, Wilbert F. *Christianity according to St. John*. London: Duckworth, 1943.

Hunt, Steven A., D. Francois Tolmie, and Ruben Zimmermann, eds. *Character Studies in the Fourth Gospel: Narrative Approaches to Seventy Figures in John*. WUNT 314. Tübingen: Mohr Siebeck, 2013.

Hurtado, Larry W. *How on Earth Did Jesus Become a God?* Grand Rapids: Eerdmans, 2005.

———. *Lord Jesus Christ: Devotion to Jesus in Earliest Christianity*. Grand Rapids: Eerdmans, 2003.

———. *One God, One Lord: Early Christian Devotion and Ancient Jewish Monotheism*. 3rd ed. London: Bloomsbury, 2015.

Janowski, Bernd. *Konfliktgespräche mit Gott: Eine Anthropologie der Psalmen*. 3rd ed. Neukirchen-Vluyn: Neukirchener Verlag, 2009.

Jaubert, Annie. "Jésus et le calendrier de Qumrân." *NTS* 7 (1960/1961): 1–30.

———. *La Date de la Cène*. Paris: Gabalda, 1957.

Jeremias, Joachim. *The Eucharistic Words of Jesus*. Translated by Norman Perrin. Philadelphia: Fortress, 1966.

———. *Neutestamentliche Theologie: Erster Teil: Die Verkündigung Jesu*. 3rd ed. Gütersloh: Gerd Mohn, 1973.

Jewett, Robert. *Romans*. Hermeneia. Minneapolis: Fortress, 2007.

Jülicher, Adolf. *Einleitung in das Neue Testament*. Tübingen: Mohr 1894. 5th/6th ed., 1906.

Kähler, Martin. *Der sogenannte historische Jesus und der geschichtliche, biblische Christus*. Edited by E. Wolf. Munich: Kaiser, 1953.

Käsemann, Ernst. *Jesu letzter Wille nach Johnannes 17*. Tübingen: Mohr Siebeck, 1966. English translation: *The Testament of Jesus according to John 17*. Translated by Gerhard Krodel. London: SCM Press, 1966.

Katz, Steven T. "Issues in the Separation of Judaism and Christianity after 70 C.E.: A Reconsideration." *JBL* 103 (1984): 43–76.

Keener, Craig S. *The Gospel of John: A Commentary*. 2 vols. Peabody, Mass.: Hendrickson, 2003.

Kierspel, Lars. *The Jews and the World in the Fourth Gospel: Parallelism, Function, and Context*. WUNT 2/220. Tübingen: Mohr Siebeck, 2006.

Kimelman, Reuven. "Birkat Ha-Minim and the Lack of Evidence for an Anti-Christian Jewish Prayer in Late Antiquity." Pages 226–44 in vol. 2 of *Jewish and Christian Self-Definition*. Edited by Ed P. Sanders, Albert I. Baumgarten, and A. Mendelson. London: SCM Press, 1981.

Kirchschläger, Peter G. *Nur ich bin die Wahrheit: Der Absolutheitsanspruch des johanneischen Christus und das Gespräch zwischen den Religionen*. HBS 63. Freiburg im Breisgau: Herder, 2010.

Klein, Christian, and Matias Martinez, eds. *Wirklichkeitserzählungen: Felder, Formen und Funktionen nicht-literarischen Erzählens*. Stuttgart: Metzler, 2009.

Kloppenborg, John S. "Disaffiliation and the ἀποσυνάγωγος of John." *HTS* 67 (2011): 159–74.

Knöppler, Thomas. *Die theologia crucis des Johannesevangeliums: Das Verständnis des Todes Jesu im Rahmen der johanneischen Inkarnations- und Erhöhungschristologie*. WMANT 69. Neukirchen-Vluyn: Neukirchener Verlag, 1994.

Koch, Dietrich-Alex. "Der Täufer als Zeuge des Offenbarers: Das Täuferbild von Joh 1,19–34 auf dem Hintergrund von Mk 1,2–11." Pages 1963–84 in vol. 3 of *The Four Gospels*. Festschrift Frans Neirynck. Edited by F. van Segbroeck et al. 3 vols. BETL 100. Leuven: Leuven University Press, 1963–1984.

Koestenberger, Andreas J. "Early Doubts of the Apostolic Authorship of the Fourth Gospel in the History of Modern Biblical Criticism." Pages 17–47 in *Studies on John and Gender: A Decade of Scholarship*. Studies in Biblical Literature 38. New York: Peter Lang, 2001.

———. *Encountering John: The Gospel in Historical, Literary, and Theological Perspective*. Grand Rapids: Baker, 1999.

———. *John*. BECNT. Grand Rapids: Baker, 2004.

Koester, Craig A. *The Gospel of John: A Commentary*. 2 vols. Grand Rapids: Hendrickson, 2003.

Koester, Helmut. *Ancient Christian Gospels: Their History and Development*. Philadelphia: Trinity, 1990.

Kriener, Tobias. *"Glauben an Jesus"—ein Verstoß gegen das zweite Gebot? Die johanneische Christologie und der jüdische Vorwurf des Götzendienstes*. Neukirchen-Vluyn: Neukirchener, 2001.

Kuhn, Karl Georg. "Die in Palästina gefundenen hebräischen Texte und das Neue Testament." *ZTK* 47 (1950): 192–211.

Kysar, Robert. "The Dehistoricizing of the Gospel of John." Pages 75–102 in vol. 1 of Anderson, Just, and Thatcher, *John, Jesus, and History*.

———. "Expulsion from the Synagogue: A Tale of a Theory." Pages 234–45 in *Voyages with John: Charting the Fourth Gospel*. Waco: Baylor University Press, 2005.

Labahn, Michael. "'Blinded by the Light': Blindheit und Licht in Joh 9 im Spiel von Variation und Wiederholung zwischen Erzählung und Metapher." Pages 453–504 in *Repetitions and Variations in the Fourth Gospel: Style, Text, Interpretation*. Edited by G. van Belle, M. Labahn, and P. Maritz. BETL 223. Leuven: Peeters, 2009.

———. *Jesus als Lebensspender: Untersuchungen zu einer Geschichte der johanneischen Traditionen anhand ihrer Wundergeschichten*. BZNW 9. Berlin: de Gruyter, 1999.

Lagrange, Marie-Joseph. *Évangile selon Saint Jean*. 2nd ed. *EBib* 16. Paris: Gabalda, 1925.

Landmesser, Christof. *Wahrheit als Grundbegriff neutestamentlicher Wissenschaft*. WUNT 113. Tübingen: Mohr Siebeck, 1999.

Lang, Manfred. *Johannes und die Synoptiker: Eine redaktionsgeschichtliche Analyse von Joh 18–20 vor dem markinischen und lukanischen Hintergrund*. FRLANT 182. Göttingen: Vandenhoeck & Ruprecht, 1999.

Lemitz, Bastian. "Der Tod Jesu und das Nicken des Zeus: Zur Wendung κλίνας τὴν κεφαλὴν (Joh 19,30)." Pages 241–56 in *Erzählung und Briefe im johanneischen Kreis*. Edited by Uta Poplutz and Jörg Frey. WUNT 2/420. Tübingen: Mohr Siebeck, 2016.

Leroy, Herbert. *Rätsel und Missverständnis: Ein Beitrag zur Formgeschichte des Johannesevangeliums*. BBB 30. Bonn: Peter Hanstein, 1968.

Lessing, Gotthold Ephraim. "Neue Hypothese über die Evangelisten als bloss menschliche Geschichtsschreiber betrachtet." Pages 614–35 in vol. 7 of *G. E. Lessing Werke*. Edited by P. Rilla. Munich: Aufbau, 1976.

Lieu, Judith M. "'The Parting of the Ways': Theological Construct or Historical Reality." Pages 11–29 in *Neither Jew nor Greek: Constructing Early Christianity*. London: T&T Clark, 2002.

Lightfoot, Joseph Barber. *Biblical Essays*. London: Macmillan, 1983.

———. *The Gospel of St. John: A Newly Discovered Commentary*. Edited by Ben Witherington III and Todd D. Still. Downers Grove, Ill.: IVP Academic, 2015.

Lincoln, Andrew. *Truth on Trial: The Lawsuit Motif in the Fourth Gospel*. Peabody, Mass.: Hendrickson, 2000.

Loisy, Alfred. *Le quatrième évangile*. Paris: Picard, 1903.

Lücke, Fridrich. *Commentar über das Evangelium des Johannes*. 3rd ed. 2 vols. Bonn: Weber, 1840–1843.

Luther, Susanne. *Die Authentifizierung der Vergangenheit: Literarische Geschichtsdarstellung im Johannesevangelium*. Habilitationsschrift University of Mainz (2018). WUNT. Tübingen: Mohr Siebeck, forthcoming 2019.

Mackay, Ian D. *John's Relationship with Mark: An Analysis of John 6 in the Light of Mark 6–8*. WUNT 2/182. Tübingen: Mohr Siebeck, 2004.

Marcus, Joel. *Mark 1–8*. Anchor Yale Bible Commentaries 27. New York: Doubleday, 2000.

———. "Tribute to J. Louis Martyn." *NT Blog*, June 17, 2015. Online at http://ntweblog.blogspot.ch/2015/06/tribute-to-j-louis-martyn-by-joel-marcus.html.

Marguerat, Daniel. "La 'source des signes' existe-t-elle?" Pages 60–93 in *La communauté johannique et son histoire*. Edited by Jean-Daniel Kaestli et al. Geneva: Cerf, 1990.

Markschies, Christoph. *Christian Theology and Its Institutions in the Early Roman Empire: Prolegommena to a History of Early Christian Theology*. Translated by W. Coppins. BMSEC 3. Waco: Baylor University Press, 2015.

Martyn, J. Louis. "Glimpses into the History of the Johannine Community." Pages 90–121 in *The Gospel of John in Christian History: Essays for Interpreters*. New York: Paulist, 1979.

———. *History and Theology in the Fourth Gospel.* New York: Harper & Row, 1968.

———. *History and Theology in the Fourth Gospel.* 2nd enl. ed. Nashville: Abingdon, 1979.

———. *History and Theology in the Fourth Gospel.* 3rd ed. New Testament Library. Louisville: Westminster John Knox, 2003.

———. "The Salvation-History Perspective in the Fourth Gospel." Ph.D. diss. (unpublished), Yale Divinity School, 1957.

McCaffrey, G. *The House with Many Rooms: The Temple Theme of Jn 14:2–3*. Rome: Pontificio Istituto Biblico, 1988.

McGrath, James F. "'Destroy This Temple': Issues of History in John 2:13–22." Pages 35–44 in vol. 2 of Anderson, Just, and Thatcher, *John, Jesus, and History*.

Meeks, Wayne A. "The Man from Heaven in Johannine Sectarianism." *JBL* 91 (1972): 44–72.

———. *The Prophet-King: Moses Traditions and the Johannine Christology.* NovTSup 14. Leiden: Brill, 1967.

Meier, John P. *A Marginal Jew: Rethinking the Historical Jesus*. Vol. 1: *The Roots of the Problem and the Person*. New York: Doubleday, 1991.

———. *A Marginal Jew: Rethinking the Historical Jesus*. Vol. 2: *Mentor, Message, and Miracles*. New York: Doubleday, 1994.

———. *A Marginal Jew: Rethinking the Historical Jesus*. Vol. 3: *Companions and Competitors*. New York: Doubleday, 2001.

Menken, Maarten J. J. "Die jüdischen Feste im Johannesevangelium." Pages 269–86 in *Israel und seine Heilstraditionen im Johannesevangelium*. Festschrift Johannes Beutler. Edited by Michael Labahn, Klaus Scholtissek, and Angelika Strothmann. Paderborn: Schöningh, 2004.

Mercier, Robert. *L'Évangile "pour que vous croyez": Le quatrième évangile (selon Saint Jean)*. Montreal: Wilson & Lafleur, 2010.

Merkel, Helmut. *Die Pluralität der Evangelien als theologisches und exegetisches Problem in der Alten Kirche*. TC 3. Bern: Peter Lang, 1978.

———. *Die Widerspüche zwischen den Evangelien: Ihre polemische und apologetische Behandlung in der Alten Kirche bis Augustin*. WUNT 13. Tübingen: Mohr, 1971.

Merz, Annette. "Response to the Essays in Part 2." Pages 299–317 in vol. 3 of Anderson, Just, and Thatcher, *John, Jesus, and History*.

Meyer, Annegret. *Kommt und seht. Mystagogie im Johannesevangelium ausgehend von Joh 1,35–51*. FB 103. Würzburg: Echter, 2005.

Moloney, Francis J. "The Fourth Gospel and the Jesus of History." *NTS* 46 (2000): 42–58.

———. "The Gospel of John: The Legacy of Raymond E Brown and Beyond." Pages 19–39 in *Life in Abundance: Studies of John's Gospel in Tribute to Raymond E. Brown*. Edited by John R Donahue. Collegeville, Minn.: Liturgical, 2005.

———. "The Johannine Son of Man Revisited." Pages 177–202 in *Theology and Christology in the Fourth Gospel*. Edited by Gilbert van Belle, Jan G. van der Watt, and Petrus Maritz. BETL 184. Leuven: Peeters, 2005.

Moss, Candida R. "The Marks of the Nails: Scars, Wounds and the Resurrection of Jesus in John." *Early Christianity* 8 (2017): 48–68.

Nagel, Titus. *Die Rezeption des Johannesevangeliums im 2. Jahrhundert: Studien zur vorirenäischen Aneignung und Auslegung des vierten Evangeliums in christlicher und christlich-gnostischer Literatur*. ABG 2. Leipzig: Evangelische Verlagsanstalt, 2000.

Neirynck, Frans. "The Anonymous Disciple in John 1." Pages 617–49 in *Evangelica II: 1982–1991: Collected Essays*. Edited by F. van Segbroeck. BETL 94. Leuven: Leuven University Press, 1991.

———. "John 4:46–54: Signs Source or Synoptic Gospels." Pages 679–87 in *Evangelica II: 1982–1991: Collected Essays*. Edited by F. van Segbroeck. BETL 94. Leuven: Leuven University Press, 1991.

———. "John 5:1–18 and the Gospel of Mark: A Response to Peder Borgen." Pages 699–711 in *Evangelica II: 1982–1991: Collected Essays*. Edited by F. van Segbroeck. BETL 94. Leuven: Leuven University Press, 1991.

———. "John and the Synoptics." Pages 365–400 in *Evangelica: Gospel Studies—Étude d'Évangile*. Edited by F. van Segbroeck. BETL 60. Leuven: Peeters, 1982.

———. "John and the Synoptics: The Empty Tomb Stories." Pages 571–99 in *Evangelica II: 1982–1991: Collected Essays*. Edited by F. van Segbroeck. BETL 94. Leuven: Leuven University Press, 1991.

———. "The Signs Source in the Fourth Gospel: A Critique of the Hypothesis." Pages 651–77 in *Evangelica II: 1982–1991: Collected Essays*. Edited by F. van Segbroeck. BETL 94. Leuven: Leuven University Press, 1991.

Newman, Carey C. *Paul's Glory Christology: Tradition and Rhetoric*. NovTSup 69. Leiden: Brill, 1992.

Neyrey, Jerome H. "The Foot Washing in John 13:6–11: Transformation Ritual or Ceremony." Pages 198–213 in *The Social World of the First Christians*. Essays in Honor of W. A. Meeks. Edited by L. M. White. Minneapolis: Fortress, 1995.

Niemand, Christoph. *Die Fusswaschungserzählung des Johannesevangeliums: Untersuchungen zu ihrer Entstehung und Überlieferung im Urchristentum*. Studia Anselmiana 114. Rome: Pontificio Ateneo S. Anselmo, 1994.

Obermann, Andreas. *Die christologische Erfüllung der Schrift im Johannesevangelium*. WUNT 2/88. Tübingen: Mohr Siebeck, 1996.

O'Connor, Jerome Murphy. "John the Baptist and Jesus: History and Hyptheses." *NTS* 36 (1990): 359–74.

Oegema, Gerbern S. *The Anointed and his People*. JSPSup 27. Sheffield: Sheffield Academic, 1998.

Olsson, Birger. *Structure and Meaning in the Fourth Gospel*. ConBNT 6. Lund: Gleerup, 1974.

Onuki, Takashi. *Gemeinde und Welt im Johannesevangelium: Ein Beitrag zur Frage nach der theologischen und pragmatischen Funktion des johanneischen 'Dualismus.'* WMANT 56. Neukirchen-Vluyn: Neukirchener Verlag, 1984.

O'Rourke, John. "Asides in the Gospel of John." *NovT* 21 (1979): 210–19.

Painter, John. "Memory Holds the Key: The Transformation of Memory in the Interface of History and Theology in John." Pages 229–45 in vol. 1 of Anderson, Just, and Thatcher, *John, Jesus, and History*.

———. *Theology as Hermeneutics: Rudolf Bultmann's Theology of the History of Jesus*. London: Bloomsbury, 2015.

Parsenios, George L. *Departure and Consolation: The Johannine Farewell Discourses in Light of Greco-Roman Literature*. NovTSup 117. Leiden: Brill, 2005.

Pastorelli, David. *Le Paraclet dans le corpus johannique*. BZNW 142. Berlin: de Gruyter, 2006.

Popkes, Enno Edzard. *Die Theologie der Liebe Gottes in den johanneischen Schriften*. WUNT 2/197. Tübingen: Mohr Siebeck, 2005.

Poplutz, Uta. "Hinführung." Pages 659–68 in *Kompendium der frühchristlichen Wundererzählungen 1: Die Wunder Jesu*. Edited by Ruben Zimmermann. Gütersloh: Gütersloher Verlagshaus, 2013.

Porter, Stanley E. *The Criteria for Authenticity in Historical-Jesus Research: Previous Discussion and New Proposals*. JNTS 191. Sheffield: Sheffield Academic, 2000.

———. "How Do We Know What We Think We Know? Methodological Reflections on Jesus Research." Pages 82–99 in *Jesus Research: New Methodologies and Perceptions*. Edited by James H. Charlesworth. Grand Rapids: Eerdmans, 2014.

Potterie, Ignace de la. "*Jésus roi et juge d'après Jn 19,13* ἐκάθισεν ἐπὶ βήματος." *Biblica* 41 (1960): 217–47.

———. *La vérité dans Saint Jean*. 2 vols. AnBib 73/74. Rome: Biblical Institute, 1977.

Powell, Mark Allan. "The De-Johannification of Jesus: The Twentieth Century and Beyond." Pages 121–32 in vol. 1 of Anderson, Just, and Thatcher, *John, Jesus, and History*.

Rahner, Johanna. "*Er sprach aber vom Tempel seines Leibes.*" BBB 117. Bodenheim: Philo, 1998.

Rasimus, Tuomas. "Ptolemaeus and the Prologue's Valentinian Exegesis." Pages 145–72 in *The Legacy of John: Second-Century Reception of the Fourth Gospel*. Edited by Tuomas Rasimus. NovTSup 132. Leiden: Brill, 2010.

Ratzinger, Joseph (Pope Benedict XVI). *From the Baptism in the Jordan to the Transfiguration*. Vol. 1 of *Jesus of Nazareth*. New York: Doubleday, 2007.

Rebell, Walter. *Gemeinde als Gegenwelt: Zur soziologischen und didaktischen Funktion des Johannesevangelium*. BET 20. Frankfurt: Peter Lang, 1987.

Reed, Annette Yoshiko, and Adam H. Becker, eds. *The Ways That Never Parted: Jews and Christians in Late Antiquity and the Early Middle Ages*. TSAJ 95. Tübingen: Mohr Siebeck, 2003.

Rein, Mattias. *Die Heilung des Blindgeborenen (Joh 9): Tradition und Redaktion*. WUNT 2/73. Tübingen: Mohr Siebeck, 1995.

Reinhartz, Adele. *Cast Out of the Covenant: Jews and Anti-Judaism in the Gospel of John*. Lanham, Md.: Rowman & Littlefield, 2018.

———. "Great Expectations: A Reader-Oriented Approach to Johannine Christology and Eschatology." *JLT* 3 (1989): 61–76.

Rengstorf, Karl-Heinrich. "ἀποστέλλω κ.τ.λ." *TDNT* 1:398–447.

Reynolds, Benjamins. *The Apocalyptic Son of Man in the Gospel of John*. WUNT 2/249. Tübingen: Mohr Siebeck, 2008.

Rhea, Robert. *The Johannine Son of Man*. ATANT 76. Zürich: Theologischer Verlag, 1990.

Richter, Georg. *Studien zum Johannesevangelium*. Edited by J. Hainz. BU 13. Regensburg: Pustet, 1977.

Ricoeur, Paul. *Temps et récit*. 3 vols. Paris: Ed. du Seuil, 1983–1985.

Riesner, Rainer. *Jesus als Lehrer: Eine Untersuchung zum Ursprung der Evanglien-Überlieferung*. 3rd ed. WUNT 2/7. Tübingen: Mohr Siebeck, 1988.

Robinson, James M. "The Johannine Trajectory." Pages 232–68 in *Trajectories through Early Christianity*. Edited by Helmut Koester and James M. Robinson. Philadelphia: Fortress, 1971.

Robinson, John A. T. "The New Look on the Fourth Gospel." Pages 338–50 in vol. 1 of *Studia Evangelica*. Edited by Kurt Aland et al. Berlin: Akademie-Verlag, 1959.

———. *The Priority of John*. London: SCM Press, 1985.

Ruckstuhl, Eugen. "Sprache und Stil im johanneischen Schrifttum." Pages 304–31 in *Die literarische Einheit des Johannesevengeliums*. Enl. new ed. NTOA 17. Freiburg Schweiz: Uniersitätsverlag; Göttingen: Vandenhoeck & Ruprecht, 1987.

———. "Zur Chronologie der Leidensgeschichte Jesu." *SNTU* 10 (1985): 27–61; *SNTU* 11 (1986): 97–129.

Ruckstuhl, Eugen, and Peter Dschulnigg. *Stilkritik und Verfasserfrage im Johannesevangeliums: Die johanneischen Sprachmerkmale auf dem Hintergrund des Neuen Testaments und des zeitgenössischen hellenistischen Schrifttums*. NTOA 17. Freiburg Schweiz: Universitätsverlag; Göttingen: Vandenhoeck & Ruprecht, 1991.

Rüsen, Jörn. "Historisches Erzählen." Pages 43–105 in *Zerbrechende Zeit: Über den Sinn der Geschichte*. Cologne: Böhlau, 2001.

Sabbe, Maurits. "The Anointing of Jesus in Jn 12,1–8 and Its Synoptic Parallels." Pages 2051–82 in *The Four Gospels 1992*. Festschrift Frans Neirynck. 3 vols. BETL 100. Leuven: Leuven University Press.

———. "The Arrest of Jesus in Jn 18,1–11 and Its Relation to the Synoptic Gospels." Pages 203–34 in vol. 3 of *L'Évangile de Jean: Sources, redaction, théologie*. Edited by Marinus de Jonge. BETL 44. Gembloug: Duculot and Leuven: University Press.

———. "The Johannine Account of the Death of Jesus and Its Synoptic Parallels (Jn 19,16b–42)." *EThL* 70 (1994): 30–64.

———. "The Trial of Jesus before Pilate in John and Its Relation to the Synoptic Gospels." Pages 341–85 in *John and the Synoptics*. Edited by Adalbert Denaux. BETL 101. Leuven: Peeters, 1992.

Sass, Markus. *Der Menschensohn im Evangelium nach Johannes*. TANZ 35. Tübingen: Francke, 2000.

Schäfer, Peter. "Die sogannante Synode von Jabne: Zur Trennung von Juden und Christen im ersten/zweiten Jh. n. Chr." Pages 45–64 in *Studien zur Geschichte und Theologie des Rabbinischen Judentums*. AGAJU 15. Leiden: Brill, 1978.

Schleritt, Frank. *Der vorjohanneische Passionsbericht: Eine historisch-kritische und theologische Untersuchung zu Joh 2,13–22; 11,47–14,31 und 18,1–20,29*. BZNW 154. Berlin: de Gruyter, 2007.

Schnackenburg, Rudolf. *Das Johannesevangelium*. 4 vols. Freiburg: Herder, 1965–1984.

———. "'Der Vater, der mich gesandt hat': Zur johanneischen Christologie." Pages 275–92 in *Anfänge der Christologie*. Festschrift Ferdinand Hahn. Edited by Cilliers Breytenbach and Henning Paulsen. Göttingen: Vandenhoeck & Ruprecht, 1987.

———. "Die johanneische Gemeinde und ihre Geisterfahrung." Pages 33–57 in *Ergänzende Auslegungen*, vol. 4 of *Das Johannesevangelium*. HTK 4/4. Freiburg: Herder, 1984.

Schnelle, Udo. *Antidoketische Christologie im Johannesevangelium*. FRLANT 144. Göttingen: Vandenhoeck & Ruprecht, 1987. English translation: *Antidocetic Christology in the Gospel of John*. Minneapolis: Fortress, 1992.

———. *Das Evangelium nach Johannes*. THKNT. Leipzig: Evangelische Verlagsanstalt, 1998.

———. *Einleitung in das Neue Testament*. 8th ed. Göttingen: Vandenhoeck & Ruprecht, 2013.

———. "Johannes und die Synoptiker." Pages 1799–1814 in vol. 3 of *The Four Gospels 1992*. Festschrift Frans Neirynck. 3 vols. BETL 100. Leuven: University Press.

Schwank, Benedikt. *Evangelium nach Johannes: Erläutert für die Praxis*. St. Ottilien: EOS, 1998.

Schweitzer, Albert. *Die Geschichte der Leben-Jesu-Forschung*. Tübingen: Mohr, 1913. English translation: *The Quest of the Historical Jesus: First Complete Edition*. Translated by W. Montgomery, J. R. Coates, S. Cupitt, and J. Bowden. London: SCM Press, 2000.

———. *Die Mystik des Apostels Paulus*. Tübingen: Mohr, 1930. English translation: *The Mysticism of Paul the Apostle*. Translated by W. Montgomery. New York: Holt, 1931.

———. *Von Reimarus zu Wrede: Eine Geschichte der Leben-Jesu-Forschung*. Tübingen: Mohr, 1906. English translation: *The Quest for the Historical Jesus: A Critical Study of Its Progress from Reimarus to Wrede*. Translated by W. Montgomery. New York: Macmillan, 1957.

Segal, Alan F. *Two Powers in Heaven: Early Rabbinic Reports about Christianity and Gnosticism*. Waco: Baylor University Press, 2012. Orig. pub. 1977.

Skinner, Christopher W., ed. *Characters and Characterization in the Gospel of John*. LNTS 461. London: Bloomsbury, 2012.

Smith, D. Moody. *The Composition and Order of the Fourth Gospel: Bultmann's Literary Theory*. New Haven, Conn.: Yale University Press, 1965.

———. "The Contribution of J. Louis Martyn to the Understanding of the Gospel of John." Pages 275–94 in *The Conversation Continues: Studies in Paul and John in Honor of J. Louis Martyn*. Edited by Robert T. Fortna and Beverly R. Gaventa. Nashville: Abingdon, 1990. Reprinted in Martyn, *History and Theology in the Fourth Gospel*, 3rd ed. (2003).

———. "Jesus Tradition in the Gospel of John." Pages 1997–2039 in vol. 3 of *Handbook for the Study of the Historical Jesus*. Edited by Tom Holmén and Stanley E. Porter. 4 vols. Leiden: Brill, 2011.

———. *John among the Gospels: The Relationship in Twentieth-Century Research*. Minneapolis: Fortress, 1992.

———. "Judaism and the Gospel of John." Pages 76–96 in *Jews and Christians: Exploring the Past, Present, and Future*. Edited by James H. Charlesworth. New York: Crossroad, 1990.

———. "Postscript for Third Edition of Martyn, *History and Theology in the Fourth Gospel*." Pages 19–23 in Martyn, *History and Theology in the Fourth Gospel*, 3rd ed. (2003).

Smitmans, Adolf. *Das Weinwunder zu Kana: Die Auslegung von Jo 2,1–11 bei den Vätern und heute*. BGBE 6. Tübingen: Mohr Siebeck, 1966.

Stemberger, Günter. "Die sogenannte 'Synode von Jabne' und das frühe Christentum." *Kairos* 19 (1977): 14–21.

Streeter, Burnett H. *The Four Gospels: A Study of Origins Treating of the Manuscript Tradition, Authorship, and Dates*. London: McMillan, 1924.

Tenney, Merrill C. "The Footnotes in John's Gospel." *Biblia Sacra* 117 (1960): 350–64.

Thatcher, Tom. "Anatomies of the Fourth Gospel: Past, Present, and Future Probes." Pages 1–35 in *Anatomies of Narrative Criticism: The Past, Present and Future of the Fourth Gospel as Literature*. Edited by Tom Thatcher and Stephen D. Moore. SBLRBS 55. Atlanta: SBL, 2008.

Theissen, Gerd, and Dagmar Winter. *Die Kriterienfrage in der Jesusforschung: Vom Differenzkriterium zum Plausibilitätskriterium*. NTOA 34. Freiburg Schweiz: Universitätsverlag; Göttingen: Vandenhoeck & Ruprecht, 1997.

Theobald, Michael. *Das Evangelium nach Johannes*. Vol. 1. RNT. Regensburg: Pustet, 2007.

———. *Die Fleischwerdung des Logos*. NTA 20. Münster: Aschendorff, 1988.

———. *Herrenworte im Johannesevangelium*. HBS 34. Freiburg im Breisgau: Herder, 2002.

———. "Johannine Dominical Sayings as Metatexts of Synoptic Sayings of Jesus: Reflections on a New Category within Reception History." Pages 383–406 in vol. 3 of Anderson, Just, and Thatcher, *John, Jesus, and History*.

———. "'Stellt die johanneische Erzählung von der sogenannten 'Tempelreinigung' Jesu (Joh 2,13–22) eine Relecture ihrer synoptischen Parallelen dar? Kontroverse in der Forschung, nicht im Text." Pages 228–60 in *Kontroverse Stimmen im Kanon*. Edited by Martin Ebner et al. Quaestiones Disputatae 279. Freiburg im Breisgau: Herder, 2016.

Theodore of Mopsuestia. *Commentary on the Gospel of John*. Edited by Joel C. Elowsky. Ancient Christian Texts. Downers Grove, Ill.: InterVarsity, 2010.

Thompson, Marianne Meye. *The Humanity of Jesus in the Fourth Gospel*. Philadelphia: Fortress, 1988.

———. *John: A Commentary*. NTL. Louisville: Westminster John Knox, 2015.

Thyen, Hartwig. *Das Johannesevangelium*. HNT 6. Tübingen: Mohr Siebeck, 2005.

———. "Die Erzählung von den Bethanischen Geschwistern (Joh 11,1–12,19) als 'Palimpsest' über synoptischen Texten." Pages 2021–50 in vol. 3 of *The Four Gospels*. Festschrift Frans Neirynck. Edited by F. van Segbroeck. BETL 100. Leuven: Peeters, 1992. Reprinted in "Die Erzählung von den Bethanischen Geschwistern (Joh 11,1–12,19) als 'Palimpsest' über synoptischen Texten." Pages 182–212 in *Studien zum Corpus Iohanneum*. WUNT 214. Tübingen: Mohr Siebeck, 2007.

———. "Ich bin das Licht der Welt: Das Ich- und Ich-Bin-Sagen Jesu im Johannesevangelium." *JAC* 35 (1992): 19–42. Reprinted in "Ich bin das Licht der Welt: Das Ich- und Ich-Bin-Sagen Jesu im Johannesevangelium." Pages 213–51 in *Studien zum Corpus Iohanneum*. WUNT 214. Tübingen: Mohr Siebeck, 2007.

———. "Ich-bin-Worte." *RAC* 17 (1995): 147–213.

———. "Johannes und die Synoptiker." Pages 81–107 in *John and the Synoptics*. Edited by Adalbert Denaux. BETL 101. Leuven: Peeters, 1992. Reprinted in "Johannes und die Synoptiker." Pages 155–81 in *Studien zum Corpus Iohanneum*. WUNT 214. Tübingen: Mohr Siebeck, 2007.

Treloar, Geoffrey L. *Lightfoot the Historian: The Nature and Role of History in the Life and Thought of J. B. Lightfoot (1828–1889) as Churchman and Scholar*. WUNT 2/103. Tübingen: Mohr Siebeck, 1998.

Trudinger, Paul. "The Cleansing of the Temple: St. John's Independent, Subtle Reflections." *ExpTim* 108 (1997): 329–30.

Tuckett, Christopher. "Sources and Methods." Pages 121–37 in *The Cambridge Companion to Jesus*. Edited by Markus Bockmuehl. Cambridge: Cambridge University Press, 2001.

van Belle, Gilbert. *Les parenthèses dans l'évangile de Jean*. SNTA 11. Leuven: Leuven University Press, 1985.

———. *The Signs Source in the Fourth Gospel: Historical Survey and Critical Evaluation of the Semeia Hypothesis*. BETL 116. Leuven: Peeters, 1994.

van Belle, Gilbert, and Sydney Palmer. "John's Literary Unity and the Problem of Historicity." Pages 217–28 in vol. 1 of Anderson, Just, and Thatcher, *John, Jesus, and History*.

van der Watt, Jan G. *Family of the King: Dynamics of Metaphor in the Gospel of John*. BIS 44. Leiden: Brill, 2000.

van Henten, Jan Willem, and Friedrich Avemarie. *Martyrdom and Noble Death: Selected Texts from Graeco-Roman, Jewish and Christian Antiquity*. London: Routledge, 2002.

VanderKam, James C. "The Origin, Character, and Early History of the Qumran Calendar: A Reassessment of Jaubert's Hypthesis." *CBQ* 41 (1979): 390–411.

Verheyden, Joseph. "The De-Johannification of Jesus: The Revisionist Contribution of Some Nineteenth-Century German Scholarship." Pages 109–20 in vol. 1 of Anderson, Just, and Thatcher, *John, Jesus, and History*.

———. "P. Gardner-Smith and the 'Turn of the Tide.'" Pages 423–52 in *John and the Synoptics*. Edited by Adalbert Denaux. BETL 101. Leuven: Peeters, 1992.

von Ranke, Leopold. *Geschichten der romanischen und germanischen Völker von 1494 bis 1514*. Vols. 33 and 34 of *Sämmtliche Werke*. 2nd ed. Leipzig: Duncker und Humblot, 1874.

von Wahlde, Urban C. "Archaeology and John's Gospel." Pages 523–86 in *Jesus and Archaeology*. Edited by James H. Charlesworth. Grand Rapids: Eerdmans, 2006.

———. *The Earliest Version of John's Gospel: Recovering the Gospel of Signs*. Wilmington, De.: Michael Glazier, 1989.

———. *The Gospel and Letters of John*. 3 vols. Grand Rapids: Eerdmans, 2010.

Watson, Francis. *Gospel Writing: A Canonical Perspective*. Grand Rapids: Eerdmans, 2013.

———. "Reciprocity, Mimesis and Ethics in 1 John." Pages 257–76 in *Erzählung und Briefe im johanneischen Kreis*. Edited by Uta Poplutz and Jörg Frey. WUNT 2/420. Tübingen: Mohr Siebeck, 2016.

Weiss, Bernhard. *Das Johannes-Evangelium*. 9th ed. KEK 2. Göttingen: Vandenhoeck & Ruprecht, 1902.

Weiss, H. "Foot Washing in the Johannine Community." *NovT* 21 (1979): 298–325.

Weissenrieder, Annette. "The Infusion of the Spirit: The Meaning of ἐμφυσάω in John 20:22–23." Pages 119–51 in *The Holy Spirit, Inspiration, and the Cultures of Antiquity: Multidisciplinary Perspectives*. Edited by Jörg Frey and John R. Levison. Ekstasis 5. Berlin: de Gruyter, 2014.

Welck, Christian. *Erzählte Zeichen: Die Wundergeschichten des Johannesevangeliums literarisch untersucht: Mit einem Ausblick auf Joh 21*. WUNT 2/69. Tübingen: Mohr Siebeck, 1994.

Wellhausen, Julius. *Das Evangelium Johannis*. Berlin: Reimer, 1908.

Wendt, Hans Hinrich. *Die Lehre Jesu*. 2 vols. Göttingen: Vandenhoeck & Ruprecht, 1886.

Wengst, Klaus. *Das Johannesevangelium*. 2 vols. THKNT 4. Stuttgart: Kohlhammer, 2000/2001.

Westcott, Brooke Foss. *The Gospel according to St. John: The Greek Text with Introduction and Notes.* 2 vols. London: John Murray, 1908.

Wheaton, Gerry. *The Role of Jewish Feasts in John's Gospel.* MSSNTS 162. Cambridge: Cambridge University Press, 2015.

White, Hayden. *The Content of the Form: Narrative Discourse and Historical Representation.* Baltimore: John Hopkins University Press, 1987.

———. "The Fictions of Factual Representation." Pages 21–44 *The Literature of Fact.* Edited by Angus Fletcher. New York: Columbia University Press, 1976.

Williams, Catrin H. *I Am He: The Interpretation of* 'Anî Hû' *in Jewish and Early Christian Literature.* WUNT 2/113. Tübingen: Mohr Siebeck, 2000.

Willis, Wendell. "The Discovery of the Eschatological Kingdom: Johannes Weiss and Albert Schweitzer." Pages 1–14 in *The Kingdom of God in 20th Century Interpretation.* Edited by Wendell Willis. Peabody, Mass.: Hendrickson, 1987.

Windisch, Hans. *Johannes und die Synoptiker: Wollte der vierte Evangelist die älteren Evangelien ergänzen oder ersetzen?* UNT 12. Leipzig: Hinrichs, 1926.

Witherington, Ben, III. *John's Wisdom: A Commentary on the Fourth Gospel.* Louisville: Westminster John Knox, 1995.

Wrede, William. *Charakter und Tendenz des Johannesevangeliums.* Tübingen: Mohr, 1903.

———. *Das Messiasgeheimnis in den Evangelien: Zugleich ein Beitrag zum Verständnis des Markusevangeliums.* Göttingen: Vandenhoeck & Ruprecht, 1901. English translation: *The Messianic Secret.* Translated by J. C. Greig. London: James Clark, 1987.

Yee, Gale A. *Jewish Feasts and the Gospel of John.* Wilmington: Michael Glazier, 1989.

Zahn, Theodor. *Einleitung in das Neue Testament.* 2nd ed. 2 vols. Leipzig: Deichert, 1900.

Zangenberg, Jürgen. *Frühes Christentum in Samarien: Topographische und traditionsgeschichtliche Studien zu den Samarientexten im Johannesevangelium.* TANZ 27. Tübingen: Francke, 1998.

Zimmermann, Johannes. *Messianische Texte aus Qumran.* WUNT 2/104. Tübingen: Mohr Siebeck, 1998.

Zimmermann, Ruben, ed. *Kompendium der frühchristlichen Wundererzählungen 1: Die Wunder Jesu.* Edited by Gütersloh: Gütersloher Verlagshaus, 2013.

Zumstein, Jean. *Das Johannesevangelium.* Translated by K. Vollmer-Mateus. KEK. Göttingen: Vandenhoeck & Ruprecht, 2016.

———. "Johannes 2:13–22 im Plot und in der Theologie des vierten Evangeliums." Pages 275–88 in *The Opening of John's Narrative (John 1:19–2:22).* Edited by R. Alan Culpepper and Jörg Frey. WUNT 385. Tübingen: Mohr Siebeck, 2017.

———. "Story, Plot, and History in the Johannine Passion Narrative." Pages 109–18 in vol. 3 of Anderson, Just, and Felix, *John, Jesus, and History.*

INDEX OF ANCIENT SOURCES

Early Jewish Authors and Texts

Early Christian Authors and Texts